FUNDAMENTALS *of* BASIC READING INSTRUCTION

MILDRED A. DAWSON
PROFESSOR OF EDUCATION
SACRAMENTO STATE COLLEGE

Second Edition

NEW YORK
1963

HENRY A. BAMMAN
PROFESSOR OF EDUCATION
SACRAMENTO STATE COLLEGE

FUNDAMENTALS *of* BASIC READING INSTRUCTION

DAVID McKAY
COMPANY, INC.

FUNDAMENTALS OF BASIC READING INSTRUCTION

FIRST EDITION JANUARY 1959
REPRINTED SEPTEMBER 1959
FEBRUARY 1960
AUGUST 1960
SECOND EDITION MARCH 1963

LIBRARY OF CONGRESS CATALOG CARD NUMBER: 63-9327

MANUFACTURED IN THE UNITED STATES OF AMERICA

Preface

THIS BOOK IS INTENDED FOR THE STUDENT WHO IS preparing to teach, for relatively inexperienced teachers, and for those teachers who are returning to the classroom and wish to acquaint themselves with the modern philosophy and practices in the teaching of reading. It has been written with the intent of being specific and practical. The philosophy and techniques are in alignment with the findings of research and observations of successful practice.

A program in elementary reading is geared to the developmental characteristics of children; therefore, it constantly promotes readiness at each level of the curriculum, incorporates a skills-development program which includes reading and study skills for each content subject, and emphasizes reading for both personal and educational growth. It provides for meeting individual differences which exist among all children in all classrooms, for careful evaluation which indicates the effectiveness and worth-whileness of instruction, and for close liaison with the parents of children who are seeking means of developing their skills.

MILDRED A. DAWSON
HENRY A. BAMMAN

June, 1962

Contents

FUNDAMENTALS *of* BASIC READING INSTRUCTION

1

A Modern Reading Program

Reading undergirds the entire curriculum. In every subject, pupils' learning activities involve reading. Lessons in the content subjects call for the use of textbooks, reference books, and related library reading. Even in handwriting and art, children often read from printed guides and manuals. The teacher writes assignments and informal records on the chalkboard, to be read by the children. They also write productions of their own to be read later on. Reading is truly a basic means of learning in all subjects.

This first chapter presents a preliminary and brief discussion of the following phases of a modern reading program: the nature of reading, stages in development at the elementary school level, goals of instruction, types of reading activities serving to achieve these goals, ways of providing for individual differences, interrelationships among the language arts (listening, speaking, reading, written language), and the place of reading in the general curriculum. Each of these phases will be more fully developed in ensuing chapters.

The nature of reading. Reading is a many-sided, very complex activity. It has been variously described as a process, a mode of thinking, a kind of real experience, a type of vicarious experiencing, an aspect of communication, and a tool subject. It is possible that reading is all of these, but not necessarily at one and the same time.

As a *process* reading involves many skills: the ability to focus the eyes on printed materials, to move them from side to side in following lines of print, to hear and to see the differences in words that resemble one another in sound and appearance (*pan, pen, pin*), to figure out the pronunciation of a new word by dividing it into parts, to select main points and the major supporting details, to adjust reading rate to suit different kinds of materials or to satisfy different purposes, and the like. In learning to read, the child must master such skills if he is to read well.

As *thinking*, reading requires that the reader follow the line of thought which the author has expressed. In so doing, the former must (1) recall pertinent previous experiences and already learned facts that will help him understand the printed materials, (2) follow the writer's development and organization of ideas, (3) evaluate the accuracy and appropriateness of information and conclusions, (4) see how the printed data can apply to a problem the reader may be trying to solve, (5) select the facts that are important to his purposes, and so on. Unless the reader does understand the writer's message and think along with him, there is actually little or no reading. Mere word-calling is not reading.

Reading may be considered as *real an experience* as swimming or typing. It is a part of our living in a civilized world. We read the label on a new detergent or fabric; we scan the ads in the morning newspaper to see if there are appealing bargains; we pore over the directions for making out income tax reports; we watch road signs or study a road map as we drive through unfamiliar territory. On every side, we are surrounded with reading that is an integral part of our everyday experiences. Purposeful reading is and should be a very real experience.

On occasion, however, reading becomes *vicarious experiencing* as, for instance, when we pick up a book or magazine and share the adventures or problems of fictitious or real-life characters. The young child, in particular, identifies himself with the persons and animals in the stories that are read to him or that he reads for himself. The reading of literature, history, and biography or a scientist's following of the description of a new experiment is vicarious experiencing.

Like the other language arts, reading is a form of *communication.* Just as we speak in order that others may listen, just so does a writer put his ideas into writing or print in order that others may read what he has to say. He may wish to define or clarify a problem, prove a point, share newly acquired information, win others to his point of view, or possibly amuse and entertain. The exchange of ideas is the ultimate goal of reading.

In certain respects, reading is a *tool subject* since it is an essential instrument for learning in all subjects in the curriculum. Children read books in history and geography, health and science, arithmetic and language. Learning how to use such books efficiently while studying is a necessary part of the reading program. Reading lessons should give training in study skills and work-type reading.

To the extent that learning to read demands the mastery of specific skills, reading is a *process.* Only as such skills are acquired can a child efficiently use reading as the *tool subject* it must be when he is studying his lessons in various subjects. Whenever a person enjoys literature and books dealing with biography and travel, he is indulging in *vicarious experiences;* whenever he reads as part of his everyday living, he is utilizing reading as *real experience.* It is only as a person understands the words or passages before his eyes, only as print *communicates* the writer's message to the reader, that he is really reading. Reading is always *thinking,* never mere word calling. W. S. Gray has well described the reading process:

> Reading is no longer defined as a unique ability which functions uniformly in all situations but rather as a series of complex mental tasks which vary widely with the kind of material read and the purpose for reading. Detailed studies show also that there are at least four dimensions of the reading act, namely: the perception of words, including both meanings and pronunciations; a clear grasp of the sense meaning of a passage and of the supplementary meanings that are implied but not stated; appreciative, imaginative and critical reactions to what is read; and the use or application of the ideas acquired.[1]

This is possibly as complete a definition of reading as can be found in professional literature, one that embraces the concepts that various authorities in the field have enunciated.

Stages in development. Because reading is such a complex task, it takes years for a child to master the skills that are involved, to mature to the successive levels necessary for doing the kinds of thinking that are demanded when reading increasingly difficult materials. Experts in reading have studied the course of child development and the stages through which children pass as they gradually progress toward the level where they can read efficiently and easily. A description of the successive stages follows.

The first stage is that of being prepared to learn to read, or *initial reading readiness.* In order to attain this stage, the young child must gain a multitude of experiences, acquire a sizable vocabulary and control over sentences, develop con-

[1] William S. Gray, "Improving Reading Programs," *Education,* LXXI (May, 1951), p. 536.

siderable auditory discrimination so that he hears sounds in words accurately and speaks them precisely, learn to enunciate well, improve in muscular coordination and the ability to see objects quite close to the eyes, and build up an interest in looking at books and listening to stories. Varied types of growth and experience are needed if the child is to become ready to learn to read.

In the second stage, the child receives his *initial instruction* —first through the use of chalkboard, charts, labels, and other teacher-prepared materials, in addition to commercially prepared introductory materials. Gradually the child learns to start at the left of the top line, to read from the left and from top to bottom; he acquires a growing stock of words he knows at sight because he has often seen them in meaningful situations. Always he gains meaning from everything he reads. Eventually he is ready to read from the first simple little readers called preprimers, but still needs much supplemental reading from charts and the chalkboard.

Once having started this task of reading simple materials, the child passes into the third stage, that of *rapid progress* in mastering the basic reading skills. On the basis of a constantly increasing sight vocabulary, the pupil learns varied ways of figuring out new words for himself and can read materials of appropriate difficulty fluently and comprehendingly, with due appreciation and enjoyment. During this stage, the child progresses through primers, then first and second readers—sometimes at corresponding grade levels but, for slow-developing pupils, in a higher grade than the label on the reader indicates. During this period of rapid progress, most of the reading materials deal with activities and experiences familiar to the typical child and are phrased in the language customary in the speech of children his age (short sentences using familiar words).

Next, the pupil progresses into the fifth stage in which he refines the skills which he has been using in a relatively crude and rudimentary way. In this period of *refinement,* he learns to adjust his way of reading to the difficulty of the materials and to his purpose for reading (he may skim, read casually, peruse carefully, or actually study); he gradually masters the techniques of outlining and summarizing simple selections; he learns to use efficiently books of different kinds, such as parallel readings, reference books like the dictionary and encyclopedias, and various kinds of textbooks; his silent and oral reading becomes smoother; he uses the several techniques of word analysis with considerable ease and effectiveness.

At the two successive stages that normally fall in the junior and senior high school years, pupils become increasingly evaluative and critical. They mature to the stage where they can, under proper guidance, learn to follow the thread of thought in complex and detailed accounts; they can read in depth so that they see the underlying significance of statements and note bias or lack of proof in them; they can organize their readings from several sources into one well-organized report; they begin to feel true appreciation for artistic writing.

Goals of reading instruction. For each stage in reading development, there are specific aims to be accomplished. These will be developed in the chapters to follow. The general aims common to all stages in reading instruction are these:

1. To stimulate strong motives for, and lasting interests in, reading for both enlightenment and entertainment
2. To help children to understand and appreciate more and more the place and values of reading in a world where mass media are so prominent
3. To enrich and extend children's experiences through their

reading abundantly materials suited to their maturity, learning capacity, and background

4. To promote interests and tastes that will induce children to become habitual readers of better types of reading materials in books, bulletins, and periodicals
5. To provide measures for determining and building reading readiness at each successive stage in the reading program
6. To build habits and skills that will permit efficient reading of all the varieties of reading materials that children will meet throughout life
7. To teach children to use books and other study aids effectively in their independent endeavors

Kinds of reading activities. As has already been shown, reading is thinking the thoughts that some writer is communicating to his readers by way of the written or printed word. In most reading activities, ideas are the central concern; but there is need for some lessons for developing and improving reading skills as such, for instance, in learning how to find the main idea in a paragraph or to make an outline of a lengthy passage. In this section of the chapter will appear a brief discussion of activities concerned with (1) reading to get information and to seek enjoyment, and (2) training to improve a specific reading skill. Such activities may be either silent or oral.

At the readiness stage of reading, there is much listening. The teacher reads directly from a delightful book or tells the story as she displays the pictures in it. She reads verse and helps the children enjoy the rhymes, alliteration, and rhythm. On the chalkboard and on labels respectively, she records the children's plans and gives credit for their contributions to the bulletin board or the science center. At this stage, children do not actually read but they do become aware that printed or written words can convey the same meanings as the words they are accustomed to hearing and speaking. There should be a reading corner where children can sit and browse through picture books and "read" each story by means of looking at the pictures. Such activities build a desire to read and also make reading seem a meaningful process.

At the stages of initial instruction and rapid progress (normally first and second grades), the teacher continues to read and tell many stories to her pupils and to make liberal use of the chalkboard, bulletin board, and charts. The pupils themselves begin to read under her close guidance. In the introductory lessons, the reading activities include the following: conversation and discussion by the pupils that will eventually be pulled together into a chart story as the pupils dictate sentences to the teacher; this they later read, sentence by sentence, in response to guiding questions by the teacher. She similarly guides the children's reading of sentences in simple reading books. In all cases, the children listen to the question, read the corresponding sentence or sentences *silently*, then read orally. Always there is silent reading of a passage *before* it is read orally.

At the period of rapid progress, children are similarly guided, not sentence by sentence, but by units of increasing length. They still should read silently before trying to read any part orally. In fact, there are many lessons in which all the reading is silent, the teacher's check-up being by means of discussion or dramatization. Sometimes parts or all of a story will be read orally on the day following the silent reading lesson. Parallel to such silent and oral reading is instruction in word-attack skills so that children can acquire the ability to read independently in both textbooks and library books.

During the upper primary and middle-grade years, there is still considerable guidance in reading. Before reading stories in their readers, the pupils will engage in discussion on their pertinent experiences and will give close attention to the teacher's introductory questions that are designed to promote understanding and appreciation of the story. Often she will present new words in a preliminary phrase drill so as to prevent the pupils' being balked by unidentifiable vocabulary as they read. In handling very difficult materials, she will have them read a selection a little at a time, and will preface the reading of each part with a guiding question. Such carefully guided lessons are called *directed reading*.

Too, there may be specific *training lessons* in which the pupils are taught how to use an index, select the main idea or the topic sentence in each of several paragraphs, identify the three or four main ideas in an entire selection, make an outline or a summary, use the dictionary for each of the several purposes it can serve, use contextual clues, make efficient use of the topical headings in their textbooks, read graphs and maps, and utilize all suitable study aids. Reading as a tool subject needs training lessons.

Along with lessons that feature guidance and instruction in specific reading skills should come many opportunities to read simpler materials independently for *recreational* purposes. Such reading is individual, self-selected, enjoyable, fluent, because the child is following his personal tastes, and because the books and selections are simple enough for him to read without any outside guidance. Of course, recreational reading materials can be informational as well as entertaining.

As pupils read these relatively simple materials that they enjoy most, they will find many materials they wish to share with their fellows through oral reading. Here we find genuine *audience situations* in which the oral reader offers something unfamiliar to his listeners and thus is assured of their interest. It is possible, however, to have audience situations by reading from a story in a basal reader; for example, a pupil may read aloud some portion which a group of his listeners will pantomime. Such oral reading must be well prepared in several preparatory silent readings to insure familiarity and fluency and there may possibly be an additional oral rehearsal (if the materials present any difficulty in interpretation or enunciation). In the elementary school, few pupils are able to do *sight reading* in which they effectively read at sight materials they have never seen before. Unless passages are read silently ahead of time, the pupils may read haltingly without due attention to the ideas and mood to be stressed in their oral reading.

Interrelationships among the language arts. Effective reading instruction takes advantage of the relationships among the four language arts: listening, speaking, reading, and written language. In the first place, there are sequential relationships inasmuch as the language arts develop in a definite order: The child first learns to listen, then to speak, later to read, eventually to write. Each form of communication in turn forms the basis for learning the one to follow. By the age of seven, most children have made a good beginning in learning the four language arts; but, even so, teachers of older pupils should still keep in mind the sequence in which listening and speaking should precede reading or in which these three language arts ought to precede writing. For instance, before pupils can read comprehendingly materials in a completely new field of knowledge, they should have an opportunity to *listen to and talk over* introductory ideas that will help them interpret the unfamiliar concepts they are to meet in their reading. Or, before they attempt to write on topics that are still quite new to them, they should *read* abundantly and then discuss (*talk about* and *listen to*) the ideas so as to round out and organize them. Poor reading and poor writing often result from too little preparatory listening and discussion before work begins.

There are also important working, or functional, relationships among the language arts. Listening, for instance, is basic to learning to read. As the infant looks at, listens to, smells, tastes, and handles the things that surround him, he builds up a large store of ideas. It is through listening that he learns the words to attach to his experiences and then how to fashion these words into sentences. Important, too, is auditory discrimination, the ability to hear correctly the sounds that make up words. Unless a child hears the differences between words like *pig* and *peg* or *burr* and *purr*, he will have difficulty in using phonics to figure out new words he meets in his reading. Listening provides the vocabulary, the sentence patterns, and the auditory discrimination that build a foundation for reading.

The service of speaking to reading is much the same. In early lessons in reading, the words should be those that are already in the pupil's speech. The sentence patterns must be those that the child uses in his speaking; otherwise he is likely to be blocked in trying to read. If he never says sentences in reverse order, as "Away to the house ran Jimmy," he is likely to have great difficulty in trying to read this, or any, inverted sentence. Too, if the child pronounces or enunciates words incorrectly, he may have trouble in recognizing the printed word. How can he learn to read easily such words as *mother* and *like* if he says *muvvah* and *wike?* Typically, the preschool child learns to tell his experiences and to narrate stories in good order, and thus builds a basis for following the sequence of events in stories he reads. Unless he does think and talk sequentially, he can hardly be expected to follow the sequence of ideas in the stories in a preprimer.

The place of reading in the general curriculum. Reading is used as a tool subject as children read in the various curricular fields: lessons in the content subjects, words for songs, labels and directions in art, or instructions and problems in arithmetic. One function of reading instruction, then, is to prepare pupils to read informational materials. There should be training lessons to help them acquire the skills peculiar to reading in each subject—possibly in the period devoted to reading, more often in the time devoted to teaching each particular subject. Each curricular field has its own special vocabulary, its own way of thinking, its own type of organization.

But reading activities should do more than build skills in study and reading in each of the curricular fields. Various books in the library afford background for informational lessons: biography, travel, true adventure stories, historical fiction, and newspapers in social studies; nature lore and periodicals in science; encyclopedias for general information. It is such reading that enriches the content and builds interest in lessons in all subjects. Reading instruction serves to build work-study skills; individual reading takes advantage of these skills and makes the whole curriculum come alive.

Organization of the reading program. Basically, child development determines the proper organization of the reading program. In the first place, child development is *sequential,* and consequently the reading program is organized into stages that roughly correspond: initial reading readiness, initial instruction, rapid progress, and finally increasing efficiency and refinement. These stages are largely concerned with the sequential development of skills in reading; but children's interests, too, affect the sequence of the reading program. For example, the interests of a young child revolve about the real, live things in his immediate environment; but nine-year-olds like factual accounts that concern past time and distant places. Girls and boys in the early primary grades generally agree in their reading tastes; while older children disagree quite widely, they still have many significant tastes in common.

Even though children pass through the same successive stages of development, they are characterized by *individual differences* in rate and level of growth; the reading program is likewise organized in terms of individual differences. Pupils who are bright, quick-developing, and richly experienced are ready for reading sooner than are their duller, slow-developing, less experienced classmates; the former typically progress through the successive stages in reading much more rapidly than the latter. Therefore, some pupils should be introduced to book reading sooner than others; at each grade level, there must be a variety of reading materials so that each child can find materials of suitable difficulty. Differences in reading tastes also demand many types of books so that each child can find those books that appeal most to him.

Because the general pattern of child development is basically similar, it is possible for the reading program to provide for *group instruction;* but, because there are significant individual differences, there must also be a measure of *individualized teaching.* In crowded classrooms with large enrollments, it is economical of the teacher's time and effort for her to assemble her pupils into groups that are at approximately the same stage in their reading achievement, that have similar instructional needs, or that share similar interests. For instance, several children may be ready to read at the second-reader level at the same time, or may need help in syllabifying long words, or may like animal stories. In the course of a week, the same pupil may be in several different groups: in Billy's group in the reading lesson proper, in a special group that needs help in noting the *s, ed,* and *ing* endings on words like *help* and *work* (these children may be in different reading groups), in a quartet that is working on a dramatization of "The Three Bears," and in a still different group which is using its free time to read through the experience charts that have been developed during the semester.

As a teacher works with her pupils in groups, she will be aware of the individual differences. She will note that Bobby has difficulty with *went;* that Molly shows evidence of noticing that *back* begins with the same letter as do the familiar words *big, boy,* and *baby;* or that Jill is suddenly making very rapid progress and should be shifted to a more advanced group. Bobby is asked to read several sentences that contain *went;* Molly is encouraged to notice other beginning sounds now that she shows an awakening awareness of word similarities; Jill is given a few days of experience in the early pages of the reader used by the advanced group before she is shifted (she and a member of that group sit together and read cooperatively).

Some reading instruction is completely individualized. Each day there may be an afternoon free-reading period in which each pupil selects a book of suitable difficulty and appeal. Some expert teachers manage to do all their reading instruction individually by making detailed plans with their pupils so that every child will have a definite reading task to do, while the teacher calls one at a time to discuss the stories that have been read silently and hears some oral reading. These skilled teachers, however, find opportunities for group instruction as pupils read aloud to several classmates, as a number of children show need for help on the same reading skill, or as several pursue interests they hold in common.

Probably no reading program should be conducted always in groups or always by individual instruction. A good program is balanced, varied in approach, adjusted to the children's current needs and interests. Children like to work together in groups; they appreciate and profit from individual instruction whenever it is especially needed.

Summary

Reading is the process that enables a reader to think the thoughts of a writer, to experience vicariously with him; it is a useful tool for other subjects in the curriculum; it is a useful element in real living. In learning to read in mature and efficient ways, the child passes through a series of developmental stages, each with its particular goals that are consistent with the general goals of building skills, developing interests and tastes, as well as broadening and deepening each reader's experiences. In the elementary school, all materials are read silently before a pupil attempts to read orally; there should be no sight reading, except by the most able pupils in the middle grades who may be able to read comparatively simple passages on sight. There should be much recreational reading; but all pupils need direct instruction in essential reading skills that enable them to use books efficiently and to read independently. Since children vary in intelligence, general background, and rate of development, the reading program must provide for individual differences by pacing instruction, providing a variety of materials, and giving a certain amount of individual instruction. Learnings in each of the language arts reinforce learnings in the others, listening and speaking being especially important in building a background for intelligent, purposeful reading—not only in reading classes but in the work-study reading activities throughout the curriculum.

Selected References

(* recommended)

*ANDERSON, IRVING, and DEARBORN, WALTER. *Psychology of Teaching Reading*. New York: Ronald Press, 1952. Pp. 203–94.

*Association for Supervision and Curriculum Development. "Research Helps in Teaching the Language Arts." Washington, D.C.: National Education Association, 1955.

*BURTON, WILLIAM H. *Reading in Child Development*. Indianapolis; Bobbs-Merrill Co., 1956. Pp. 5–165, 587–94.

*GRAY, WILLIAM S. "Objectives for the New Reading Program," *The Evaluation of Reading*. Chicago: University of Chicago Press, 1958. Pp. 9–14.

HARRIS, ALBERT J. *How to Increase Reading Ability*. New York: David McKay Co., Inc., 1961, Pp. 63–84.

HEILMAN, ARTHUR W. *Principles and Practices of Teaching Reading*. Columbus, Ohio: Charles E. Merrill Books, Inc., 1961. Pp. 1–19.

HILDRETH, GERTRUDE. *Teaching Reading*. New York: Holt, Rinehart and Winston, 1958. Pp. 1–14, 64–82.

*MCCULLOUGH, CONSTANCE. "Changing Concepts of Reading Instruction," in *International Reading Association Conference Proceedings*, Vol. 6: *Changing Concepts of Reading Instruction*. New York: Scholastic Magazines, 1961. Pp. 13–22.

RUSSELL, DAVID H. *Children Learn to Read*. 2nd ed. Boston: Ginn and Co., 1961. Pp. 97–137, 141–66.

TINKER, MILES A., and MCCULLOUGH, CONSTANCE. *Teaching Elementary Reading*. New York: Appleton-Century-Crofts, Inc., 1962. Pp. 3–16.

YOAKAM, GERALD. *Basal Reading Instruction*. New York: McGraw-Hill Book Co., 1955. Pp. 77–90.

2

Reading and Child Development

FROM BIRTH THROUGH ADOLESCENCE, BOYS AND girls are growing and developing in their passage to maturity. The changes that are taking place have a strong influence on their progress in learning to read. If a child is a "slow-developer," this fact indicates that his eyes and motor coordination may not be fitted for the intricate movements of the reading act as soon as for his more rapidly developing classmates. If at six years of age a child is not yet at an equivalent mental age, he can scarcely be expected to launch into the reading program and to make as rapid progress as his classmates who have a higher mental age. All aspects of his growth and development have a strong influence on his potential success in learning to read. The reading program, therefore, must be closely geared to the child's course of general development.

General Relationships

Teachers need to understand the nature of individual differences in children and the need for adjusting the reading program to the varying developmental patterns of the pupils in their care. On the other hand, they need to realize that children are much more alike than they are different and that there are general policies and procedures suitable for use with all children—possibly at different times and at varying rates of progress.

Reading as part of the general growth pattern. Psychologists have established the fact that children's growth tends to be unified; that is, the curves of growth for physical, mental, emotional, and social functions tend to rise or level off together. Usually a child's developmental curves are high in all aspects of growth, average in all, or consistently low. As would be expected, the curve of reading achievement falls within the general area of a child's total pattern of growth. This shows that a child's progress in reading is strongly influenced by the forces that determine his over-all course of development. There is an occasional child whose growth curves fan out, whose growth is uneven. This child is likely to be one of the pupils who adjusts poorly to the educational program.

Teachers can profit greatly from knowing details of the pupil's preschool history. If a child has been late in learning to walk and to talk, slow in dentition, and retarded in developing a hand preference, he may well prove to be slow in manifesting reading readiness and in acquiring the various skills demanded in reading. We should not consider this slow-developing child a remedial case. Rather, he should be given a very gradual approach to the step-by-step program in reading and may normally learn in third grade what his more precocious classmates learned with ease in first grade. Every child should advance in reading at his own rate and according to his general pattern of growth; but he should stay with his own age group if he is to develop good social traits and to be well adjusted emotionally. The curriculum should be shaped to the child, not the child to a fixed curriculum.

Sex differences. In general, girls mature more rapidly and earlier than boys. At birth, girls are several months ahead of boys on the average, and, at the age for entering first grade, six-year-old girls are about a year more advanced in their physiological maturation than boys are. This advantage has grown to almost two years by the time the pupils reach sixth-grade age. Boys, therefore, tend to be slower in all language functions and may be ready for the introduction to the various phases of reading at a somewhat later age than girls are. This fact should not be overemphasized, however, since a rapid-growing boy of high intelligence and excellent home background may be a leader in the most advanced reading group in his class.

Individual differences. Every parent or teacher knows that children vary in height, weight, and rate of physical growth. There are similar differences in school learnings. It would be a miracle if all the children in any single class were ready for reading instruction at the same time and were to continue to progress together. Individual differences are a nature-ordained fact, not only because of inborn variations but also because children have different experiences and develop different interests.

In the accompanying graph, the relationship between chronological age and reading age is shown. Data for girls and boys have been recorded separately. The first fact revealed by the graph is that individual differences tend to increase with age. Six-year-old boys, for example, range from a reading age of six to almost ten years, while eleven-year-olds vary from about seven to seventeen years in reading age; that is, a range of four years has grown to one of about ten years.

A comparison of the reading ages of boys and girls brings out further facts. The slower-growing girls at each age level (see the left of each bar) are less retarded than boys of the same age; but the fast-advancing boys tend to have a higher

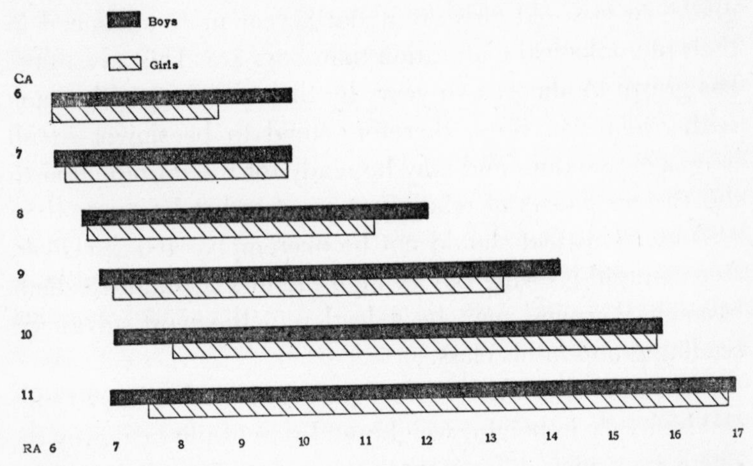

Range in Reading Achievement of Boys and Girls at Various Chronological Age Levels. (Adapted from Anderson and Dearborn, *The Psychology of Teaching Reading*. Copyright, 1952, The Ronald Press Company.)

reading achievement than the most advanced girls. It is evident, then, that girls are less variable than boys: slow-developing girls at any particular age tend to be less retarded than their boy peers and precocious girls likewise to be less advanced. It is apparent that sex differences are much smaller than individual differences among children, regardless of sex.

In these facts lie several implications for reading. (1) Every teacher should expect the pupils in her group to vary in reading achievement, and to be reading at different levels. Probably more of the boys will be in the slow-advancing groups. (2) Middle-grade teachers should plan to use primary methods and very simple materials for their less mature pupils. (3) No remedial program can "bring an immature pupil up to grade" in his reading, since his pattern of growth has ordained that he should normally learn his reading skills later than his more rapidly maturing classmates. (4) Every classroom needs a wide variety of reading materials so that each pupil can read at his current level of advancement.

Psychologists have confirmed the fact that child growth is sometimes uneven. It is possible for an occasional bright child to make somewhat slow progress in learning to read because he is immature in other ways. If no "fuss" is made over his retardation and if he is allowed to move along at a natural rate, this child is very likely to develop into an excellent reader before he reaches high school. "Accept each child as he is and help him to progress at his natural rate of development" should be the slogan of every teacher.

Specific Relationships

Certain phases of physical, intellectual, social, and emotional development strongly affect the child's chances of success in learning to read.

Physical development. Motor coordination plays an important part in the act of reading. The child must be able to focus his eyes on the words he is reading; he must be able to follow the line of print and to make a return sweep to the beginning of the next one. The very young child has made a beginning toward such abilities as he learns to make his two eyes work together and to turn them in the direction he wishes to look. In reading, such movements are very small and call for very fine coordination of small muscles.

Eye-hand coordination, too, is important. Through it, the

child learns to reach accurately for the objects he sees, to place his crayon or paintbrush at the spot where he wishes it to be, and to gain control over eye movements that enable his following a line of print.

Another crucial phase of physical development is the change in the eye as the infant grows into childhood. In the early years, the eyeball is relatively flat and the child consequently farsighted. It becomes more rounded as he grows into his school years; the child is consequently less farsighted, and his eyes gain the ability to do the close work demanded in reading. Somewhere between the ages of six and ten, the typical child's eyes attain the roundness that permits reading from books without undue eyestrain. Slow-developing children may have difficulty in reading from books all through first grade because of eyestrain caused by their continuing farsightedness. The large size of the print in first-grade reading materials helps to compensate for this deficiency; the gradual reduction in the size of print in subsequent books at higher grade levels is in line with child maturation.

Intellectual development, including language. The child grows as a whole. Until maturity is reached, his intellectual, or mental, age thus progresses with his chronological age. The hypothetical "average" child of six years has a mental age of six, while his duller six-year-old classmate is less than six mentally and his brighter companion of the same age has a mental age of seven or more. Many authorities in reading believe that a mental age of six or six and a half is very advantageous in promoting reading readiness. For one thing, the attention span of a relatively mature child tends to be longer than average and is favorable to learning.

Another phase of intellectual growth is concerned with the child's mastery of language. The infant listens to the words of his companions and learns to associate meaning with their speech; at the same time, his babbling is leading to control over his vocal organs so that he can form the sounds that make up the words he wants to say. Thus is language born. Before entering kindergarten or first grade, the child has progressed far: he knows and uses a large stock of words; he strings them into meaningful sentences; he typically can enunciate and pronounce most of his words clearly and correctly; and he can follow the sequence of ideas in a story or a recounted even he himself is relating or to which he is listening. Except for very dull or foreign-language-speaking children, most pupils in first grade have advanced far enough in their language growth to be ready to learn to read—so far as language development determines such readiness. (An extremely barren or an unhappy home life may occasionally retard language development and interfere with the acquisition of reading readiness.) In later school years, too, a child's language mastery is a factor in deciding how well he can read. If the vocabulary and sentence structure in reading materials vary widely from his customary usage, he may fail to comprehend and may experience considerable difficulty in attacking his reading tasks.

Intellectual interests, too, show a typical pattern of development and are factors in deciding an appropriate reading program. Preferences for literature change. For instance, the very young pupils' liking for talking beast stories, like "The Three Bears," and accumulative tales, such as "The Little Red Hen," soon disappears. Likewise the penchant for tales of fantasy, like "The Elves and the Shoemaker," which upper primary children feel, lasts but a year or two. On the other hand, stories about truly lifelike animals have a constant appeal through the years. It is such facts about children's interests that teachers should know and utilize in the reading program.

Social development. In kindergarten and first grade, children are naturally egocentric, preoccupied with "me and mine." Among their developmental tasks are learning to share, to take turns, and to assume responsibilities set up by group living. These children observe the adults about them, imitate their behavior and, through dramatic play, identify themselves with the activities of their elders. Much of their informal reading (found on chalkboard and charts) features these social learnings; many of the stories they hear or read should concern children like themselves, children who are learning developmental tasks like their own.

From these egocentric and adult-imitating characteristics, children gradually pass into a phase where "otherness" is more prominent, where the approval of one's peers is more important than the opinion of adults, where clubs and gangs are typical, where the child strives to evade the domination of adults, where he seeks the privilege of independent thinking and action. In years to come, these children as adolescents resume the characteristic interest in adults: they look discerningly at their grown-up associates, select the ideals and behavior that appeal to them, and assimilate into their personalities and conduct those characteristics that have made the deepest impression. As children pass from one phase of their social development to the next, they tend to like the stories that reflect their current stage of social growth. On the progressing road of reading, the children learn to like tales of clubs, scouting, camping, adventure, heroic exploits, lives of social service and civic leadership, and successful home life.

Sex differences influence children's choices in literature. In young children there is little or no variation based on being a boy or a girl. However, differences do appear and grow during the later primary and intermediate grades. Girls like fantasy, sentiment, and mild adventure, while boys prefer the realities of science and history or the rough-and-tumble kind of adventure stories.

Emotional development. The relationships between reading and a child's emotional development are influenced by his basic needs: security, status, approval, and affection. To children and their parents, school is a place where girls and boys learn to read. Success in his reading endeavors leads to the child's feeling of security or status among his fellows. Success brings approval from parents and his teacher and assures him of affection within his family circle, an assurance he might lack if his parents were to show strong concern for, and disapproval of his lack of progress in learning to read well.

It is important, then, that the program in reading be constantly adapted to each child's capacity to learn, his current readiness for learning reading skills, and his special interests. The pupil who "takes to reading" and makes steady and rapid progress will develop favorable attitudes toward reading, feel secure in his reading endeavors, achieve status among the members of his group, and receive the approval of his family and teacher. The slow-developing child, too, can be fully as favored if he is introduced to his reading tasks gradually but steadily, if he feels that he is attaining mastery and is making progress, if he knows success at his level. Then he will feel secure, confident, successful, sure of his family's approval and affection. On the other hand, if his parents and teacher put on pressure in an attempt to make him keep with his more mature and gifted classmates, the slow-developing child may grow to dislike reading, to become worried or defiant or withdrawn. He is on the way to becoming a remedial case, something he need not be.

The young child is dependent on his elders. One of his

developmental tasks is to work toward personal independence, toward the ability and the privilege of making his own decisions and acting for himself. Learning to read is part of this process of attaining self-sufficiency. As the child acquires a sizable sight vocabulary, gains skills in figuring out unfamiliar words for himself, and learns to abstract essential meanings from printed materials, he is truly gaining independence and self-assurance. He is performing his basic developmental task of becoming a person on his own.

Reading can be of further aid in a child's emotional life. Every child has problems of his own, issues he must meet. Sometimes he is confused. He may find a book or a story that deals with this problem and helps in the solution of his own. His life may seem somewhat tame; books will give him vicarious adventures. He may have difficulty in building a system of sound values and setting his life goals; in books he may find an enunciation of ideals, an account of heroic and altruistic deeds that will help him formulate his own life purposes. There is such a thing as bibliotherapy, or the use of books to solve personality difficulties and to help build a system of worthy ideals.

Summary

A child's progress in learning to read is generally parallel to his pattern of growth curves. While the growth and development of some children are uneven, typically his developmental curves rise, fall, or even out together. Growth that begins slowly tends to continue to be slow; a precocious beginning usually indicates that a child will develop at an accelerated rate. Consequently, differences between individuals tend to increase with age during the period of childhood and early adolescence; and the reading program must be sufficiently varied to suit the widening differences in children as they progress through school.

Physically, it is important that the child's eyes have lost their farsightedness, which is characteristic of the flattened eyeballs of the preschool child, and that he has learned to coordinate his eye movements. Intellectually, the child builds up a store of concepts and a mastery of oral language that will form a background for learning to read; and his interest will expand from egocentricity to civic interests in community and world-wide affairs. A child's success in learning to read is intimately related to his feelings of security and status, or to the lack of them.

Selected References

(* recommended)

ANDERSON, IRVING, and DEARBORN, WALTER. *Psychology of Teaching Reading.* New York: Ronald Press, 1952. Pp. 3–49.

*GANS, ROMA, *et al. Teaching Young Children.* Yonkers, N.Y.: World Book Co., 1952. Pp. 16–50.

HARRIS, ALBERT J. "Reading and Human Development," in *Development in and through Reading,* Sixtieth Yearbook, Part I, National Society for the Study of Education. Chicago: University of Chicago Press, 1961. Pp. 17–34.

HAVIGHURST, ROBERT J. *Human Development and Education.* New York: Longmans, Green and Co., 1953. Selected pages.

HERRICK, VIRGIL, and JACOBS, LELAND. *Children and the Language Arts.* Englewood Cliffs, N.J.: Prentice-Hall, 1955. Chapter IV.

*HILDRETH, GERTRUDE. *Readiness for School Beginners.* Yonkers, N.Y.: World Book Co., 1950. Pp. 19–41.

Language Arts for Today's Children (Commission on the English Curriculum of the National Council of Teachers of English.) New York: Appleton-Century-Crofts, Inc., 1954. Chapter II.

LODGE, WILLIAM J. "Developmental Characteristics of Childhood Related to the Language Arts Curriculum," *Elementary English* (February, 1953), pp. 106–15.

RUSSELL, DAVID H. *Children Learn to Read.* 2nd ed. Boston: Ginn and Co., 1961. Pp. 69–93.

3

Children's Interests and Tastes in Reading

WHILE IT IS IMPORTANT THAT CHILDREN LEARN to read, it is fully as important that they *do read* voluntarily and appreciatively. It is only as people turn to newspapers, periodicals, bulletins, and books for information and pleasure that the ultimate goals of reading instruction have been reached, especially if the choices of reading matter reflect good taste and discrimination. Radio and television are strong rivals of printed sources for facts and enjoyable activity; yet books have something to offer in the way of depth and contemplative search for the truth that only they can give. We want our children to like to read worth-while types of materials regularly.

Under what circumstances do children come to enjoy reading? What are the factors that will exert a favorable influence in building reading interests and developing desirable tastes? What kinds of materials appeal to children at successive age levels, of different sexes and native ability, from various types of homes and neighborhoods? It is such questions that this chapter is designed to answer.

Underlying Needs and Interests of Children

Fundamental personality needs. Psychologists identify four basic needs felt by children and adults alike. These are those of security, status, affection, and independence. In whatever way reading can help to satisfy these needs, it serves a child well. Whenever a child's reading experiences bring him insecurity, loss of status, disapproval, and a feeling of personal inadequacy, they do him harm.

To meet these basic needs, learning to read must be a successful experience. Only then can a child feel secure and hold status among his fellows; can he expect approval from his teacher, his classmates, his parents; is he able to read for himself. Thus success in reading can meet basic human needs if the materials are suitable in topic (interesting in content and treatment) and difficulty. On the contrary, any child who tries to read materials unsuited to his abilities and interests will tend to feel insecure because he lacks the ability to work successfully by himself and does not have the approval of either himself or his companions; consequently he lacks status. A liking for reading results only as it serves to meet his basic needs through satisfying successful reading activities.

Developmental interests in literature. While pupils in any group will vary in their preferences for reading materials, an underlying similarity in their interests is still likely. This is true because there is a general developmental pattern in the waxing and waning of children's preferences for literature.

Children in kindergarten and first grade tend to enjoy stories of children like themselves whose activities and problems with playmates, pets, and toys resemble their own.

They like realism. Investigations of decades ago indicated that these young children do not care for fantasy because reality is so wonderful in itself that they cannot discriminate between the true and the make-believe. However, more recent studies show that these children do enjoy fantasy and are not especially likely to be confused, probably because television and radio have broadened their knowledge of the real world and because many children travel widely and share their knowledge with their peers. Besides, they hear and view many programs featuring fanciful tales. There seems to be little likelihood that they will become confused. They do like stories with "talking beasts," swift action, suspense, the humor of the physically ludicrous (an unexpected fall or a cow that says, "Bow-wow"), and the repetition of phrases in an accumulative tale. Picture books have a special place in the classroom, since young children get very favorable attitudes toward reading as they follow the story by looking at the pictures and gradually pick up the ability to read the simple text.

At seven or eight, tales that feature fairies, elves, giants, pixies, and brownies begin to have appeal. Recent studies of children's preferences for reading materials show that pupils in grades three to five enjoy fables and fairy stories. There is a shift to myths, legends, and hero and folk stories in grades five to seven. Arbuthnot believes that the readers gain feelings of security from fanciful tales where the good are always rewarded, the bad punished; where there is an underlying universal truth and where justice prevails.

According to recent investigations, children in grades four to eight turn to mystery, recreation, and sports, and manifest less enjoyment in reading cowboy and fairy stories.

In the middle grades, the liking for fantasy turns to tall tales such as those about Paul Bunyan or Pecos Bill. The preadolescent gets a "real kick" out of the exaggeration and impossibility of such tales. At the same time, he likes to get acquainted with actual people and places far away—in both time and space; that is, books of travel and biography or history that are dramatically told have great appeal. Stories that feature adventure, lively action, and animal characters have steady appeal through the years of the elementary school.

The upper-grade child begins to establish the interests of his lifetime. The diversity of the intermediate-grade child's reading tends to narrow down to individually preferred types: adventure, travel, biography, mystery, detective stories, or the classics—whatever has been proving most satisfying in earlier years. There is increasing interest, too, in political and civic problems, patriotic themes, vocations, and hobbies. Fiction that features adventure and mystery continues to be a favorite.

While the reading interests of boys and of girls are parallel to a considerable degree, differences begin to appear in the primary grades and increase as the children progress into junior high school. While both sexes like adventure stories, girls reject the violence and bloody struggles that may appeal to boys. All children enjoy animal stories; but girls prefer books about domestic animals and pets and do not care for stories that feature the fierce wild beasts about which boys like to read. Children of both sexes seek out books about human characters but girls do not want the children in the stories to be younger than themselves, and boys prefer not to read stories about girls.

In some ways, girls and boys differ greatly in their likes and dislikes. Girls prefer stories of home and school life, love and romance, sentiment, and the supernatural. They avoid accounts that feature bitter conflict, violence, and goriness;

at the same time, boys do not care for love and romance, sentiment, fairy stories, or physical weakness. The latter do like accounts of physical struggle, hero tales, sports and games, humor, and the factual accounts of history and science—in particular modern tales about space ships, motors, and atomic devices.

Factors That Influence Reading Interests and Tastes

While, in the large, the patterns of child development determine what will interest children at successive age levels, there are other factors that help to influence individual choices of reading matter. The amount and kind of reading characteristic of the members of a child's family help to color his preferences and even more to decide how well he will like to read. If there is little reading done in the home, if there are actual statements of indifference or dislike for reading made there, he is likely to be predisposed to dislike reading. Of course, favorable attitudes equally can be a good influence.

Another potent factor in determining a child's preferences for reading is the accessibility or availability of books. A home or a classroom that offers an abundance of varied reading materials gives the child an opportunity to sample liberally and to build up preferences that are best suited to him personally; but if materials are not varied or are scarce, then he cannot sample sufficiently and may develop narrow interests far below his potential. Too, there must be school time regularly available for individual free reading.

The nature of the school curriculum may also be a force in determining what children select and enjoy in their reading. An interesting unit in the social studies or science may call for outside reading that proves so intriguing that the most interested readers will look for more books along the same line. A trip to the public library may be necessary and there the rich and varied offerings may induce the pupil visitor to become a regular card-carrying patron. A barren curriculum, on the contrary, can fail miserably to bring about enjoyable and fruitful supplementary reading.

The teacher herself is almost surely an important factor in determining whether children like to read and whether they will habitually turn to reading as a form of recreation and a source of information. If she is ever on the alert for "the right book for the right child" and deliberately but tactfully brings it to his attention, she may make of almost every pupil an avid reader. It is essential that she tailor each recommendation to the reading achievement-level and established interests of each child. No one enjoys reading a book that is extremely difficult for him; nor will anyone enjoy reading regularly books that are far too easy. The teacher should read parts aloud, tell enticing excerpts, and in many other ways use "teasers" that will pique the pupils' interest. Her own obvious and *genuine* enthusiasm for personal reading, as well as her enjoyment of the juvenile books, is likely to be contagious. Interests are very often caught, never forced, seldom taught explicitly.

In the middle and upper grades, pupils are much concerned about the approval of their peers. Consequently these children's interests and tastes in reading are strongly influenced by the recommendations of their classmates. The most potent recommendation for a story that the writers have experienced came from Alfred, a rather reluctant and retarded reader in sixth grade. He had found, in a magazine supplied by the teacher, an exciting and humorous story about a bear cub. He read it with evident relish and then wrote his opinion on the margin (as had been suggested): "Boy! This is swell!" As the result of Alfred's chuckling and enthusiastic recommendation, the magazine was hustled from hand to hand and this story became the "story of the month."

Children's outside activities and interests also do much to guide their reading selection. Ward and his pal in eighth grade spent their spare time working with their chemistry sets; their favorite reading was the chemistry textbook that a sister had brought home after her freshman year in college. Freddie was interested in guns, and thoroughly enjoyed poring over the relevant pages of a mail-order catalog. Douglas began to collect caterpillars; consequently he sought out every science book and encyclopedia in the school so as to find out about their life cycle, life habitats, and eating habits. Soon he knew exactly the kind of leaves to feed each kind of caterpillar he had collected.

Are radio, movies, and television taking time and interest away from reading? Possibly, sometimes. Yet various library surveys have shown that there have been more book withdrawals, a greater maturity of choice in areas where television has newly come. Librarians cannot supply the demand for books like *Peter Pan* or *Moby Dick* after the movie or television show featuring these books. Interests aroused by these forms of entertainment can and often do carry over into reading. On the other hand, cheaply sensational programs might not lead into reading, but take away from it.

The teacher's inventory. Knowing the factors that are operative in determining pupils' interests in reading, the teacher needs to make a study of which factors are most potent for each child and just what interests are being established. She will keep eyes and ears alert as she *observes* each child. During intermissions in the classroom and on the playground, what are his favorite topics of discussion? What does he bring to show his classmates? From the wealth of books, to which does he first turn? How prone is he to ask the recommendations of his classmates as he looks for something new to read?

Further inventory is possible if she makes a check list of the factors that determine the pupil's interest and *checks* each pupil off, point by point, as she *interviews* him. What parts of the newspaper does he read at home? What kinds of reading do his parents do? What magazines are taken at home? When choosing a book to read, what does he look for? Such are the points that may come up in the interview. (The check list may be carefully worded and written up in the form of a *questionnaire,* instead of a check list.) [1]

Much can be learned from the school library or the juvenile librarian in the public library as the teacher interviews her or checks through the list of *borrowings* on the part of her pupils. The trained librarian can, besides, suggest many titles similar to those that certain children are reading so that the teacher can help to confirm a budding preference or suggest books at a somewhat higher quality but of similar type.

Much can be learned incidentally through the pupils' *club work.* For example, as the teacher studies the significance of each member's offerings for "hobby club" programs, she may get much insight into what might be liked by a reluctant reader. She may also watch to see what type of stories appeal to "problem" pupils (indifferent to reading for themselves) as she reads parts of books that she believes to be easy enough and likely to have appeal for such pupils. Visits to the home and *conferences* with parents may also be enlightening.

[1] The check lists that follow are an adaptation in greatly curtailed form of a check list used by E. Culver *et al.* in studying the interests of many children in grades four through eight (Yolo County area, California). The original check list had a number of sections devoted to details of several of the subcategories in the check lists presented on the next two pages.

INVENTORY OF CHILDREN'S INTERESTS
(For younger pupils)

Put a plus (+) before the things you do most or like the most. Put a check (√) before those you do sometimes or like fairly well. Be ready to tell or write points that are not listed here.

1. *During the school year, what do you do at home?*

___ Play
 ___ By myself (what?)
 ___ With pets
 ___ With children (what?)
___ Watch TV
___ Listen to radio
___ Read
___ Study
___ Play an instrument
___ Help (how?)
Do what else? ___________
____

2. *What do you do in vacation?*

___ Play (what?)
___ Help (how?)
___ Travel
___ Go visiting
___ Read
___ Watch TV; listen to radio
___ Go to camp
___ Go to movies
___ Have water fun
Do what else? ___________

3. *What TV programs do you watch?*

___ Cartoons
___ Westerns
___ Comedies
___ Musicals
___ Family situations
___ Adventures
___ Detective stories
___ Science fiction
___ Travelogs
___ Fairy stories
___ Animal stories
Others ___________

4. *What do you like to read about?*

___ Pets
___ Wild animals
___ Other children
___ Fairies; giants
___ Funny happenings
___ Other lands; travel
___ History; famous people
___ Adventure
___ Mystery
___ Things to do
Others ___________

5. *What hobby do you enjoy?*

___ Collecting (what?)
___ Raising animals (what?)
___ Drawing; painting
___ Making models
___ Riding (what?)
___ Coloring
___ Gardening
___ Sports; games
___ Reading

What else? ___________________________

INVENTORY OF CHILDREN'S INTERESTS
(For older pupils)

Put a plus sign (+) before things you do most or like most.
Put a check mark (√) before things you do sometimes or like fairly well.
Put a minus sign (−) before those you do not care for.

1. *During the school year, what do you do outside school?*

___ Enjoy sports and games
  ___ Take part (what?)
  ___ Watch (what?)
___ Play indoor games (what?)
___ Build models
___ Sew
___ Cook
___ Garden
___ Read
___ Study
___ Watch TV
___ Listen to radio
___ Play on instrument
___ Draw; paint
___ Earn money (how?)

Do what else? ___________________________

2. *How do you spend vacations?*

___ Play; enjoy sports (what?)
___ Watch TV; listen to radio
___ Work away from home (what?)
___ Read
___ Help at home
___ Travel
___ Go visiting
___ Go to camp
___ Go to movies
___ Have water fun (what?). Do what else? ___________

3. *What TV programs do you enjoy?*

___ Sports	___ Family situations	___ Travelogs
___ Westerns	___ "Who-done-its"	___ Documentaries
___ Comedies	___ Science fiction	___ Adventures
___ Musicals	Others? ______	

4. *What do you like to read?*

___ Mysteries	___ Detective stories	___ Biography; history
___ Westerns	___ Animal stories	___ Travel
___ Adventure	___ Romance	___ Home; family
___ Tall tales	___ Humor ___ News	___ Comics
Others? ______		

5. *On the back, list the magazines you read. What parts?*

6. *What hobbies do you enjoy?*

___ Collecting (what?)	___ Raising animals	___ Creative writing
___ Gardening	___ Making models	___ Dramatics
___ Reading	___ Drawing; painting	___ Watching TV
___ Sports; games	___ Sewing; knitting	Others ______

Promoting Interests and Good Taste in Reading

Recent studies indicate that children do read voluntarily after they have learned to read for themselves, but that they tend to spend more time with television than with books. According to the San Francisco study, there is an increase in the amount of reading from grade one to grade six, girls in general doing more than boys do. On the average, children were found to read from one-half to an entire book per week. The combined study by Northwestern University and the Office of Education showed that children read about 1.1 hours daily, their choices being largely restricted to fiction and stories of famous people. Bright pupils read more than their classmates and watch television programs less. But how good are the books they are reading? This is a matter of real concern.

If a child's tastes have developed at a low level, what then can be done? Perhaps the experiences of shoppers can give some clues. In grocery stores, they frequently find a demonstrator who is offering free sampling of some newly devised food product. Children can similarly be given samplings of good books that they will almost surely like if they find out that such intriguing reading is available. Or consider the lady who is shopping for a dress and, in the process, tries on a beautifully tailored but simple gown of high-quality material. She is almost sure to find no cheaper model that is as chic or becoming as the more expensive dress. Her tastes have been elevated by her experience with high quality. In books, too, children are sensitive to the differences between trash and well-written stories, and they come to prefer books that represent a wholesome and realistic portrayal of life to the Horatio Alger or Diamond Dick type of literature. The availability of reading materials of suitable difficulty, with appealing topics and illustrations, and of skilled craftsmanship is one essential feature of a program designed to build interest in worth-while literature; measures for making children aware of these accessible materials are another essential. There follow suggestions on procedures for increasing accessibility and making pupils aware of the potentially appealing books which are available.

Making reading materials readily accessible. Pupils should be surrounded with books, varied in topic and difficulty, attractive in appearance. Each child should be able to leaf through a number of books and find just the right one for him. This means that (1) there must be an abundant and varied offering—many possible choices; (2) the classroom itself must provide shelving sufficient for numerous books at all times; and (3) there should be a reservoir of books upon which the classroom teacher may draw so that she can supplement her necessarily restricted set of classroom-contained books from a library or bookmobile, as well as check out fresh books to replace those it is time to return because the children have read the ones which interested them.

In making books available in attractive ways, the classroom may have a reading corner where a low table and chairs of proper size are placed near the book cupboard. Here any pupil may repair in his free time and read to his heart's content. Going to this corner should be considered a privilege. There may be the New Books Shelf where each week or fortnight a few new books may be displayed and offered for withdrawals; or it may be My Favorite Book Shelf where each child may take a turn in placing a well-liked book, possibly brought from home.

Many schools provide a weekly library period at which time a class is scheduled to go to the central library and, with the possible assistance of the librarian, each pupil may locate exactly the book he will most enjoy reading. At unscheduled times, too, individual pupils and specific committees should have the privilege of going to the library and looking up information or finding literature connected with on-going units in the social studies or other curricular areas. The library should be an accessible, helpful, interesting place for children to go.

Books should be available for home reading, too. The teacher may lead an excursion to the public library where the children are shown the location of the different types of reading materials and are helped in getting a library card. Also parents may be helped to make good choices of books to be given their children. For example, the school may hold an exhibit of suitable books during the November Book Week festival; the parents may come after school to inspect the books and get the teacher's advice on which ones would be best for their particular children. The pupils themselves may put on a book fair for their parents and act as "barkers" to promote the books that they wish to recommend for purchase by their classmates' parents; or a local bookshop may put on an exhibit so that pupils may come, one class at a time, to hear the presentations of an expert salesman and to inspect the books for themselves (with clean hands and due care to keep the books in good condition). On this basis, each child may make up his individual shopping list to turn over to his parents just before the Christmas shopping is to begin. Also a parents' group may form into committees responsible for examining standard book lists (*Children's Catalog* or lists put out by the American Library Association, for instance), inspecting the most highly recommended books and making up a selective list of books for purchase.

Bringing books to the pupils' attention. In making books accessible to children, a teacher is doing much to bring them to the pupils' attention. Consequently, some of the activities already mentioned are repeated in the list to follow, which is organized under the following categories: oral reading, dramatics, exhibits, bulletin board displays, social activities, and radio-television programs. The list does not necessarily include all the possible ways of bringing books to children's attention. Teachers can devise others currently more appropriate and effective.

Oral reading

- By the teacher
  - Excerpts from a new book
  - Selected portions from a neglected choice book
  - Whole book by installments because interesting but difficult

By the pupils
  Excerpts from favorite books
  Portions to reflect humor, exciting adventure, suspense
  Interesting descriptions as of Georgie, the friendly ghost
  Original riddles about widely read books

Dramatics
  Short story pantomimed as one child reads it
  Dialogue that reveals liveliness and/or humor (a pupil per character)
  Puppet show developed and shown to class or assembly
  Book parade in costumes, as for Red Riding Hood

Exhibits
  New or favorite books
  Pupil-made figurines of literary characters
  Dolls dressed in "period" costumes
  Peep shows that show scenes from stories
  Dioramas that give settings for specific books
  Drawings and paintings illustrating a story
  A picture-strip, pupil-made "movie"

Bulletin board displays
  Jackets from new books
  Posters
    Advertising individual books
    Slogans to encourage reading
  Announcements of arrival of bookmobile or group of new books
  Personally written recommendations for books
  Frieze featuring a single book or several related books
  Literary map

Social activities
  A story party one day a month
    Storytelling based on favorite books
    Recorded stories
    Guest storytellers
    A pupil-written book

School assembly featuring books
"Book shop" where make-believe clerks "sell" a book to prospective readers

Radio and television programs

Recommended use of network literary programs for children
Pupils appearing on local programs

Some of the foregoing activities give opportunity for much creative effort on the part of pupils. The entire class may plan and carry out a book parade, for instance. It may feature riddles, telling or reading orally significant excerpts from popular books, pantomiming, and costuming. In one book parade, two boys sent their audience into gales of laughter when they used an old buffalo robe and enacted the pushmi-pullyu of Dr. Doolittle's menagerie. A little girl in a cross-striped costume and carrying a tiny umbrella puzzled the watchers until she said:

> I live in a great big forest.
> One day a little boy in fine clothes came along.
> I was going to eat him.
> He gave me his little umbrella.
> Then I was the finest beast in the forest.
> Who am I?

Many other enticing activities may be worked out by teachers and their pupils. Anything that can bring children's attention to worth-while books is likely to lead to interest in reading that tends to crowd out the cheap kinds of stories that pupils may have been reading. It is good for every teacher, experienced or inexperienced, to remember each day that *her own* enthusiasm for, and genuine interest in, reading good books is a prime factor in awakening interests in children.

Selected References

(* recommended)

AMATORA, S. M., and EDITH, S. M. "Children's Interest in Free Reading," *School and Society*, LXXIII (March, 1951), 134–47.

ARBUTHNOT, MARY HILL. *Children and Books.* Chicago: Scott, Foresman and Co., 1957. Selected pages.

*DAWSON, MILDRED A. "Lodestones in Children's Books," in *International Reading Association Conference Proceedings*, Vol. 6: *Changing Concepts of Reading Instruction.* New York: Scholastic Magazines, 1961. Pp. 183–86.

GANS, ROMA. *Reading Is Fun: Developing Children's Reading Interests.* New York: Bureau of Publications, Teachers College, Columbia University, 1949. Selected pages.

GRAY, WILLIAM S. (ed.). "Basic Instruction in Reading in Elementary and High Schools," *Supplementary Educational Monographs*, No. 65. Chicago: University of Chicago Press, 1949. Pp. 179–95.

HARRIS, ALBERT. *How to Increase Reading Ability.* New York: David McKay Co., Inc., 1961. Pp. 466–502.

HILDRETH, GERTRUDE. *Teaching Reading.* New York: Holt, Rinehart and Winston, 1958. Pp. 503–29.

LARRICK, NANCY. "Making the Most of Children's Interest," *Education*, LXXIII (May, 1953), 523–31.

*NORVELL, GEORGE W. *What Boys and Girls Like to Read.* Morristown, N.J.: Silver Burdett Co., 1958. Pp. 19–54; selected pages.

ROBINSON, HELEN. "What Research Says to the Teacher of Reading," *Reading Teacher*, VIII (February, 1955), 173–77.

*RUSSELL, DAVID H. *Children Learn to Read.* 2nd ed. Boston: Ginn and Co., 1961. Pp. 362–406; 409–53.

"San Francisco Study of Children and Mass Communication, The," Report IV (mimeographed). Palo Alto, Calif.: Stanford Institute for Communication Research, 1959.

Study of the Interests of Children and Youth, A (A study made cooperatively by Northwestern University and the Office of Education, U.S. Department of Health, Education and Welfare). Washington, D.C.: Government Printing Office, 1960. Selected pages.

TINKER, MILES A., and MCCULLOUGH, CONSTANCE. *Teaching Elementary Reading.* New York: Appleton-Century-Crofts, Inc., 1962. Pp. 274–87.

WITTY, PAUL. "The Role of Interest," in *Development in and through Reading, Sixtieth Yearbook,* Part I, National Society for the Study of Education. Chicago: University of Chicago Press, 1961. Pp. 127–43.

*WITTY, PAUL, *et al.* "Studies of Children's Interest—a Brief Summary," *Elementary English,* XXXVII (November, 1960), 469–75.

4

Readiness for Learning to Read

WHEN THE EXPERT OBSERVER SAYS, "THIS YOUNG bird is ready to fly," what does he mean? Probably he has such factors as these in mind: the bird is big enough, has sufficient motor coordination, has seen its parents flitting here and there and flying to it with welcome food, and has a consequent desire to fly for itself. Or, what is meant by saying the adolescent Indian boy is ready for the endurance tests that will prove he can take his place with the men in hunting and fighting? His readiness involves his having arrived at the suitable stage of physical and social development, his feeling a compelling desire to become a man and willingness to go through strenuous ordeals to prove his fitness, a sense of confidence in his having had the requisite experiences and training that fit him to go about the duties of an adult.

"Reading readiness" similarly suggests that the child is all set to go, developed to the stage where he is ready to learn to read. Physically, intellectually, emotionally, socially—in every way the child's whole being is poised, attuned to the demands of the reading task, completely prepared for learning. (Actually, perfect readiness is hardly to be expected. Nearly always any particular child is deficient in one or more phases of his development and needs supplementary experiences or more time to grow in order to be fully ready.) His readiness may be that of a first-grade child who is all set for the first step in learning to read; or it may be that of an older pupil who is ready to learn how to figure out an unfamiliar word by syllabication, or of a still older child who has progressed to the stage where he can learn to outline a four-page informational article.

Often the term *reading readiness* is used to refer only to that period when the child is ready for initial reading instruction, when he is ready to begin learning to read. In reality, this term should be *initial* reading readiness. When a child has developed initial readiness, he is sufficiently mature, sufficiently experienced, and sufficiently interested to assure his making the best possible response to introductory reading lessons. He is all set to go and to succeed in his initial attempts to learn how to read.

Throughout the elementary school years, pupils are ever moving toward some more advanced phase of reading readiness. Month by month, year by year, the program expands as it calls for increasingly refined and precise thinking, or demands new and more intricate skills. The reading program goes by stages, each stage being essential to learning the skills and requiring understanding of the stage to follow. That is, each child must develop a readiness for each of the successive phases of the reading process. For this type of readiness, the term *developmental reading readiness* seems appropriate. Developmental reading readiness is constantly building up in the elementary school years, probably through high school as well, as the pupil arrives at the point where he is ready for each successive phase of reading.

Readiness for Initial Reading Instruction

Part of being ready to learn to read is the child's being old enough, mature enough, for this type of activity. Another part of his readiness is his having gained a rich and varied store of knowledge from many experiences, a knowledge made evident through the child's mastery of language—a large vocabulary and complete sentences, for instance. Still another aspect of initial reading readiness consists of his having gained attitudes favorable to learning to read and thus having developed a desire to learn to read.

Maturation. As was shown in an earlier chapter, the act of reading demands a certain degree of physical maturation. (See page 21.) Muscular coordination and the rounding out of the eyeball are essential if the eyes are to fixate properly as they progress along each line of print.

Another phase of physical maturation that affects initial reading readiness concerns the child's ability to speak his words clearly and correctly. (See page 23.) He may have particular difficulty with all words that contain *r* and *th* elements. His poor enunciation may be the result of baby talk that has been encouraged by doting parents who think baby talk is "cute." Then the teacher has the relatively simple task of helping the child learn the more mature speech patterns for which he was actually ready before entering school. However, he may be a child who is still physically immature and who does not yet have the vocal coordinations necessary for forming certain speech sounds. Such a child needs time to mature before he goes too far into the introductory reading program. According to Davis [1] the following speech ages are normal:

[1] Irene Poole Davis, "The Speech Aspects of Reading Readiness," *Seventeenth Yearbook of the Department of Elementary School Principals.* National Education Association, Washington, D.C., 1938.

6.5 years: *l, sh, zh,* and *th* (as in *them* and *think*)
8.0 years: *r, wh, s,* and *z* (relearned after second dentition)

Mental maturity is an important element in initial reading readiness. Many children of six or six and a half years are ready to learn to read, but others are not. If a child is so immature that he cannot keep his hands off other children, cannot pay attention more than two or three minutes at a time, or is constantly flitting from one activity to another, the teacher may suspect that he is too immature for formalized reading instruction. Then it is really important that the child be given a standardized test to determine mental maturity. If the mental age is low, he should have many enriching real experiences, look at picture books, hear countless stories, and even watch his teacher use the chalkboard in recording sentences which he and classmates dictate to her—not so much that he is actually learning to read as that he is getting an idea of what reading is like and is building up an interest in learning later for himself. Meanwhile he is growing older, maturing, getting mentally ready to read.

While no one level of mental maturity is absolutely essential for learning to read, many authorities recommend that a child be six or, better still, six and a half in *mental age* before reading instruction is introduced. He is then likely to have acquired a considerable span of attention, to have become quite observant in learning from his environment and his experiences in it, to have acquired thereby a rich background of information and wide vocabulary, and to be able to think sequentially. He will probably take to reading as a duck does to water and should make rapid progress. He tends to enjoy reading and soon is ready to read widely from simple books in the library corner.

On the other hand, teachers also know that many children of a somewhat lower mental age can and do learn to read satisfactorily—*if* teachers plan and provide a painstaking introductory program that fills in gaps in these pupils' readiness, that permits the children to go at their individually appropriate rates, that insures thorough learning before new phases are introduced. These pupils need to be worked with, and must be allowed to move along at a slower rate than their more mature classmates. Even so, children who are genuinely slow-learning or slow-developing (though bright) should go into the reading program at a considerably later chronological age than their peers; they usually advance at a slower pace.

Psychologists emphasize the importance of mental maturation in a program of initial reading readiness. Olson and Anderson, for instance, maintain that it is useless to try to teach any skill before the child is ready to learn it. All the explanations, activities, and drills that teachers and parents give in order to produce readiness that is not maturationally appropriate are useless when given prematurely. Likewise it is wrong to wait too long after the child has attained readiness. It is, therefore, a mistaken policy to have a school regulation that forbids the use of reading books in the early part of first grade, inasmuch as some children will be ready then. It is equally a mistake to insist that all first-grade children be introduced to book reading before midyear. "Strike when the iron is hot," not before, not after.

Background of experiences. Maturation alone is not enough to produce initial reading readiness. A child living in a vacuum could hardly get ready to read without exercise for his muscles, sunshine and milk for his blood and bones, and experiences for feeding his mind. His development comes as the result of the interaction of his environment and his maturing inborn capacity to learn. For instance, the child gains the eye-hand coordination essential to reading as he matures and manipulates objects. Taste, smell, hearing, feeling, sight, and kinesthetic impressions gained through manipulation are the avenues by which the child takes in his environment. As he observes and handles things, the child builds a growing stock of ideas which become formulated through discussion with his elders. Experience along with language is an essential element in reading readiness.

A child's language development does much to determine his initial readiness for reading. How can he read sentences if his spoken sentences are fragmentary or incorrectly phrased? How can he follow the sequence of events in a story if he cannot tell an experience of his own in good sequence? How can he read English if he hears and speaks a foreign language at home? It is important that a child's spoken language be far advanced if he is going to be able to read printed language. The so-called prerequisites for learning to read involve the following aspects of language:

A wide listening and speaking vocabulary
Ability to speak in complete sentences
Ability to pronounce and enunciate words correctly
Ability to hear the differences and likenesses in the sounds that make up spoken words (*m* vs. *n; d* vs. *t*)
Ability to follow the sequence of ideas in a story

Actually, the various phases of language do not present much of a problem in reading readiness at the first-grade level. Most six-year-old children speak in sentences; they have several thousand words in their speaking vocabulary and know many thousands more which they have met in their listening; their speech is usually quite adequate. It is in the area of *auditory discrimination* (the ability to hear the differences and similarities in the sounds of various words) that many children need supplementary experiences after they enter first grade. Hearing and saying nursery rhymes and other simple poems can be so guided that the pupils will begin to note both the alliteration and the rhyming words in "Peter, Peter Pumpkin Eater" and "Sing a Song of Sixpence." Listening to rhymes and word sounds is not enough; the children should also have many opportunities to enunciate them. It is as a child deliberately gets his tongue and lips into position for making a desired sound that he becomes truly aware of the sounds that constitute any particular word.

Introductory reading readiness books for the pupils' use abound in interesting exercises that will help children become alert to the sounds that make up spoken words. Teachers' manuals that accompany sets of readers give careful guidance in the materials and methods that will best cultivate auditory discrimination in children. Every teacher should avail herself of the helps that such manuals provide. Since many teachers do not fully understand auditory discrimination and ways to develop it, they must use manuals for this very fundamental aspect of reading skills.

Another important element in reading readiness is *visual discrimination,* or the ability to see the differences and likenesses in words. The typical child has made a crude beginning in acquiring such discrimination as he decides which of two cookies is the bigger, which of several boards is the longer, or which of his playmates is the taller. Because the beginning reader soon has to discriminate between such words as *boy* and *toy* or *was* and *saw,* he needs experience in making visual discriminations. Many reading readiness books have exercises in which a row of five objects has four that are just alike, and one that is a little bigger or that faces the opposite way or that has a part missing. The child then selects the one that is not like the others. Other beginning workbooks have similar exercises that involve only letters or words, the principle being that children should learn the kind of discrimination that reading actually calls for. Here, too, teachers' manuals give helpful suggestions for teaching children to develop visual discrimination.

The home and school should provide other kinds of experiences that are directly related to reading, namely, many activities that involve reading materials. Children should observe their elders reading books, magazines, and newspapers, as well as traffic signs and the "come-on" signs in store windows. They should listen to stories read from books and interpret the stories which picture books show. Reading ought to seem a natural and important part of living in the world today. Thus favorable attitudes toward reading can be nurtured.

To a certain degree a child's social and emotional development can affect his initial reading readiness, such development having been shaped by the experiences he has had with other people. If he is accustomed to playing with children of his own age, he is more likely to fit easily into the group life of the classroom and to "put his mind to his reading activities" than is the child who has not had playmates and is consequently preoccupied with the problems and pleasures of mingling with his fellows. A first-grade teacher in a school where there is no kindergarten may find several socially inexperienced children in her group and may have to give considerable time to activities that stress cooperation, taking turns, sharing, and carrying on other socially adjustive activities. If a child is to do his best in beginning reading, he must be able to give it his full attention and not be diverted by personal problems.

Occasionally a child comes to school with an emotional problem serious enough to interfere with his learning to read. He may have been overprotected at home and be too dependent; he may have been spoiled and be subject to tantrums whenever he does not get his way; or he may feel unloved and unwanted because a brother or sister seems preferred in the family circle and he consequently comes to school withdrawn and disinterested. Such a child needs an understanding teacher who will give him school experiences that act as a needed supplement: small and gradually increasing responsibilities for the too dependent, firm and kindly insistence that the spoiled child consider the decisions of his group, recognition and friendly praise for the insecure and withdrawn child. Consultation with the school psychologist and conferences with the parents may help to get at the bottom of the emotional problem that is interfering with progress in learning to read. Certainly scolding is not the answer when a child is emotionally disturbed.

Attitudes toward reading. Unless the child is genuinely interested in learning to read, he will make very little progress even if he is ready in every other aspect. In general, it may be said that children in first grade manifest one of three attitudes: enthusiasm, reluctance, or indifference. With an enthusiastic attitude, a child will bend every effort toward learning to read and is likely to make rapid progress even if poorly taught. A child with a reluctant attitude tends to resist any reading instruction and to put up a block against learning. Little Mary, for instance, had been embarrassed by a tactless teacher in the second week of first grade because she had no news for the show-and-tell period. This child did not speak or make a gesture toward participation in any reading activity for a whole semester. When transferred to another teacher in January, she blossomed forth in all reading activities. Twelve-year-old Ralph, who had made fair progress in his reading, developed a distaste for books when his second-grade brother became an avid and skillful reader.

The parents had unwisely commented on the relative superiority of the younger child's reading and had tried to prod Ralph into greater effort. The humiliation and jealousy that the older boy felt was expressed through his strong dislike for reading activities. Indifference may result from one of many causes: mental immaturity, parents who do not read much and who are not much in favor of schooling, or emotional problems that block other interests. The reluctant child must be won over by interesting, success-building activities; the indifferent child must have the cause of his indifference removed, whether by being given time to mature or by activities that will alleviate his problems.

Most children think of first grade as a place where they are supposed to learn to read, and, typically, desire to learn. If the teacher's prereading inventory reveals that certain children have unfavorable attitudes toward learning to read, she should be alert to any reliable clues that will point to the causes of such reluctance or indifference.

For the child who has had meager contacts with reading, the teacher should provide a rich reading environment: a corner with many intriguing picture books; a bulletin board with announcements, posters, and captioned pictures that will arouse curiosity; a chalkboard that daily features committee listings and plans, news stories dictated by the pupils, and other current notices. There should be almost daily periods when she reads to the children. Here the teacher must provide abundantly what the home has failed to give.

The immature child mainly needs time—time to grow. He must gain the requisite physical coordination, better near-vision, mastery of his vocal organs; he needs a widening range of experiences that will afford a rich background and a basis for language growth. He, too, should handle picture books and listen to many stories. When he has sufficiently matured, he will probably acquire a desire to learn to read.

As has been said, the child who is preoccupied with problems that interfere with his developing an interest in learning to read needs to have his problems solved. Sometimes, however, the introductory reading program can be made so appealing that the problems are forgotten, and the desire to read is awakened or sufficiently strengthened.

A check list for determining initial reading readiness. With so many elements to keep in mind, the teacher should have at hand a comprehensive but simple check list to aid her in her study of her pupils' relative readiness for learning to read. The following check list is suggestive.

Physical Readiness

Motor development

1. Are his bodily movements well coordinated?
2. Does he hold a book and turn pages well?
3. Is his eye-hand coordination sufficiently developed to enable him to pick up articles accurately, cut, and follow a line?

Auditory development

1. Does he seem to hear what you read and say to the group?
2. Does he listen attentively? What are the audiometer results?
3. Can he pass the 20-foot low-voice test, and the 15-inch whisper test?
4. Does he hear and enunciate words accurately?

Visual development

1. Are there signs of eyestrain (blink, squint, watery eyes)?
   a. At a distance
   b. Near eyes
2. Does he tend to hold the book too close or too far from his eyes?
3. Does he see likenesses and differences in objects, letters, words?
4. What does any available clinical or oculist's test show about vision?

Speech

1. Does he use baby talk, or other immature speech patterns?
2. Which sounds does he not yet enunciate accurately?

General health

1. Does he tire too easily?
2. Are there evident physical handicaps (eyes, ears, nose-throat, coordination)?
3. Are there signs of poor health and malnutrition?

Social Development

1. Does he like to work and play with his fellows?
2. Does he show leadership?
3. Does he cooperate and follow decisions of the group?
4. Does he like to hear his peers express their ideas?
5. Is he learning to be polite?

Ways of Working

1. Does he stick to a task or a voluntary activity?
2. In taking directions, does he listen attentively and respond promptly?
3. Is he a neat, systematic, careful worker?

Mental Development

1. Can he pay careful attention for several minutes?
2. Does he have a good memory?
3. Is he resourceful in solving his problems?

Emotional Development

1. Is he withdrawn, shy, or overly aggressive?
2. Is he at ease in the school situation?
3. Is he self-reliant and confident?
4. Is he a happy, alert child?

Background of Experience

1. Does his family customarily speak English?
2. Is the child included in family planning and conversation?
3. Do both parents work?
4. Do they take the child on trips?
5. Do they discuss pictures and read to him?
6. Does he have playmates, pets, toys, books, tools?

Language Development

1. Does he enunciate and pronounce words clearly and correctly?
2. Does he have a reasonably wide vocabulary?
3. Is it based on well-understood concepts?
4. Does he speak in full sentences?
5. Does he tell a story in good order?

Prereading Interests and Skills

1. Does he pretend to be reading when by himself?
2. Does he voluntarily go to books and look through them?
3. Can he read the story that a picture tells?
4. Does he notice and recognize common signs and labels?
5. Does he know numerous stories and rhymes?
6. Is he curious about new notices that the teacher has put up?

Standardized tests on reading readiness. There are available several reading readiness tests that yield definite evidence concerning children's readiness to learn to read, especially in the area of concepts and auditory and visual discrimination. (See Appendix B.) As the preceding check list indicates, there are areas which these tests do not touch; and carefully directed observation by the teacher provides valuable supplementary data. The chapter devoted to evaluation in reading will describe the various published tests of reading readiness.

Developmental Reading Readiness

Learning to read resembles climbing a ladder a rung at a time. Step by step, the child masters the various skills and understandings that make up the complete reading program. There is little use in doing so-called "remedial teaching" of retarded readers who are doing as well as their current maturation and native abilities make possible. Much of the drill and practice that teachers give slow-learning pupils is all in vain because the children are being taught skills for which they have not yet developed readiness.

Sight vocabulary. One of the first developmental tasks of the reading process is the acquirement of a sight vocabulary —words so familiar that they are recognized immediately at sight. Here readiness involves an awareness that there is meaning in the passages where the words to be learned are being used: listings, sentences, whole stories. The basic words should be learned in context and used repeatedly in meaningful situations. In addition, the child must have the visual and auditory discrimination that will enable him to see and hear the differences or likenesses in the words he is meeting. Interest in reading, too, is an essential. Until a child has a considerable sight vocabulary, he can do little independent reading and has little basis for lessons in word analysis.

Word analysis. After a pupil has mastered an initial sight vocabulary, he has a basis for noting the similarities between new words and already familiar words. For example, if he has already learned *baby, boy, ball,* and *big,* he is likely to notice that all begin with the same sound and he is on his way toward figuring out the new word *bed.* Word endings are similarly impressed, as the *s, ed,* and *ing* that may be added to the word *walk.* Thus, a knowledge of initial consonants and word endings begins to develop.

Before a child can read well in a reader used by average sixth-grade students, he goes through a succession of steps in word recognition: recognizing the internal short vowel in a word like *hat,* the long internal vowel in words that have a double vowel or end in *e* (*gate, gait*), the blending of two consonants as *tr* or *cl,* the digraph whose consonants yield a sound different from either letter (*th* or *ph*), the dividing of words into syllables, the use of prefixes and suffixes, and so on. For each of these successive steps in word attack, the child must have developed readiness to learn by mastering the skills antecedent to it.

Growth in independence. The mastery of a sight vocabulary and the acquisition of word-attack skills partially account for the child's progress toward independence in reading. There are, however, additional elements. In the beginning, the teacher raises a question to direct the pupil's thinking as he attacks his reading, a sentence at a time. Each question promotes the child's readiness not only to get the idea in each sentence but also to recognize any new or difficult word through its context.

Gradually the teacher increases the length of the passages which she introduces through a thought-provoking question: two sentences, three sentences, a half page, several related paragraphs, one or two pages, a whole selection. Constantly the pupils are developing readiness to read more and more materials independently. They have been developing and mastering such intrinsic skills as following the line, reading from left to right, swinging the eye back to the beginning of the next line, guessing a new word from its context, seeking meaning from what is read, and the like.

Use of books. In learning to use books, the child goes through many and varied stages in developmental readiness. As he gains the ability to read for himself, he is reaching the stage where he needs to learn to use books efficiently: the table of contents and index for locating desired information; chapter titles and topical headings as a means of forecasting main ideas and later reviewing them; the captions of pictures to facilitate their interpretation; legends so that lines and shadings on maps or graphs have meaning; the figures in tables so that their significant ideas will be abstracted. Through the intermediate grades, children typically become ready for learning the successive steps in using a dictionary:

locating words according to their alphabetical arrangement; determining the correct spelling or pronunciation of a word; selecting the meaning that best fits the context in which a word is used, and so on. Children should be shown how to use encyclopedias, atlases, card catalogs, the *Reader's Guide* in the library, and other reference books as soon as they are ready.

Such information is rather mechanical. There are also ideational elements for which readiness gradually develops. Through careful teacher guidance, the child progresses through stages such as finding the topic sentence or main idea in a paragraph, determining the major points in a passage of several pages, outlining these points, recognizing the details which support each major point and allocating proper placement in an outline, and making a summary, or stating the theme. As the child accumulates a wealth of information, he develops readiness for detecting inconsistencies in printed statements, bias, incompleteness, false premises, loaded statements, jumping to conclusions, and other faulty presentations of ideas.

Certain study skills, too, become appropriate at successive stages of learning to read: skimming to locate a desired bit of information or to determine its pertinence; surveying topical headings to determine the line of thought which an author pursues or to fix the main ideas in a passage for a subsequent report or a test; raising questions that the reader wishes to have answered through his independent reading; rereading any section that seems obscure, controversial, or especially important in settling an issue; underlining or marking in some way the key sentences (providing the reader owns the book!). As the child develops mentally, he gets ready to do more and more complex thinking, to note the relationships between ideas, to be intelligently critical of what he reads, and thus to become selective. Such development underlies the progressively complicated thinking the child is ready to do as he reads.

Developmental reading readiness is partially a function of the nature-ordained inner growth of the child's mind. It is also a function of the kinds of reading experience the child gets as he develops a sight vocabulary, the ability to figure out new words independently, a thoughtful attitude as he reads increasingly lengthy passages, skill in utilizing the study aids in the books, the ability to adjust its rate of reading to his purposes, and discriminating evaluation of the ideas in his reading materials.

Summary

The development of reading readiness is a continuous process. The child must first become ready to learn to read, or develop *initial reading readiness;* subsequently, he progresses from one stage of reading to the next, and he is continuously developing readiness for each successive phase of reading. Such readiness may be called *developmental.*

Initial reading readiness calls for adequate language development in the way of rich concepts, a wide vocabulary, ability to speak in well-constructed sentences, and clear enunciation. Mental maturity of six or six and one half years is advantageous, though possibly not essential. Auditory and visual discrimination, or the ability to hear and see similarities and differences in words, is a necessary component in readiness. Most important of all is the child's genuine desire to learn to read. Since initial reading readiness is a complex of many elements, the teacher may advisedly use a check list so that her evaluation may be inclusive and significant.

The aspects of developmental reading readiness were defined as (1) learning a sight vocabulary, (2) gradually mastering a series of word-attack skills, (3) becoming independent in comprehending what is read, (4) learning how to use books efficiently, and (5) acquiring a critical, evaluative attitude. Each of these aspects goes through a series of developmental steps.

Selected References

(* recommended)

ANDERSON, IRVING, and DEARBORN, WALTER. *Psychology of Teaching Reading*. New York: Ronald Press, 1952. Pp. 50–100.

BETTS, EMMETT. *Foundations of Reading Instruction.* New York: American Book Co., 1954. Pp. 103–281; 291–373.

BURTON, WILLIAM H. *Reading in Child Development.* Indianapolis: Bobbs-Merrill Co., 1956. Pp. 166–208.

CARTER, HOMER, and MCGINNIS, DOROTHY. *Teaching Individuals to Read.* Boston: D. C. Heath and Co., 1962. Pp. 27–39.

HESTER, KATHLEEN. *Teaching Every Child to Read.* New York: Harper and Bros., 1955. Pp. 17–135.

*HILDRETH, GERTRUDE. *Readiness for School Beginners.* Yonkers, N.Y.: World Book Co., 1950. Pp. 3–17; 42–63; 88–201; 224–323.

———. *Teaching Reading*. New York: Holt, Rinehart and Winston, 1958. Pp. 159–84.

MCKIM, MARGARET. *Guiding Growth in Reading in the Modern Elementary School.* New York: The Macmillan Co., 1955. Pp. 33–115.

*MONROE, MARION. *Growing into Reading.* Chicago: Scott Foresman and Co., 1951. Entire book.

RUSSELL, DAVID H. *Children Learn to Read.* 2nd ed. Boston: Ginn and Co., 1961. Pp. 167–98.

*TINKER, MILES A., and MCCULLOUGH, CONSTANCE. *Teaching Elementary Reading.* New York: Appleton-Century-Crofts, Inc., 1962. Pp. 51–117; 377–93.

YOAKAM, GERALD. *Basal Reading Instruction.* New York: McGraw-Hill Book Co., 1955. Pp. 103–19.

5

Early Primary Reading Instruction

SYSTEMATIC READING INSTRUCTION MAY BEGIN AS soon as a child shows definite evidence of readiness for learning to read. He should have developed facility in his use of language: a rich store of concepts reflected in a wide vocabulary, ability to speak in complete sentences with his ideas arranged in good sequence, clear and accurate enunciation of words. If at home he has not learned to see and hear the likenesses and differences in the objects and sounds around him (visual and auditory discrimination), the instructional program in reading readiness should have made a good start in developing such discrimination. Through his handling books, looking at their pictures, and listening to stories, he should have become interested in learning to read for himself. This interest should have been further encouraged by the teacher's using the chalkboard and bulletin board to record pupil "committees" who are to do certain classroom jobs, simple plans, brief news stories, and accounts of classroom activities—not so much that the pupils can yet read these as that such activities yield an idea of what the nature of reading materials and of the reading act is.

This chapter will be divided into three sections: preparatory informal reading, introductory book reading, and progress toward independence in reading. It covers the period in which children proceed through preprimers, primers, and first readers. Quick-learning children will accomplish this reading in first grade; but average pupils should probably use first readers in second grade and slow learners may need materials at the first-reader level as late as third or even fourth grade. The topics for such materials should be more mature than those in the typical first reader.

Preparatory Informal Reading

By *informal reading materials* are meant those that are teacher-prepared, often at the pupils' dictation, sometimes by her own initiative. These may be script-printed on the chalkboard, on chart paper, or on long strips of paper; and for individual use they may be prepared with a primer typewriter or script-written on 9″ by 11″ sheets of paper.

Types of introductory informal materials. In general, informal materials are divided into two classes: the *experience type,* which is usually dictated by the pupils, and the *parallel-reading type,* which the teacher prepares for the purpose of teaching a definite vocabulary or a particular skill. These will be discussed in turn.

Some teachers start the school day with a show-and-tell period on any morning when a pupil brings to school an object which he wishes to display to his classmates. It may be something he has made himself, a gift he has received, a souvenir from a week-end trip, or an article brought from home to illustrate current lessons in science, social studies, or literature. Frequently the ensuing discussion will bring out interesting statements which the teacher will record on the chalkboard. An example follows.

Betty has a new doll.
It is as big as a baby.
It can walk and talk.

Sometimes a child will bring news of great interest to him, but he will have nothing to display. After a general exchange of news, the group will suggest the items of greatest general appeal and dictate sentences like these to the teacher.

Ted's father gave him a bicycle.
Ted is learning to ride it.

Jerry's dog has three puppies.
They are white with brown spots.

We have a new girl today.
Her name is Phyllis.

Unlike the summary report above, the news story may feature only one item which is reported in several short sentences. As classroom activities proceed, the teacher may also record the announcements and the plans that the children are making; for instance:

We will give a party for our mothers.
We will make grape jelly.
We will buy crackers and milk.
We have some stories to read.
We have a good play about goats.

News stories and plans that are of more than temporary interest may be transferred from the chalkboard to charts for later reference.

The bulletin board may also be used as a medium for displaying informal reading materials, such as announcements, records of plans and classroom activities, and various listings. Whenever pupils' drawings are posted, each young artist will wish to dictate a label for his picture and to sign his name for classmates to read.

These are entries found on one first grade bulletin board:

The bookmobile comes today.
You may get a picture book.
You may take it home.
You may read to Father and Mother.

Our Furniture

We need furniture for the play corner.
We will make it from apple boxes.
This is what we need.
2 chairs–2 boxes
1 couch–2 boxes
1 table –1 box, 4 boards
We need 5 boxes and 4 boards.
Bill will get boxes from the store.
Mr. Bates will give us the boards.

Often the teacher in early first grade will prepare some experience reading materials that are designed to pique the children's curiosity. One teacher daily put a one-sentence secret on the bulletin board; for instance, she wrote one morning: *Miss Snow will come today.* Miss Snow was the very popular art teacher. What fun the pupils had as they tried to figure out the secret of the day! Another teacher wrote a short letter on the chalkboard each morning. This she read to her pupils while moving a pointer smoothly along each line as she read it. (She never pointed to any single word, but kept the pointer in motion.) A third teacher intrigued her pupils by occasionally making up a story paralleling one that they had dictated and read the previous day. The children got great enjoyment out of making their best possible guess as they attempted to read the story on the basis of recognizing their names and the meaningful words that had impressed them most vividly. The teacher, if need be, phrased a helpful question to aid in reading each of the more puzzling sentences.

All the preceding types of informal reading materials have no vocabulary control. The purposes for presenting them are to arouse interest in reading, to make reading meaningful through association with the pupils' experiences, to enhance the children's sentence sense, and to help them realize that reading should proceed from left to right along each line and from the top line to the bottom one in serial order. On the other hand, the vocabulary of parallel reading is strictly held to that in the basal reader. Its initial purpose is to teach the vocabulary of the first preprimer before the children are introduced to book reading.

The teacher may get large pictures of people and pets somewhat similar to those featured in the first preprimer. Each will be labeled with the corresponding name, which the pupils will come to recognize through seeing it frequently. Then she will devise stories that contain exclusively the words that are contained in this preprimer, for instance, such words as *come, go, run, up,* and *down.* A picture of a boy running may have the sentence label, *Run, Tim.* Simple chart stories may be prepared in duplicate so that one copy may be divided into sentence strips which may then be matched with the corresponding sentences on the complete chart. This chart story, for instance, grew out of seeing a picture of a dog chasing a kitten up a tree.

Run, Snowball, run.
See Tip come.
Run, Snowball.
Go up, up, up.

Both the chalkboard and print-script charts will be used in presenting such parallel materials.

Fundamental teaching techniques. All series of basal readers have a teacher's manual for each book, with detailed directions for introducing, teaching, and following up each story. The beginning teacher should study her manual and follow its suggestions. Thus can be assured her use of effective and usually well-rounded teaching procedures. An experienced teacher should also go through the manual to find supplementary or improved ways of teaching.

This section of Chapter 5 presents only major fundamental techniques for teaching informal reading. In introductory reading, sentences must be kept short so that each one takes only a single line. Thus the eyes gain skill in following one line at a time, from left to right, and in returning to the next line in order to read the sentence that follows.

In every instance, a sentence is read "with the eyes" before a pupil reads it aloud. The teacher prefaces the reading with a question so that reading is a thought-getting process. Then the child is prepared to read orally in a fluent, conversation-like manner. In order to facilitate the silent reading, the teacher asks a leading question to help the child read correctly. The question is so phrased as to suggest the wording of the sentence, especially any new word that is being introduced. Note the illustrations that follow. (The reading comes after the teacher has printed on the chalkboard the sentences which her pupils have dictated.)

The first sentence tells what Molly has. Read it with your eyes. Who can read it to us?

Molly has a new dress.

What color is it?

It is red and white.

Who made the dress?

Her grandmother made the dress.

When will Molly wear it?

Molly will wear it next Sunday.

Who can read us all of the story now? I'll help you by asking you a question about any sentence you find hard. Be sure to read each sentence with your eyes before you read it out loud. Then you can read as if you are talking.

In order to improve children's visual discrimination and—in the case of parallel reading materials—to build a basic sight vocabulary, many chalkboard stories are transferred to charts prepared in duplicate. One of these is cut into sentence strips so that the pupils can match each strip to the corresponding portion of the chart story. At first, the matching may be in the serial order of the sentences; but often the sentences will be matched in mixed order so that the pupils have to look carefully. (It is wise at the start to have the sentences begin differently and to be of varying lengths. The preceding story about Molly's doll illustrates this point. At the latter part of this period for introducing pupils to reading through parallel charts, the sentences in the story may be cut up into phrases to be matched with the identical ones in the complete chart story.)

In planning parallel reading, the teacher should make an effort to include each new introduced word several times, since repetition is one of the chief ways in which a child learns his basic reading vocabulary. After listening to Dorothy Baruch's "Seesaws," the pupils may make up a chant of their own that features only the basic words: *up, down, and,* and *go,* for instance.

Up and down,
Up and down!
Go up.
Go down.
Go up and down.

In parallel reading, which is introduced after weeks of work with experience stories, it is not necessary to have the sentences begin differently because, through experience reading, the children should have learned to look quite discriminatingly at their reading materials and to follow the line without confusion. The purpose now is to provide many repetitions of the basic words so as to attain mastery of them. Parallel charts may precede the book story so as to introduce new words; or they may follow book reading whenever pupils need additional practice on hard words.

Class organization. During the readiness and introductory informal reading periods, the teacher is constantly observing to see which pupils are making rapid progress, which are definitely acquiring the abilities and interest that are essential but are doing so more gradually and slowly, and which need considerably more time and preparatory activities before attaining reading readiness. Most first-grade teachers find it convenient to divide a class into three groups: one that will soon enter books and progress quite rapidly from one to another, with some informal reading and seatwork to reinforce learnings; another that will start book reading some weeks later and that will need much more of the informal reading and seatwork so as to make sure of mastery as they proceed; a third group whose members will need months of preparation before they are introduced to book reading. From time to time, the teacher will plan to have pupils come one at a time and read individually or will give any single pupil any extra informal reading he may need. Though such individual attention will always be essential, reading in groups gives pupils social experience and, moreover, they learn from one another as they read together. While there are individual differences among the pupils in each group, grouping reduces the *range* of differences represented in the class as a whole. The grouping should be flexible so that any pupil can be transferred to a different group as soon as he comes to fit into another that is progressing more slowly or more rapidly than his has been going. (The chapter on organizing for reading instruction treats these matters in greater detail.)

Introductory Book Reading

As has been said, introductory informal reading builds a basis for fluent reading in the first preprimer. The pupils have been taught to start at the top and to read each line from left to right. They have learned to read for meaning and to be fluent so that they read in conversational style and do *not* call out one word at a time. The parallel reading lessons have already introduced the vocabulary of the preprimer so that all the words in it are fairly well known. Even so, there are new learnings demanded by the first book reading.

New skills demanded by book reading. When pupils read from the chalkboard and chart, they focus their eyes to see at a distance and their eye movements are relatively wide. Book reading, on the other hand, calls for focusing on materials close to the eyes and the eye movements across the line and to the next line are diminutive. Unless a child is mature enough to have lost the farsightedness typical of the preschool child, there may be considerable eyestrain, or the still uncoordinated movements of the eyes may cause some children to lose their place on a line or, in the return sweep, to shift to the wrong line. The demands for coordinated movements of eye muscles are considerable.

Many teachers follow the practice of providing each child with a "marker" to help him keep his place in preprimer reading. This is a 1″ by 5″ strip of oaktag or stiff construction paper which the pupil can place under each line as he reads it. Thus his eyes can more easily follow the line.

Preprimers are printed in large bold type so that eyestrain can be reduced. The demands on the still immature eye are further lessened by the pupils' periodic looking up at the teacher as she gives the question that will direct the reading of the next sentence and as the group discusses what has just been read.

Teacher guidance in preprimer reading. All through the period of preprimer reading, the teacher will continue to provide experiences in parallel reading—sometimes to introduce new words, often to give follow-up practice on those which have proven difficult in the book reading. On the chalkboard she may print-script two or three sentences which contain the words that need attention; or she may develop a parallel story which the children are to illustrate with a drawing as, for instance, the following:

See Joe run.
Run to the house, Joe.
Run, Rover, run.
Run with Joe.

Most preprimers have an accompanying workbook that will help to introduce and review the basic vocabulary. Even so, the teacher will usually have to prepare further seatwork that will help the children note the likenesses or differences in words or will further impress their sight vocabulary. For instance, she may prepare exercises such as these.

Find the word that is different in each row.

look	run	ball	go
look	can	ball	go
book	run	baby	go
look	run	ball	do

Find two words in each row that begin with the same letter.

ball	good	look	take
doll	give	book	here
big	jump	like	tell

In using the workbook, the pupils need very close direction and supervision if they are not to *practice and learn mistakes.* The teacher should make sure that every new kind of exercise is thoroughly understood before the pupils start to work independently at their seats. She should either work out several illustrative items at the chalkboard, or she should direct the group in doing the first two or three workbook exercises before they start independent work. Whenever exercises are actually difficult for them, she should keep herself free to supervise their work. This may be necessary because the exercises are completely unfamiliar and complicated or because a slow-learning group of pupils is still uncertain and confused. Whatever happens, pupils should be prevented from practicing mistakes or making wild guesses.

All through their preprimer reading, pupils should read every sentence silently before reading it orally. There can be no sight reading at this stage because it would be too halting and could induce word calling. Too, the teacher must encourage thoughtful and fluent reading by continuing to use a preliminary question to guide silent reading. Children who have an easy time learning to read may be able to read two or three sentences at a time, the teacher's question being directed to the main idea in the group of sentences and often concerning the last of the sentences so that the pupils will learn to read until they actually find the answer to the question. Most children at the preprimer level, however, will do much of their reading one sentence at a time—silently first, later orally. Often a page will be read as a whole *after* it has been read silently and orally by individual sentences. (There are usually only two to four sentences to a page.) Such follow-up reading of a page as a whole encourages fluency.

It is easy for children to memorize a story. For this reason there may be follow-up reading which is done out of order. For instance, the teacher may call for the third sentence by saying, "Find this sentence: Joe ran and jumped"; or, for more fluent readers she may direct: "Find the sentence that tells what Joe did."

Supplementary reading. Parallel stories and charts as well as workbooks and teacher-prepared seatwork have already been mentioned as essential types of reading to supplement the preprimer. In connection with the show and tell period, units in the social studies and science, the morning news period about personal happenings, and the organization of classroom collections, there should still be much experience reading. Children should continue to use the reading corner as they look at picture books or browse through simple supplementary preprimers or very easy storybooks.

When children are reading fluently as the result of reading through several basic preprimers and the accompanying informal reading, they are ready to progress into primers and eventually first readers. Quick learners can progress through all these materials in first grade; but average and slow learners will use first readers sometime later.

Rapid Progress toward Independence

In this period children progress from the primer stage through second readers and into third readers. Sight vocabulary grows continuously while, at the same time, pupils go far toward mastering the word-attack skills that apply to words of one syllable (with their inflectional endings like *ed* and *ing*). The teacher continues to use informal reading, both parallel and experience types, to reinforce the book reading so that the children may become fluent readers who are mastering their reading skills as they go along. There should be much free, individual reading of simple materials of high interest because true fluency comes only as the children read abundantly.

Transitional guidance. All through the primary grades, the teacher takes care that pupils do not bog down because they are developing a backlog of unmastered words. Children must learn newly introduced basic words thoroughly as they go along, either as sight words or as words they can recognize through contextual clues or by word analysis. Before they read new stories, the teacher should introduce unfamiliar words by one of the following means: (1) using a parallel chart story; (2) talking over the illustrations in the reader; (3) recalling some experience that involves the meaningful inclusion of the new words; (4) listing these words on the chalkboard as they enter the discussion; (5) listing and saying each new word, then having the pupils skim a specified paragraph that contains it and having them point to it; or (6) making a large word card for each new word and having the pupils match it with the same word in the parallel chart. These are a few ways of introducing new words meaningfully before book reading takes place. By some such means, the teacher should prepare pupils for fluent reading of stories that contain unfamiliar words.

Despite the most careful and thoughtful introduction of new words, most pupils will need follow-up attention on them. The teacher needs to script-print supplementary sentences on the chalkboard; she should give matching exercises; increasingly she should follow up with exercises in word analysis by way of *phonics, visual analysis* that involves seeing likenesses and differences in similar words, or *structural analysis* as in noting *ed* and *ing* endings. Almost daily the teacher will conclude the reading lesson by giving attention to difficult words through some such follow-up activity. All word-attack skills should be learned in connection with new words found in current reading lessons.

Possibly the most important way of recognizing a new word is through its context. There may be picture clues that help; but the teacher should stress activities in which the children figure out a new word by noticing how it is used in the sentence; for instance, *bow-wow* might be guessed correctly in this sentence: *The dog said, "Bow-wow."*

In terms of reading vocabulary, teacher guidance should gradually shift from emphasis on sight vocabulary to stress on the ability to use contextual clues and word analysis to figure out words independently. There is careful transition, too, in the guidance given to help the child to read comprehendingly. While the teacher always sees that the children have a question in mind as they read in directed reading lessons, her questions will apply to longer and longer passages, for instance, a part page in the primer, a page or more in the first reader, and so on. The more difficult the selection, the shorter the passage which a question should cover; the more able the reading group, the longer the passage. The most advanced readers may read an entire first- or second-reader selection without stopping; but they should have had preliminary discussion or looked at pictures so as to raise questions to induce thoughtful reading.

Continued supplementation. Whether at the primer or the third-reader level, children should have considerable experience reading. Some of the informal materials may be the outcome of a show and tell or a news period; but more of them will be the result of the planning and evaluating of activities in the social studies and science. Often they will be of transitory value and be confined to the chalkboard; others should be kept for reference and transferred from the chalkboard to charts that can be tacked to the bulletin board or hung from a regular chart holder.

Also there will be many listings: personnel on each of several working committees, jobs to be done, materials to secure or to prepare, data collected through reading or observation during trips, or vocabulary lists. Some of the words will be so unusual that only the most able readers will master them for future reading; however, used in context, most of these words will be recognized by less able readers.

Much of the informal reading will be in the form of memoranda. There may be sentences to remind the children of jobs to be done before the close of the school day, suggestions of activities for filling spare time profitably, facts learned through individual reference reading or a simple experiment, and plans for projects that will consume a considerable period of time. One third-grade class became much interested in the Indians of the Southwest after one of its members returned from a six-weeks' trip to New Mexico. In talking over possible resources for learning more about these Indians, the pupils developed the following memorandum:

We think these people can help us.
Judy's mother has some souvenirs to send us.
The librarian will lend books.
The music teacher knows some Indian chants.
The art teacher says she will show us how to make pottery.
The PE teacher will teach us dances.

Slow-learning pupils will also need much parallel reading. Real experiences, movies and slides, and still pictures can provide a background of information for making concepts clear and easing the burden of new terms in book reading.

In addition, the teacher should often prepare paragraphs that incorporate unfamiliar words in a meaningful way. (Informal materials should not give away the ideas in the book stories to be read later.) Very often the teacher will give follow-up practice on troublesome words—sentences to reinforce meaning, lists to use in practicing word-attack skills.

Increasingly, children in the primary grades become able to read library materials independently. In the early stages, picture books with a minimum of simple text are appropriate. There may also be single copies of primers and eventually more advanced readers of a supplementary type, especially for the slow-learning pupils who need a controlled vocabulary. There should be many attractive trade books on a variety of topics and at various levels of difficulty so that each child can find just the right book for him. It is wise to change the books from time to time so as to meet awakening interests and suit the growing competencies of the child readers. It is intriguing, besides, to find fresh materials in constant supply.

Growth toward independence. At the end of the period of rapid progress, pupils will have become fairly independent in their reading. They should have gained a sizable sight vocabulary; they should have learned the mechanics of following a line of print quite smoothly; reading should consistently be a thought-getting process. Particularly important is the children's growing ability to figure out new words for themselves in each of several ways.

Once pupils have become familiar with the sounds of beginning consonants, they should proceed to initial consonant blends like *tr* in *tree* or *str* in *string,* and digraphs like *ch* in *child* and *wh* in *while.* Terminal blends, like *rt* in *start* and *nd* in *wind,* eventually should become familiar and help in attacking new words. Vowels, too, should come under control: the sound of an internal vowel in words like *hat, met, hit, hot,* and *hut;* in words ending with *e* like *mate, kite, note,* and *mute;* in words with paired vowels like those in *stream, raid,* and *road.* Pupils should also have learned to divide compound words like *milkman* and *afternoon* into their two main parts, and to find the base word in derivatives like *growing* and *quickly.*

Chapter 10 will explain the techniques and procedures for teaching pupils to use the various word attack skills.

Summary

All through the period of early primary reading instruction, the use of informal reading materials is important for the purposes of introducing the process of reading, of preparing the child for the vocabulary of a particular story in the reader, and of following up and reinforcing learnings that have been introduced. Some are dictated to the teacher by the pupils as they plan, evaluate, and report on their activities; others are prepared by the teacher with the express purpose of teaching basic vocabulary.

Much of children's reading in first and second grades is closely supervised and directed by the teacher. Preliminary discussion calls up the concepts introduced in the reading materials; a question is raised before the pupils read a passage which may vary in length from a single sentence to a page or more; discussion, dramatization or oral reading follows the first silent reading. Important to the pupils' progress and to a keen interest in reading is the opportunity to read independently materials appropriate in difficulty and topic. Library offerings should be rich and varied.

Selected References

(* recommended)

*Betts, Emmett A. *Foundations of Reading Instruction.* New York: American Book Co., 1954. Pp. 373–473.

Carter, Homer, and McGinnis, Dorothy. *Teaching Individuals to Read.* Boston: D. C. Heath and Co., 1962. Pp. 41–70.

*Gray, Lillian, and Reese, Dora. *Teaching Children to Read.* New York: Ronald Press, 1957. Selected pages.

*Gray, William S. (ed.). "Basic Instruction in Reading in Elementary and High Schools," *Supplementary Education Monographs,* No. 65. Chicago: University of Chicago Press, 1949.

Heilman, Arthur W. *Principles and Practices of Teaching Reading.* Columbus, Ohio: Charles E. Merrill Books, Inc., 1961. Pp. 73–132.

*Hildreth, Gertrude. *Readiness for School Beginners.* New York: Harcourt, Brace and World, Inc., 1950. Pp. 292–323.

———. *Teaching Reading.* New York: Holt, Rinehart and Winston, 1958. Pp. 196–247.

*Lamoreaux, Lillian, and Lee, Dorris. *Learning to Read through Experience.* New York: Appleton-Century-Crofts, Inc., 1943. Pp. 145–81.

McKim, Margaret. *Guiding Growth in Reading in the Modern Elementary School.* New York: The Macmillan Co., 1955. Pp. 117–47.

**Primary Reading,* Set I (films). Wilmette, Ill.: Encyclopaedia Britannica Films, Inc., 1952.

Russell, David H. *Children Learn to Read.* 2nd ed. Boston: Ginn and Co., 1961. Pp. 200–20.

Tinker, Miles A., and McCullough, Constance. *Teaching Elementary Reading.* New York: Appleton-Century-Crofts, Inc., 1962. Pp. 395–428.

*Witty, Paul, and the Educational Research Staff of the Encyclopaedia Britannica. "It's Fun to Find Out; Film-Story Books." Boston: D. C. Heath and Co., 1952.

6

Later Primary Instruction

CHILDREN WHO HAVE MADE AT LEAST AVERAGE progress in second grade are ready to finish off most of the skills that bring independence in word recognition, to read through stories of considerable length as a whole, and to begin work-type reading in textbooks and simple references. They are well on the road to independence. However, their slower-learning classmates will still need directed reading in which the teacher poses questions before they read short portions of their stories. Some will be reading at the primer level and will need the types of guidance discussed in the previous chapter; others will be in first readers or simple second readers and should be given the guidance that children at that stage of learning should have.

Materials written at the third-reader level typically make demands somewhat different from those met in the simpler selections and books that the children have been using. Instead of treating experiences that are current and close to children's actual experiences, the topics begin to reach outside the pupils' immediate environment into the wider community and even far-off countries, as well as into the past. Increasingly the pupils meet with unfamiliar concepts and unknown words. Therefore, the upper primary teacher has a growing responsibility to be on the alert for any concepts that may prove to be vague or perplexing, and to make sure that the children can understand what they are reading. She will use various means of introducing new ideas before the children read and of teaching her pupils to use contextual clues that will help them pick up meanings independently.

In many schools third-grade children are introduced to textbooks in the various school subjects. Reading the narrative selections in readers does not prepare the pupil fully for reading the informational matter and the specific directions in textbooks. The kind of thinking which the latter books require is quite different from that demanded in reading a lively and dramatic story, and pupils must have additional specific training in the skills which textbook reading calls for. This chapter presents the instructional procedures for lessons in both readers and textbooks.

Basic Procedures in Using Readers

Instruction at the later primary period is varied. It includes much informal reading, directed reading in books, free reading, supplementary lessons for building word-attack skills, and much attention to meaning vocabulary.

Organization for instruction. A balanced reading program calls for both grouped and individual instruction. Part of the individualized opportunities arise in the free reading period when children select books in terms of their reading proficiency and their special interests. Often the teacher will help the more dependent pupils find suitable books. Also she will frequently sit down with individual pupils so as to check on their mastery of sight vocabulary, their ability to read smoothly or to figure out new words for themselves, their general comprehension, and their relative understanding of new terms. Especially will she give such individual attention to pupils as soon as they show signs of having difficulty in order that she may explicitly locate and promptly remove the source of trouble. Even in the midst of group instruction, a skilled teacher gives much individual attention: seating hard-of-hearing pupils next to her, giving help in a quiet aside to a pupil who is not quite "up to par" and yet needs but a small boost, calling on a child whose attention is beginning to wander, or having some supplementary informal reading for any individual or small group that needs additional practice on sight vocabulary. A little help at a critical moment can do wonders. "A stitch in time" should be the slogan of every reading teacher.

If children's needs and interests are to be properly considered, grouping for reading must be flexible. Typically classrooms are divided into three groups: the fast-advancing, the average, and the slower-learning; but the teacher must be ready at any time to move a child into another group as soon as he will fit better into the work of that group. Flexibility has another connotation; namely, that pupils will join different groups as they join in their various enterprises. At times, a group will be formed for those pupils who need help in learning some particular reading skill, such as mastering the blend *cl,* its members possibly being drawn from all three of the regular reading groups. Or after three or four pupils have prepared individual stories to read aloud, the remaining children may choose which of these readers they want to hear and thus form groups. Still another basis for grouping is used when part of a class develops a dramatization while the others are making crayon illustrations to be assembled on a picture-strip movie. Several times a week the teacher will find occasion for taking a small group aside to teach some new skill (such as using an encyclopedia) and to give help on a partially familiar skill which is poorly used (syllabication, for instance). During any one day, a particular pupil may work in three or more different reading groups. Besides, there are many other groupings that develop as the children plan and carry out learning activities in the social studies and elementary science. Grouping is almost necessarily flexible.

Some authorities object to the "nondemocratic" practice of grouping in reading because, they maintain, a child in the slow-advancing group may be made to feel "dumb." Flexible grouping that allows each child to mingle with several groups each day can do much to obviate such a possibility. Also, a child can get genuine satisfaction out of successful learning experiences in a group working with materials at a level suited to his ability to learn; he can be a leader in that group; he is learning along with his group mates and, indeed, learns much through observing them and working along with them. In classes as large as are typical in many schools today, there are economy and efficiency in grouping for reading instruction.

Some very skilled teachers are effective in individualizing their primary reading instruction. In one school system, for instance, each child is reading in a completely individualized program. The day begins with careful planning to determine who will meet with the teacher that day to read orally and to discuss what has been read silently. The order in which each is to report is definitely worked out so that five children can be seated near the teacher at all times: one working with her, the others reading silently but ready for their turns. When one completes his work with the teacher, he leaves and the others move up as a replacement takes the fifth chair. Meanwhile, the remaining pupils are reading in self-selected books, working in their workbooks, or engaging in free reading activities such as reading games, review of reading charts, enjoyment of simple storybooks in the reading corner, or quiet oral reading of a choice story to an interested classmate. Each child is busy with fruitful reading endeavors until his turn to meet with the teacher comes—at least once a week for all, oftener for those who need very close supervision.

Such individualization requires that the teacher be thoroughly familiar with a wide range of reading materials, that she plan painstakingly, and that she organize the reading activities most effectively if each child is to get the guidance that he will need from time to time in selecting books and in acquiring the skills that his constantly advancing reading activities demand. Such guidance must be given at the "teachable moment," or time of readiness. Some teachers who do not plan their individual instruction carefully and who are poor managers only succeed in having the pupils waste their time in futile and superficial endeavors while they are on their own, or else the pupils "cut up" deplorably. A rich supply of reading materials, a systematically planned program of independent study and reading, and a relatively small class are essential to successful individualization.

Variety in the program. Since learning to read is a complex task, there must necessarily be a varied program of instruction. In the first place, there should be both *directed and free reading*. The directed instruction will explicitly provide the following kinds of guidance: meaningful introduction of new and unfamiliar concepts and vocabulary, preliminary discussion and questions to provoke curiosity and interest, occasional help with a hard word during reading, follow-up discussion that calls for an organization of ideas and selection of data that will prove a point, and finally informal reading exercises that will constantly add to sight vocabulary or build ability to figure out new words independently. Directed reading should be based on materials that are just a little too hard for the pupils to read fluently by themselves—materials that call for the learning of entirely new skills (as using an index), or mastering a more advanced stage of a skill (as learning to recognize a beginning blend like *gr* after mastery of the single *g* or *r* sound), or improving a skill that is still handled clumsily (as opening a book to approximately the right page at the first try).

Free reading is often recreational, though it may also be a search for information. It is individual, independent, voluntary, satisfying. The materials should be relatively simple, but suited to the current interests of the child reader. If, however, a child is very narrow in his interests or is unaware of the intriguing topics that are available, the teacher should call attention to the pictures in a book, tell an enticing bit, or read an alluring page or two so as to introduce the child to pleasures of which he might otherwise be oblivious; or she may have other pupils encourage the less advanced readers by similar activities. It is children's free reading that builds a permanent interest in reading; it also contributes to fluency and ease in reading.

Second, there should be both *silent* and *oral reading*. At the later primary level, children should continue to read silently before they read orally. There should be no sight reading. Usually pupils should read through an entire story silently, discuss it, and possibly dramatize it; at the end of a silent reading lesson, choice bits may be read orally. Or there may occasionally be an entire lesson devoted to oral reading on the day after silent reading of a story that is unusually lively or humorous. (See audience situations in the chapter on oral reading.)

In the third place, *informal reading* should supplement that in books. There will be experience stories and reports that are written on the chalkboard as pupils relate personal and community news or tell of their observations on trips or during home experiments. Learning activities in the social studies, health, and science call for many committee listings, records of plans and accomplishments, sets of standards, and original stories based on the pupils' learnings.

For slow-learning children, in particular, the use of parallel reading should be continued. If the story next to be read has many unfamiliar concepts, a parallel story can be devised to introduce the new concepts, which should be further clarified through pictures, board sketches and diagrams, stories of personal experiences, or slides and film strips. Whenever the book story has relatively few new hard words, these may be listed on the board before reading begins; they should be pronounced clearly and explained, or the pupils may be asked to skim designated paragraphs to locate the new words. Many teachers prefer not to list new words singly, but to select a phrase that includes each of the words; for instance, instead of listing *surprised,* she will lift the phrase *boys were surprised* from the story. This latter practice encourages the use of contextual clues and the perception of words in groups rather than one by one.

Attention to vocabulary. Meaning vocabulary needs careful and constant attention. For instance, the teacher may relate experiences or call for those of the pupils, tell stories, and give explanations that bear on the new words and concepts; the pupils may discuss related pictures in their books, on the bulletin board, or in slides or film strips. Often the teacher may utilize recordings or refer to relevant radio or television programs. Whenever new words are listed on the chalkboard, their meaning should be stressed even more than pronunciation, especially for silent reading lessons. No teacher can do too much to insure the children's understanding and meaningful use of the new words they constantly meet in their reading activities.

Word recognition. In their early primary reading, pupils make a bare beginning in learning how to attack new words. The most important period for extending and mastering the skills of word analysis is this period of later primary reading instruction. Pupils who are reading in second, third, and fourth readers need a systematic and thorough program for teaching the skills of independent word attack. Proficient, quick-learning pupils tend to pick up word-analysis skills with little direct teaching or to recognize words without any detailed analysis; but most pupils profit from daily help in ways of attacking new words and will suffer unless such instruction is provided. Chapter 10 gives a detailed account of a developmental word-attack program.

Lessons in word recognition must be a closely knit part of the total reading program. Long ago phonics taught as a separate phase of reading was proven to be ineffective; instead, the words that children learn to analyze must be drawn from their current reading lessons. (Suppose that *just* is a new word. The pupils may attack it by comparing *just* to already familiar words like *jump, dust,* and *must* which either begin or end similarly to the new word.) Usually at the close of a reading lesson, the teacher will list on the board any words that have proven difficult and will take about five minutes to work with these words: comparison with familiar words that begin or end in the same way, attention to the inflectional endings (as *ing*), single and paired internal vowels, blends and other common letter combinations. Nonphonetic words will be incorporated in repetitious sentences so as to lead to mastery through thought-inducing repetition, since such words are actually sight words.

In addition to word analysis, the use of contextual clues is essential. Such clues involve meaning and help the child to reason his way to understanding and possible recognition. Especially when words are not spelled the way they sound, contextual clues help the young reader to recognize words already in their speaking vocabulary, for instance, *sewing* or *colonel.* Often the setting in which such words are used is a potent clue that leads to recognition.

Fundamental steps in a directed reading lesson. The introduction of a reading lesson should prepare the pupils by building background or arousing curiosity and interest. In case there are unfamiliar concepts in the selection, the teacher may tell an illustrative story, relate an experience, show samples or pictures, list the new words and explain them, or otherwise lay a foundation for good comprehension. Often a lesson will begin with the discussion of pupils' past experiences or learnings that are related to the ideas in the reading selection, with a look at some of the illustrations to whet curiosity, and with questions that will give purpose to the reading. It is especially important that the introduction establish a definite purpose for reading so that pupils will know whether to read in rather cursory fashion for enjoyment or in a more careful manner so as to find definite information. A good introduction builds on-the-spot *readiness for reading,* an essential at all levels.

The reading lesson proper may be handled in many ways. If the selection is fairly easy and not too long, the pupils may read through without interruption. Afterwards they may discuss the questions that were raised in the introduction of the lesson; they may dramatize or read orally. If the story is long, difficult, or complicated, it may be read by installments. In extreme cases, it may be read a paragraph or half page at a time, there always being prefaced a question to aid the pupils in finding the main idea in this short portion. Such detailed guidance is especially necessary for slow-learning pupils whenever they would "get over their heads" if left to read without explicit guidance. When a selection is read by installments, oral reading may be interspersed; or oral reading may follow the completion of the silent reading. (Probably such difficult materials are inappropriate for oral reading.) Oral reading should occur only when it will yield great enjoyment, add to appreciation, or clear up a vague or disputed point. Many selections are unsuited to oral reading, since they were originally designed to give information, directions, or explanations to an individual reader.

How a reading lesson should end depends on circumstances. If the selection has much humor or several exciting incidents, it may be ideal for selective oral reading. If, on the other hand, the lesson is for the purpose of helping children to organize their thinking (sequence of events, main points, or facts that supply an answer to a question raised in the assignment), discussion that yields a list of points to be listed on the board is preferable to oral reading. Whenever the episodes in a selection are very dramatic, making an informal play may be a natural conclusion; or, if certain scenes are very vivid, the children may enjoy and profit from making crayon illustrations.

One essential step in fairly difficult lessons is the follow-up attention to words that pupils have asked for. They must develop no backlog of personally unrecognizable words. Immediate attention to difficult words should come through chalkboard exercises on the spot, or through a chart devoted to each of several word-attack elements, such as words featuring common blends or short internal vowels. Usually there will be seatwork that emphasizes meaning vocabulary, word analysis, or various comprehension skills—some in workbooks, much devised by the teacher to meet newly developing needs for specific reading skills. The latter type of exercises may sometimes be placed on the chalkboard and often duplicated on work sheets.

The use of seatwork. Children who make many errors in their seatwork or who guess wildly in their responses are learning mistakes and unintelligent ways of working. Their reading proficiency is being damaged whenever they do their seatwork poorly. The teacher must always be sure that her pupils understand what they are to do and how to do it; she should similarly make sure that no pupil is being asked to do exercises that are so easy and familiar that no learning is taking place. Whenever a new type of exercise is being introduced or the pupils are to try again on an assignment which they previously failed to understand, the teacher should do one of the following: have the pupils open their workbooks (or consult work sheets) and work out the first two or three items under her direct supervision; work out a similar set of exercises on the chalkboard; or supervise the work of the handful of pupils who did not know how to do the exercise on the previous day while the remainder work by themselves.

Seatwork should be truly educational, never mere busywork. Whatever the children are asked to do should have the definite purpose of introducing some new skill in a simple way or of reinforcing the learning of one that has been only partially mastered. Often there will be occasion to have different pupils do different exercises on the same day because their needs and abilities vary.

There follow several illustrations of educational seatwork in reading. The manuals that parallel basal readers suggest dozens of other types of helpful seatwork. It is wise, in fact, for the teacher to consult her manual in connection with each selection she teaches so that she may take advantage of the suggestions appropriate for the pupils' learning at their current stage of reading: exercises on meaning vocabulary, selection of main points, word building or word analysis, and the like.

Exercise A (To teach similar word endings, with emphasis on short internal vowels)

Find the words that rhyme. Draw a line between them. The first one is done for you.

sick	dig	fun	bell
big	fit	tell	sun
leg	quick	got	ring
hit	beg	sing	lot

Exercise B (To teach the division of a compound word into its component parts)

Each sentence has a double word. Draw a ring around this word; then write its parts. The first one is done for you.

1. Give me something to eat. some thing
2. Please let me have another cookie.
3. This is my birthday.
4. Did you come to my party without a present?
5. Mother gave the party this afternoon.
6. I liked everything I got.

Exercise C (To teach comprehension of a series of sentences related to a book story; to clear up new concepts, such as *span*)

Draw the picture that these sentences tell about. Read all of the sentences before you start to draw.

1. There is a long bridge across a river.
2. The bridge has two spans.
3. Under the bridge is a boat with a sail.
4. Two men are in it.
5. One man is fishing with a fishpole.
6. The other man has a net.
7. The men are landing a big fish.

Exercise D (To teach comprehension of individual sentences; to stress exact following of directions)

Do just what each sentence tells you to do.

1. Write your first and last names.
2. Draw a line under your first name.
3. Draw a ring around your last name.
4. Find each *a, e, i,* and *o* in your two names.
5. Put an *X* through all of these letters.
6. Draw a picture of yourself.
7. Color it to show how you are dressed today.

Exercise E (To stress the meaning of new words through matching each one with its synonym)

Look at the first word in each row. Then find the word in the same line that means the same as the first word. Draw a line under it. The first one is done for you.

little	like	small	ball	big
start	stop	string	card	begin
happy	glad	grow	funny	heavy
near	clear	clean	close	far
fast	finish	quick	stick	last
noise	note	speak	pound	sound

Recreational Reading

Pupils do much of their recreational reading during their free reading periods, though oral reading in audience situations gives frequent opportunities for enjoyment. As older primary children gain independence in their reading, they should visit the library and check out books to read at home and in their spare time at school. The classroom or school library should afford rich offerings for children's voluntary reading; and, whenever possible, the teacher should take her pupils to a near-by public library to help them get acquainted with the setup there, to look through suitable books, and to sign for personal library cards. Many city and county school systems and some public libraries run bookmobiles that serve schools and homes in their communities. Whatever the source, children should have easy access to library offerings. It is as pupils find themselves in an environment rich in reading materials that they acquire a deep interest in reading as a source of entertainment and knowledge.

Since children vary so widely in their reading proficiency and in their preferences for reading materials, library offerings should be rich and varied. Probably, for classroom use, the teacher should arrange to check out thirty to forty books at a time and to make frequent changes so that fresh books will always be available and so that the pupils' newly awakening interests and growing abilities may be served. While each classroom should probably have a limited number of basic library books as a permanent resource, it is still advisable to supplement generously from a central school library, the public library, and possibly favorite books which children offer to bring from home. The last mentioned may need to be censored.

Work-Type Reading

All through their school life, children do much of their learning through reading informational materials. Special skills are required if they are to use books effectively and to read comprehensively and evaluatively. In the later primary grades, they should make a good beginning in learning such skills.

One galaxy of skills is involved in learning to handle books and to locate materials in them. In the beginning stages of book reading, the pupils should have learned how to hold a book properly, how to turn pages, how to use a simple table of contents, and how to turn quickly to a desired page. For instance in connection with using preprimers, they will have learned to turn pages by carefully lifting the upper right hand corner first, to skim the table of contents until a specified title of a story is found, then to turn as nearly as possible to the correct page in their first try. In order to turn accurately to a desired page, the children should be given practice exercises such as these:

1. Open to the back of the book. How many pages are there in the book?
2. What would be the number of the middle page? (Help the group figure this out.) See if you can turn to this page in your first try.
3. Similarly turn to the pages at the first fourth and the third fourth of the book.
4. Look at the numbers on the board. See if you can turn to the pages having these numbers. Do this one at a time.

Such abilities may need review in the later primary grades. In addition, children need to learn to use the index or glossary found in their school books. To use either, they must become familiar with alphabetical order and learn to locate any specified topic or word according to alphabetical arrangement. In using an index, the pupil later turns to the page or pages on which the desired topic is discussed, then skims until the sought-for information is located. Learning how to perform such acts skillfully calls for a series of lessons that give opportunities for using an index and locating desired information.

Another group of skills is demanded in the reading of the information-packed textbooks and references involved in social studies and science. By asking pointed questions *before* the children read, the teacher can help them get the central idea in a paragraph or select the two or three or four main points in a several-page lesson. Too, the children should learn to take a forward look through the bold-faced topical headings that appear on the pages of their textbooks so as to get an idea of what they are about to read. In fact, the teacher may so guide third-grade children that they learn the three major uses for the topical headings in their textbooks: (1) to make a preliminary survey of a lesson by skimming the topical headings, thus getting oriented for the reading to follow; (2) to look carefully at each topical heading before reading the paragraphs that follow, to think what hint the heading gives of the main ideas to be expected, and often to change it into a question that should be answered in the ensuing reading matter; and (3) to review a lesson the next day by skimming the topical headings and quickly recalling the information they suggest. Thus, the children should learn that each topical heading gives a strong hint of the "big ideas" to be presented in the paragraphs under it and that they should formulate a question on the basis of each topical heading and then read thoughtfully in an attempt to answer this question.

The pupils should similarly utilize contextual clues in figuring out the meaning of a new word. Another skill essential to skillful reading is the ability to suit the rate and manner of reading to the purpose for reading and to the nature of the materials to be read. At the later primary stage, children can make only a bare beginning at learning when to skim, when to read in a cursory manner, or when to "dig in" and truly study. These children, for instance, can skim to locate the exact passage that proves a point, look through a chapter in a simple reference book to see whether it seems to bear on a topic for which they are searching, and read carefully a paragraph that explains exactly how to plant a bulb in the school garden.

In Chapter 14 will be found a systematic account of work-type reading.

Selected References

(* recommended)

*BROOM, M. E., *et al. Effective Reading Instruction.* New York: The Macmillan Co., 1951. Pp. 158–215.

GRAY, LILLIAN, and REESE, DORA. *Teaching Children to Read.* New York: Ronald Press, 1957. Selected pages.

HEILMAN, ARTHUR W. *Principles and Practices of Teaching Reading.* Columbus, Ohio: Charles E. Merrill Books, Inc., 1961. Pp. 171–206.

*HILDRETH, GERTRUDE. *Teaching Reading.* New York: Holt, Rinehart and Winston, 1958. Pp. 249–333.

*MCKIM, MARGARET. *Guiding Growth in Reading in the Elementary School.* New York: The Macmillan Co., 1955. Pp. 151–259.

Phonics: A Key to Better Reading (filmstrips). Chicago: Society for Visual Education, 1951.

Primary Reading, Set II (films). Wilmette, Ill.: Encyclopaedia Britannica Films, Inc., 1952.

Reading in the Elementary School, Forty-eighth Yearbook, Part II. National Society for the Study of Education. Chicago: University of Chicago Press, 1949. Pp. 93–126.

TINKER, MILES A., and MCCULLOUGH, CONSTANCE. *Teaching Elementary Reading.* New York: Appleton-Century-Crofts, Inc., 1962. Pp. 431–57.

WITTY, PAUL, and the Educational Research Staff of the Encyclopaedia Britannica. "It's Fun to Find Out; Film-Story Books," Boston: D. C. Heath and Co., 1952.

7

Reading in the Intermediate and Upper Grades

MANY PUPILS, BY THE TIME THEY ENTER THE fourth grade, are approaching independence in several of the basic reading skills; but there are several important skills that should be stressed for pupils making normal progress, and there are new skills to be learned at each succeeding level of the school. Other boys and girls, because of late maturation, low ability, lack of motivation, or any of several other causes, may still be struggling with skills typically taught in the primary grades. There is no doubt that a planned, sequential program for pupils of every level of achievement in the intermediate grades is an important aspect of the curriculum; that such a program should be extended into grades seven, eight and nine is just as important. The emphases at succeeding stages and for different levels of ability may vary; but many students if they are to become good readers need all the aid we can give them for as long as they are in school.

Truly, children in the intermediate and upper grades are approaching the "golden age" of reading. For those who have gained independence in word-attack skills and the introductory skills of comprehension, this is a period of extension and refinement. Interests deepen and become more refined; children read at greater and greater depth; the language of print is more and more challenging; and there can and should be an awakening awareness of how authors write and of the differences between well-written and poorly written stories, articles, and books. Oral reading may become an art to be practiced for the benefit of others. Also, silent reading skills can be applied to all types of materials, as the child senses and identifies different purposes for reading.

It has often been stated that the primary grades represent a period of *learning to read* and that the intermediate and upper grades represent *reading to learn*. This is not a particularly sound distinction. From the beginning, children *read to learn;* we have evidence from studies of relative maturity in reading that we are *learning to read* for the rest of our lives. Each level of maturity should bring a further refinement of the complex skills which we use in reading. Consequently, the formal reading program in the intermediate and upper grades is of the utmost importance.

The challenge to teachers. Reading in the intermediate and upper grades is characterized by the wide range of skills and abilities among the pupils and the wide variety of tasks which must be accomplished through reading. The teacher of reading in these grades has a heavy responsibility and should feel genuinely challenged.

Methods of teaching reading to pupils in the intermediate and upper grades are well outlined in any good series of basal readers. But, as any teacher knows, a reader designed for the sixth grade does not contain all of the suitable materials nor all of the necessary related practice for a heterogeneous class. There will be need to use primary methods and materials for those pupils who lack skills in word attack and vocabulary; while, on the other hand, an extension of some familiar skills and the introduction of really advanced ones are necessary for those pupils who are capable of reading independently above the grade level.

Fortunately, some of the most recently published basal readers are organized in units, or clusters of stories, which are directly related to social studies and science units which are commonly taught at each grade level. The wise teacher will correlate the teaching of reading skills with reading in the content subjects throughout each day. Chapter 15 gives suggestions for teaching reading in each of the major content subjects.

Materials for instruction in the intermediate and upper grades are usually developed with less carefully controlled vocabularies than at the primary level. Consequently, the child is required to rely more on word analysis skills and on context clues for determining pronunciation and meaning of words which may not be in his speaking or listening vocabularies. Even so, the teacher should constantly place emphasis upon the review and the introduction of basic vocabulary as new units in the content subjects are undertaken.

The task of the teacher in these grades is threefold: to *introduce* new skills as reading demands become more complex, to provide materials and opportunities for the child to *reinforce* skills which have been learned, and to aid all children to *master* the more rudimentary and essential skills.

Organizing for instruction. Should teachers of the intermediate grades continue to group pupils for instruction in reading skills? Is there need for a separate period for reading? The answer to both questions is definitely affirmative.

As we have indicated, the range of abilities and skills in the typical classroom at this level may be very wide—typically wider than at the primary level—and skills development in the children will vary from the very weak to the very able readers. It is practical to organize the class into groups for instruction according to their respective levels of skills and to move children often into other groups as their needs are satisfied on a particular skill. In Chapter 9 we will discuss grouping practices for various purposes of instruction in the heterogeneous classroom, indicating that some grouping practices are much more appropriate for the intermediate and upper grades than they are for primary grades.

New skills which are needed in the content subjects can often be introduced to the class as a whole. Some children will need simpler and more explicit examples and prolonged practice; others will move quickly toward mastery of the new skills. Groups may be formed and may be disbanded just as soon as there is evidence that children are capable of working independently with the skills learned.

Many children are ready for individualized instruction in the intermediate grades. Brief conferences with the teacher regarding their reading, the preparation of individual reports for presentation to other class members, and work on independent assignments for study-type reading may all aid children in becoming increasingly independent. Where units are being developed in science, social studies, and other subjects, there are numerous opportunities for each child to work independently toward enrichment in his learnings and toward personal contributions that serve to complete the unit.

Variety in the program. Activities in reading in these grades should contribute toward a balanced program that involves recreational reading, directed reading for the development of particular skills, and work-type reading. It is difficult to isolate and to classify skills that are particularly pertinent to the middle and upper grades; indeed, it may be said that there is no clear-cut beginning point for any specific skill, and that all skills of reading and related language arts are developed from the very beginning of children's school experiences. However, the nature of the curriculum in these more advanced grades does call for *emphasis* upon certain skills to enable children to meet the challenge of reading in the content subjects.

1. Forming generalizations concerning word-attack skills, word-meaning skills, and comprehension skills is both possible and necessary. Through spelling, the child may form generalizations about the phonetic and structural elements of our language. In reading social studies and science, he may begin to generalize about the particular meanings of words in various contexts. Basic principles can be taught, but generalizations are formed only when the child sees essential relationships and extends his knowledge to other materials, other areas.

2. Children in the middle grades have learned to distinguish between the factual and the fanciful. They continue to learn the difference between facts and opinions and should begin to form judgments about the worth of a particular article or story on the basis of these distinctions. They learn to accept fanciful writing and to enjoy being taken on flights of fancy by a good writer; on the other hand they accept different points of view on a subject and take pride in their ability to make personal interpretations.

3. Cause and effect relationships become important as knowledge of history and science unfolds; these same relationships are seen in simple stories, and stories may be used as a basis for learning about cause and effects.

4. Reading for various purposes, "shifting gears" as one moves from simple narration to expository materials, is one aspect of the mature reader. Fundamentally, there are three

purposes for reading: to be entertained, to gain information, or to be convinced. Children need careful guidance in determining which of these purposes is to be attained, and the teacher should frequently call attention to the fact that purposes have shifted. Thus, the children will adjust the rate of their reading and the intensity of their thinking according to the purpose to be accomplished.

5. One of the most noticeable changes in children's development occurs when they begin to think logically and critically. Under careful guidance, they may learn to analyze a story or selection, to determine exactly what the author has said in a literal sense. Only after they have determined the literal meaning can they be expected to *interpret* what they read; interpretation calls for the individual's bringing to an idea his own experiences and previous knowledge. Another step in critical thinking is that of comparing and/or contrasting what one learns from reading with other sources of information. Finally, the reader must form a synthesis or a conclusion drawn from the principles and the assumptions which have been considered. Excellent suggestions for helping the child to think logically and critically are given in the teacher's manual of many of our basal reading series.

6. Children in the middle grades, and particularly in the upper grades, gradually develop an awareness of and appreciation for the techniques which authors use to tell a good story, to present a point of view, or to give information. They learn the reasons for different literary forms; many children may experiment with writing poetry, short stories, essays, or factual reports. The teacher may contribute to their appreciation for literary techniques and literary forms by providing many *models*, or selections which best represent good writing and interesting forms. The incomparable artistry of Dr. Seuss, Elizabeth Guilfoile, Mark Twain, or A. A. Milne has

brought delight and profound appreciation to thousands of children and young adults.

7. Locating information and following written directions are skills which become increasingly critical as the child learns to rely more on his own efforts in work-type reading. One of the major instructional tasks in the intermediate and upper grades is teaching children how to locate information, how to outline what they have read, how to summarize information, and how to use books and the library effectively. Chapter 13 is devoted to suggestions for helping children to develop these skills.

In the hierarchy of reading skills, skimming followed by intensive reading ranks high, particularly for the pupil who must sift through many sources to find needed information. Many lessons should be planned to give children practice in skimming for information, particularly in materials in the content subjects.

8. During the intermediate grades, the rate of children's reading should increase as they gain independence in word-attack skills, recognize and master various linguistic forms, and learn to shift the rate of reading according to the purpose for reading. In Chapter 13 suggestions are given for improving the rate of reading.

Materials of instruction. Basal readers are the framework of a good reading program in the intermediate and upper grades. Many teachers seem to be unaware of this fact; they apparently believe that since the emphasis in the teaching of reading in these grades is placed in the content subjects, there is little need for basal readers. However, basal readers should be used in these grades, for these reasons:

1. Basal readers provide a sequence and continuity of skills which otherwise may not receive attention. It is conceivable

that an experienced, well-trained teacher could teach essential reading skills through the use of textbooks in the content subjects and through encouraging children to read widely on an individual basis. However, the typical classroom teacher will do well to follow the orderly, systematic plan of the basal reader and to use the reading lesson as a means of providing transfer of learning to the content subjects.

2. Most basal readers contain a body of excellent literature, both classical and contemporary in nature. The stories in the reader should provide a good basis for follow-up wide reading on related topics, in similar types of literature or in the content subjects.
3. It is possible, through careful selection of books below and above a particular grade level, to provide concomitantly for review and practice on essential skills by slow-learning, average, and more able children.

The basal reader has never been more than the *minimum* ingredient of the reading program; it does *not* constitute the reading program itself. The teacher must extend skills beyond the basal reader, throughout the day, into all content subjects. She must make available to her classroom many, many materials which are varied in level of difficulty and interest, some easy enough that the least experienced reader can benefit from reading them and some so challenging that the most capable readers are satisfied.

Reading in Grades Seven, Eight, and Nine

The teaching of reading in the upper grades poses some difficult problems. Organization of schools for these grades varies so widely in our nation. In one instance, there may be a seventh- and eighth-grade center, where classrooms are self-contained or partially departmentalized. In the junior high school, containing the seventh, eighth, and ninth grades, all subjects may be departmentalized. Again, there may be provision for a "core" of subjects for a part of the day; a common combination is English and social studies for a "block" of two or three hours under one teacher.

Whatever the administrative organization, there has been little agreement in recent years about the formal teaching of reading in these grades. Because of an increasing number of pupils who have reading problems in these grades and in the high schools, many specialists are currently concerned with providing better training for teachers. Since the majority of teachers in the upper grades or the junior high school are trained as secondary school teachers, few of them have training in the teaching of reading.

Criteria of good programs. Certainly there must be a sequential planned program of reading skills for students in the upper grades. Too often teachers assume that students who have reached the seventh grade have been thoroughly trained in basic reading skills and that the emphasis of the upper grades should be upon developing tastes and appreciations for good literature. It is true that these students have been *exposed* to several years of training in reading skills, but in many instances the exposure simply did not result in the development of independent reading skills. To provide for the wide range of abilities and skills which are to be found in a typical class of the upper grades, we should plan a reading program in which:

1. There is a definite, planned sequence of skills, based on the scope and sequence of previous grades, but continuing toward refinement and extension of those skills.
2. Specific instruction is given in each curriculum area on how to read and study for a particular subject.
3. There is careful planning among teachers of the various subject areas to determine responsibilities for emphases of skills

and to make certain that essential skills are not being ignored by all of the teachers.
4. Thorough and continuous evaluation of the needs of students in reading is provided.
5. Provision is made for special training of the seriously disabled readers.

Organizing for instruction. Some grouping of students in the upper grades is essential if needs are to be met. Whether the teacher is working in a self-contained, a departmentalized, or a core-type organization, grouping is still advisable and possible. In a typical eighth grade, reading abilities of the students may range from third-reader level to that of a mature adult.

It is impossible to use a single textbook in a particular subject, a textbook designed for that grade level, and to expect students to read enthusiastically and accurately. Some provision must be made for materials with a wide range in difficulty, and assignment of those materials must be made to students according to their abilities. Fortunately, there is a trend today away from the type of literary anthology which contains nothing except reading selections and a few questions at the end of each selection. Recognizing the need for further extension of skills among students in the upper grades, authors of basal readers for those grades have in more recent years provided some excellent materials. The good anthology represents a balance of classical and contemporary selections; it is accompanied by a teacher's manual which gives suggestions for reinforcement and extension of basic reading skills; it gives clear, definite suggestions to the student on how to read a selection; and it is likely to provide a bibliography of related readings.

No matter how well the anthology meets the criteria we have just stated, it is not sufficient for the teaching of reading skills in the upper grades. Some of the less able students will be grouped for learning basic skills; for these students such materials as *Eye and Ear Fun* (Webster Publishing Company) or the *Be A Better Reader Series* (Prentice-Hall) are appropriate. Such practice materials should be supplemented by high-interest, low-vocabulary trade books.

Average readers in the upper grades need careful guidance in reading their anthologies and their other textbooks. They deserve a planned, sequential program which gives them opportunities to reinforce their reading skills and to master certain more rudimentary of the skills. For superior readers, the anthology is a mere beginning for reading; these students should be encouraged to follow their interests and to read widely in books that are constantly challenging to them.

Many schools are fortunate to have a reading specialist whose time is devoted to working with those students who cannot profit from regular classroom instruction. The demand for reading specialists for the upper grades or the junior high school far exceeds the supply, unfortunately. The well-trained specialist may provide training for remedial students, and special developmental courses for average or above-average students who desire to improve their skills. Unless the specialist works with classroom teachers, instructing them in the use of materials and the methods of teaching reading, this person can never satisfactorily meet all of the problems that arise at the upper-grades levels.

Summary

Reading in the intermediate and upper grades should provide for the extension and refinement of skills which were learned in the primary grades. The range of skills and abilities of our students in these grades poses some difficult problems; the reading program should be planned to provide a multitrack program of sequential, continuous development of basic skills. Major problems of instruction arise in the content areas, and it is important that skills be developed for reading in all subjects. This period of a child's development should result in his increasing independence as a reader, with broader and more refined interests, efficient study skills, and the ability to think critically and creatively.

Selected References

BAMMAN, HENRY A.; HOGAN, URSULA; and GREENE, CHARLES. *Reading Instruction in the Secondary School.* New York: David McKay Co., Inc., 1961.

JEWETT, ARNO (ed.). *Improving Reading in the Junior High School,* U.S. Department of Health, Education, and Welfare Bulletin No. 10. Washington, D.C.: U.S. Government Printing Office, 1957.

Reading, Grades 7, 8, 9: A Teacher's Guide to Curriculum Planning. Brooklyn: Board of Education of the City of New York, 1959.

SHELDON, WILLIAM D. "Reading Instruction in Junior High School," in *Development in and through Reading,* Sixtieth Yearbook, Part I, National Society for the Study of Education. Chicago: University of Chicago Press, 1961. Pp. 305–19.

TINKER, MILES A., and CONSTANCE M. MCCULLOUGH. *Teaching Elementary Reading.* New York: Appleton-Century-Crofts, Inc., 1962. Chapters 22, 23, 24.

8

Teaching Reading to the Gifted and to Low-Normal Learners

ON PRECEDING PAGES HAVE APPEARED FREQUENT references to the existence and implications of individual differences among children as they proceed through the elementary school reading program. This chapter pulls together the various administrative and curricular procedures that are currently used in various school systems in the effort to provide effectively for extreme individual differences, as represented by the gifted and the low-normal learner. First will be discussed ways of caring for very bright children who read proficiently and last, procedures for dealing with slow-learning pupils who approach average proficiency with IQs in the 80s or low 90s.

A Reading Program for Gifted Children

It has been said that the typical American school is geared to the average child so that the curriculum makes demands on slow-learning children beyond their capacity to perform and, at the same time, fails to challenge gifted pupils who tend to become bored, lazy, or mischievous. Currently there is widespread effort to devise curricula that will provide opportunities for every child to learn according to his peculiar level of ability and his special aptitudes. At present, much attention is being given to gifted children.

In a democracy where a good citizen expects himself to make a contribution commensurate with his ability to achieve, the gifted child has much to offer and should develop into a leader in community and world affairs. But qualities of leadership do not develop suddenly out of thin air; they result only as the child is given many opportunities to utilize his special abilities and discriminating guidance in leadership in his formative years. The citizen in a democracy, too, attains rich, full living as he is constantly challenged to develop his powers through diversified, stimulating, satisfying activities. Thus can he attain self-realization and personal integrity; thus can he make a contribution to his fellows and, in turn, gain a respect and appreciation for what they have to offer.

The special needs of gifted children. No matter how precocious a child may be, he shares childhood's basic needs for security, affection, companionship, recognition, and status. Despite his precocity, he may be weak in certain phases of the reading program and need systematic guidance in learning such skills as skimming or word analysis. At the same time, the gifted child has great capacity for doing independent work and should be given specific training in study-research skills that will enable him to attack individual projects on his own. Then he will be able to sample widely and delve deeply into the reading materials that various libraries afford, for the gifted child can and should develop a wide variety of interests and, at the same time, should have the opportunity to specialize his reading in any single area where he has developed great interest.

Gifted children characteristically have initiative, real potential for leadership, and creative tendencies. They should be challenged to use these qualities throughout their school life if they are to be well-adjusted, self-respecting individuals. At the same time, they should work and share with others of less ability so as to develop social sensitivity and responsibility. While they should feel pride in work well done, there should be no vainglory, no condescension. Every gifted child should expect of himself thorough, high-quality work while, at the same time, he respects whatever less able children can and do accomplish.

Criteria for a program adapted to gifted children. Havighurst and his colleagues have set up the following criteria for a program devised to meet the needs of gifted children: (1) facilities for developing a wide variety of talents; (2) a systematic program designed to discover individual talents; (3) means for motivating the children to develop and utilize their respective talents; (4) appropriate curriculum materials; and (5) effective instructional and administrative procedures.[1]

Among the talents that gifted children should be encouraged to develop are these: abilities in art or music and rhythms, mechanical aptitudes, dramatic talent, qualities conducive to social leadership, and creative propensities, such as facility in writing in an original fashion or inventiveness in science or the fine arts. Such encouragement may come through three major types of motivation: (1) enjoying the results of any worth-while achievement—what is accomplished; (2) feeling the joys of the activity itself—the fun in so doing; and (3) experiencing the pleasures growing out of

[1] Robert Havighurst, *et al.*, "A Survey of the Education of Gifted Children," *Supplementary Educational Monographs,* No. 83 (Chicago: University of Chicago, 1955), p. 3.

sharing with others—making a contribution for the group's welfare or being part of a group working on a joint enterprise. Such motivation is enhanced as the child proceeds on his own initiative, utilizes his natural powers of leadership, and expresses himself by putting his potential creativeness to work.

The more common general methods for dealing with gifted children (instructional and administrative) are three: (1) acceleration by entering school at a younger age, by skipping a grade, or by being part of a fast-moving group that will complete the curriculum in fewer years than average pupils take; (2) enrichment through supplementary materials and activities that will broaden and deepen the gifted child's experiences as he stays with his age group; and (3) special groupings of gifted pupils who work together part of the school day or the school week or who are segregated in separate rooms or even buildings. Most widely used of these methods is enrichment; part-time grouping is practiced in many school systems, while complete segregation is mostly confined to a few large cities; acceleration, once widely followed, is now being reconsidered and modified.

Acceleration. At one time, it was common practice to let pupils "skip a grade," or possibly two or three over the course of the school years. This caused the accelerated pupil to be associated with classmates older than himself and to enter high school and college very young. Often he was socially and emotionally immature in comparison with his classmates and was therefore a misfit. Consequently teachers have sought a better way to deal with the gifted child and, if a pupil does skip a grade, they make sure that he is unusually mature for his years and take measures to make up the important learnings he would miss by skipping the work of an entire grade.

Another mode of acceleration involves a degree of segregation and provides that a fast-learning group of pupils may cover the usual work of each grade in less than a year and thus progress through the typical eight-year curriculum in seven or even six years. Very large schools can provide facilities for two or more groups that have begun school at the same time and that move through the school at different rates; but there are still the problems of immaturity on reaching high school and of deprivation due to segregation from age-mates of less ability.

One type of acceleration is currently approved—that of recognizing the facts that precocious children tend to mature more rapidly than those of average ability and that they will be able to learn certain reading skills earlier and enjoy special kinds of literature (fanciful, for instance) at a younger age. So it is the curriculum that is accelerated; all children remain in the elementary school an equal number of years; but gifted children do considerably more advanced work, year by year, than do average and slow-learning pupils of approximately the same age. The principles of readiness apply here; teach a child whenever he becomes ready to learn.

Special groupings. Some well-known school systems have policies opposed to segregation and make no effort to segregate gifted chilidren from their peers even for a part day in each week. The curriculum is pretty much individualized. These schools are situated in wealthy suburban communities where most of the children will go on to college and have high IQs, where teachers are highly trained, where classes are small, and where funds are sufficient to provide a rich program for all the pupils. This situation is ideal—where all pupils profit from a much enriched program that children everywhere would welcome. But unhappily there are schools where classes are very large, where the range of the pupils' ability is extremely wide, where school funds are barely adequate to support a minimum program. It is in the latter type of schools that gifted pupils may lack the opportunities to achieve their potential.

Certain large cities follow the practice of isolating gifted pupils after they reach the middle and upper grades. These children are placed in a special room of the school building or may even be transported to a separate building, and are taught by specially trained, highly competent teachers who can deal with the special needs of the individual gifted children and can help them capitalize on their aptitudes. The program is accelerated; there is much enrichment; many opportunities for creative endeavors and leadership are afforded. In all sorts of ways, the children are encouraged to realize their potential powers. Even so, the pupils' social development may be restricted because they lack contact with children of all levels of ability, from the various socioeconomic strata. It is important that our future leaders know, understand, and appreciate all kinds of people; and total segregation of the gifted my fail to accomplish these results.

Other schools, especially in smaller cities and towns, practice only partial segregation as gifted pupils are brought together on a part-time basis, as for a half day per week or a part of every school day to work at their specialized interests and to learn skills more advanced than their classmates are currently capable of learning. These gifted children may then be taught the skills that will enable them to exercise their initiative and to work independently on projects of special interest; for example, they are taught procedures in utilizing the library resources, study skills, research techniques with simple laboratory equipment that can be used properly only if technical manuals are read with understanding, or skills of puppetry whereby favorite stories may be shared with classmates.

Among the suggestions given in a research bulletin of the University of Pennsylvania [2] are the following. Since many gifted children are already extensive readers, teachers should give special attention to the qualitative aspects of these pupils' reading. (1) They should utilize their abilities to do complex associative learning by tracing the patterns in story situations. (2) They should be encouraged to discover the generalizations underlying stories and thus develop a guide for their own daily living. (3) Since gifted children can do long-range planning, they can follow a specific theme common to several literary selections which they read over a period of time. (4) Through their propensity for independent work and self-criticism, they can constantly add to their increasingly wide and varied background as an aid to gaining further new understandings; and they consequently will profit from teacher guidance that reveals the various procedures involved in critical reading. (5) It is essential that they cultivate a social point of view and gain the desire to know about regional customs and mores as well as about other peoples, distant lands, and various civilizations. Much reading of regional literature and biography will help here. (6) Since gifted children can identify themselves with the characters in literature, they profit by pooling the ideas gained through individual reading.

This same bulletin goes on to suggest types of library study that gifted pupils may do. Among the suggestions are the following:

Study of the Dewey Decimal System; assignment of such numbers to new books in the classroom

[2] *Guiding Your Gifted: A Handbook for Teachers, Administrators and Parents,* Educational Service Bureau, School of Education, University of Pennsylvania, p. 27.

Study of library management; organization of procedures for utilizing the classroom library
Study of children's magazines; recommendations of new purchases
Analysis of the qualities that make a book a bestseller among juveniles
Study of the library budget: amount spent on new books, on rebinding and repairs; collection of fines
Analysis of book withdrawals; drive to increase and spread withdrawals

Hildreth, in discussing the education of gifted children in the Hunter College Elementary School,[3] gives a clear picture of the kind of program that gets good results with such pupils. She shows that they have a high degree of self-direction if their questions are intelligently answered and if they are supplied with the necessary resources for working out their ideas. She recommends the permissive atmosphere in a workshop setting where there is constant use of art, crafts, trips, and laboratory facilities. The emphasis should be on personal responsibility, self-identification of problems, and training to think for themselves as they set up goals, select methods of work, and try to achieve on their own. The teacher serves to set the stage for such independent endeavors and, in every way, tries to capitalize on the children's ability to reason and generalize, discover basic principles, draw conclusions from evidence, and think inductively. She also stands ready at all times (1) to give individual help in any reading skill in which a pupil is weak, or (2) to instruct a group of bright children in study and research skills necessary for carrying out any project, for instance, how to use source materials, keep notebooks, collect and file clippings, make charts and graphs, summarize,

[3] Gertrude Hildreth, *Educating Gifted Children at Hunter College Elementary School* (New York: Harper and Bros., 1952), Chap. 4.

use the dictionary and other reference books, scan newspapers and magazines for a definite purpose, put on an exhibit or demonstration, plan a lecture, or review movies, and radio and television programs in a telling way. These children are held to high standards of performance and are given systematic instruction and practice in the various reading skills just as consistently as are less gifted children; but the bright pupils need fewer repetitions or they tend to work out effective short cuts.

Enrichment. It will be noted that the previously discussed method of grouping as a means of providing for the gifted child involves much enrichment. These same enrichment procedures are likewise appropriate for bright and talented pupils who remain in the classroom with their less able peers. There follow listings of many procedures utilized in various school systems which have a definite program for guiding gifted pupils in an enriched curriculum for nonsegregated situations.

Some of these procedures are designed to develop skills that will enable a bright pupil to work effectively on individual or small-group projects or that will develop qualities of leadership. There may be experiences in word building, such as compiling lists of words based on the same stem; a sequential program for introducing the developmental reading skills (the same as any pupil needs, but learned earlier because of the naturally rapid maturation of bright children); systematic training in problem-solving procedures; acquaintance with many types of critical reading (discriminating between facts and opinions; discovering inconsistencies, anachronisms, bias, propaganda, and the like); utilizing the tape recorder in evaluating oral reading. In addition, these pupils are given training in the various library skills whenever need for each of them arises and also in the skills necessary for work-type reading that involves the use of informational materials. Too, the children are given direction in effective listening skills and are not allowed to monopolize class discussions but, rather, to show courtesy and appreciation as their classmates participate. Skills of effective leadership are also introduced and practiced; for instance, acting as club officer or committee chairman and leading in class plans for such activities as poster-making, organizing and editing a classroom newspaper or a magazine that contains the creative writing of class members, or summarizing an extensive project through a mural or booklets.

Important as skills are, avenues of expression are possibly more important for the full development of gifted children. The following list indicates some of the ways that schools succeed in giving opportunities for expression.

- Activities involving literature
  - Writing and giving skits on books
  - Organizing and directing a reading club for all class members
  - Keeping a file of book reviews to guide choices of classmates
  - Engaging in choral speaking
  - Dramatizing
    - Putting on puppet shows
    - Role-playing (especially roles involving problems like their own)
    - Putting on plays
  - Telling stories
  - Reading orally
- Performance of services to the class
  - Compiling and organizing bibliographies
  - Planning, supplying, and arranging bulletin board displays
  - Staging programs for special days
  - Making illustrative maps, charts, graphs, and posters
  - Acting as news reporter
- Projects for personal purposes
  - Keeping a notebook for supplementary individual research

Building a telegraph set, model volcano, motorized plane, and the like
Compiling a local history from newspaper files

Personal growth is encouraged through extensive reading along many lines: biography, history, travel, informational fiction, science, poetry, juvenile books that have won awards, and current events. There should be multiple opportunities to pursue specialized interests by locating all available books and pamphlets to be read to the point of satiation. The program of reading for gifted children should be both wide and deep.

Teaching Reading to the Child of Low-Normal Ability

We are not dealing here with children of exceptionally low ability, but rather with those who are dull without deviating too far below average ability. In general, the IQ will approach 80 or above. Such children are usually not placed in a special group of very retarded children and, therefore, have problems of trying to keep up with their brighter classmates—if the teacher does not wisely differentiate instruction. With proper handling, these low-normal pupils can learn to read efficiently materials of reasonable difficulty.

In practice, schools that get good results in teaching such pupils to read follow one or more of the following procedures: (1) admission to first grade at an age somewhat older than that customary for most pupils, probably not before a chronological age of six and one half or seven years; (2) an extended kindergarten program which may continue for possibly two years and thus first-grade work will begin no sooner than the age of seven; (3) part-time attendance in first grade for one year—usually during unit activities and enrichment periods—before beginning full-time attendance in a second year when reading activities will be introduced as soon as readiness is apparent; and (4) the adaptation of instruction to suit the abilities of slow-paced learners. This adaptation means a prolonged reading readiness program, slowed-down rate of progressing from level to level of the reading program, much supplementary informal reading that utilizes first-hand experiencing and pupil-dictated reports, as well as parallel charts with various matching exercises, much use of concrete and sensory learning so as to insure meaningful learning, and a great deal of practice at every stage of learning to read. Some schools, too, have a policy of retention in which retarded readers are held back a year or more, especially for children who show definite signs of immaturity. For the most part, such retentions are held to the earliest years—kindergarten or first grade, if possible. In general, the first four of the procedures mentioned here are preferred to retention, which may be a devastating experience and do permanent damage to the morale and self-respect of children.

Grade-by-grade policies. Kirk and other authorities in the area of reading instruction for children of low ability acknowledge that mental age should not be the sole criterion for determining a child's readiness for learning the skills implicit in each stage of the reading program. Yet, according to them, mental age indicates whether a slow-learning child is mature enough at each of the various stages. For instance, it is suggested that most of the work in Grade I should be given over to reading readiness activities, that Grade II should feature initial reading instruction, while Grade III should afford wide reading of easy books along with very simple and specific guidance in word-attack skills as need arises at the primer, first-reader, and possibly second-reader levels. In the intermediate grades, guidance in word recognition should be continued as the slower learners progress through relatively simple readers and are provided with many easy-to-read library materials that parallel the classroom curriculum. Here the teacher will find helpful the high-interest, low-vocabulary materials that are being developed for use with retarded and reluctant readers. (Note the bibliography of such materials in Appendix C.)

The later intermediate and upper grades should feature a gradual and closely directed program for training these slow learners how to use books and how to study. While meticulously avoiding the use of difficult materials, the teacher should help slow learners to use a table of contents, an index, and the card catalog when they are seeking specific information; she should show them how to skim the page to find a definite fact, to find the two or three main points in a lesson, to use topical headings in a simple textbook as a clue to main points to be learned, and to run through a newspaper to find articles that bear on a topic of current interest. For such skills should be provided numerous opportunities to use and practice them in practical situations. Low-normal pupils tend to gain understanding slowly and gradually; they need firsthand experiences and much use of audiovisual aids, a great deal of practicing *after* understanding is achieved, and consistent success that will be conducive to further effort, continued interest, and, eventually, independence.

There follows a table of mental ages for children of 80 and 90 IQ at the respective chronological ages of 6 to 14. By consulting this table, a teacher who knows the CA and IQ of any pupil can get a rough idea of what she can expect in reading achievement in terms of mental age.

The table on p. 125 may be interpreted somewhat as follows: A child with an IQ between 80 and 90 is unlikely to be

MENTAL AGE IN YEARS AND MONTHS, BY HALF-YEAR INTERVALS, ON BASIS OF CA AND IQ

IQ	CHRONOLOGICAL AGE								
	6	7	8	9	10	11	12	13	14
80	4–10	5–7	6–5	7–2	8	8–10	9–7	10–5	11–2
90	5–10	6–4	7–2	8–1	9	9–11	10–10	11–8	12–7

ready for systematic reading instruction when he is six years old; at the age of seven, the child with an IQ in the neighbodhood of 80 may still need extensive readiness activities and a very gradual progress into formal reading, while the child with a 90 IQ may profit from an earlier introduction of reading lessons because he is past six mentally—if environmental conditions have been favorable. At the age of 14, the pupil with an IQ of 80 will have the mental maturity of the average eleven-year-old and should be able to read materials that the latter can read; while the child of a 90 IQ will more nearly resemble, in mental maturity, a pupil approaching the age of thirteen, and should be able to read fairly difficult materials with understanding and fluency.

The primary program in reading for children of low-normal mentality. As we have shown, reading instruction should be introduced later and carried forward more gradually for slow-learning children than for average and bright pupils. There should be an extended reading readiness program rich in experiencing that builds numerous new concepts and develops an interest in books and reading. Such children are likely to have a shorter-than-average span of attention; they learn best through actual sensory experiences and profit from informal reading charts that are built around such experiences. Skills are mastered through frequent use in actual reading activities that are closely supervised and follow-up practice exercises that will help to make the skills permanent. But this frequency must be spiced with variety so that interest will be maintained; for instance, there should be many kinds of reading materials to supplement book reading.

To be specific: reading readiness activities will be prolonged, plentiful, and varied. There will be much informal reading before book reading is introduced—much of it connected with on-going activities, some of it utilizing the vocabulary of the first preprimer, all of it very simple. The first easy sentences should often lead to experiences in dramatizing of directions ("Run to the door."), drawing and coloring pictures, or finger plays. As the pupils progress through the primary grades, each phase of reading should be thoroughly mastered before a new phase is introduced: sight vocabulary, word-attack skills, following the line, reading to get meaning, and increasing length of passages to be read, for instance. Slow-learning children can attain their potential in reading only if the primary teacher at each grade level builds a firm foundation for later reading.

Reading at the intermediate-grade level. Each middle-grade teacher should take careful inventory to determine the current achievement level, needs, and reasonable reading expectancy of each slow-learning pupil: consultation of accumulative and anecdotal records, oral reading, informal tests on silent reading, and possibly newly administered intelligence tests to determine if any child's rate of development is changing. Whenever such a pupil has a special aptitude, she should capitalize on it so as to build up his interests and self-confidence. He should be treated with respect, given as much praise as possible; he should find a friendly atmosphere.

The slow-learning child has continued need for help in

word recognition, for easy books on topics currently under consideration by his more competent peers, for many experiences that lend meaning to his reading, for discussion to interpret these experiences as a means of leading into his reading. Some teachers make an attempt to guide these pupils in the use of the same textbooks that the rest of the class is using. But, when these teachers do restrict their classes to reading in the same textbook, there is a different treatment such as, for instance, letting someone (the teacher, a helpful pupil, a parent) unobtrusively read the materials aloud to them, or giving a directed reading lesson on selected parts of a lesson by raising a question to precede the reading of each paragraph (while able pupils use a worksheet to guide their independent reading of the same materials), or directing their discussion of the informational illustrations which a textbook affords. Usually, however, it is advisable to secure easier books that parallel the topics in the general curriculum or that deal with topics of a special interest (as hobbies). To the greatest possible extent, teachers should offer materials which the pupils can read independently.

Reading instruction for low-normal pupils in the upper grades. All too often pupils of low-normal ability become poor readers, in spite of the fact that most of them have the potential to become proficient in reading materials at least the typical sixth-reader level. Such retardation can usually be avoided by providing later school entry, a prolonged readiness period, and a gradual and thorough program for introducing primary and middle-grade materials, and making of reading a nontaxing and interesting activity.

It is possible to make recreational reading a highly desirable activity for older pupils of low-normal ability through activities such as the following: (1) guidance in the library so that the pupils can find books that are sufficiently easy, yet intriguing because of fast-moving action, characters and episodes related to their real experiences, and treatment of specialized interests such as hobbies; (2) discussion of appealing books, both fictional and informational; (3) procedures that will make such books easily accessible; (4) abolition of formal reports so that any sharing is completely voluntary and spontaneous; and (5) display of suitable books related to a class-wide project to which, through reading these books, the low-normal child can make satisfying contributions.

Many teachers have found that unit teaching is an effective, unforced way to incorporate the reading of pupils at many levels of proficiency. There are so many facets to a unit that every pupil can contribute to a level and in a fashion best suited to his capacities and interests. It is possible to have reading materials so varied that gifted, average, and slow-learning pupils alike can find suitable materials.

There should be continuous attention to building meaning vocabulary, introducing and using study skills as they are needed, and training in the use of the dictionary and other reference books. The teacher herself can help the slow-learners as they gradually acquire the need and ability to use various materials and to learn specific skills; or a more able classmate may assume the responsibility from time to time (under the direction of the teacher). At any rate, it is possible and even essential to make competent readers out of pupils of low-normal ability.

Summary

There is no panacea for the reading program as we attempt to provide for individual differences. Gifted children have many needs which are at a level far above the other children in a particular grade; on the other hand, the slow-learning child is incapable of participating at a level commensurate with his grade placement. In general, schools are using one or other of the following practices in dealing with gifted children: (1) acceleration of these children or of the curriculum they follow; (2) separate grouping, either part-time or full-time, with a specially tailored curriculum; and (3) extensive enrichment activities and materials. To provide for slow-normal pupils, many schools choose from the following policies: (1) later entrance to first grade; (2) delayed introduction of systematic reading instruction; (3) slower, more thorough introduction of pupils to the successive stages in learning to read; and (4) more concrete, more repetitive, and simpler lessons.

Selected References

Reading for Gifted Children

Challenging the Rapid Learner in the Elementary School. Houston, Tex.: Houston Independent School District, 1954. Selected pages.

De Haan, R. F., and Havighurst, R. J. *Educating Gifted Children.* Chicago: University of Chicago Press, 1961. Selected pages.

Educating the More Able Children in Grades Four, Five, and Six. U.S. Office of Education Bulletin No. 1. Washington, D.C.: Department of Health, Education and Welfare, 1961.

French, Joseph C. *Educating the Gifted.* New York: Holt, Rinehart and Winston, 1959. Selected pages.

Gallagher, James J. *Gifted Children in the Elementary School.* Washington, D.C.: Department of Classroom Teachers, National Education Association, 1959. Selected pages.

"Gifted Reader, The," *International Reading Association Conference Proceedings,* Vol. 6: *Changing Concepts of Reading Instruction.* New York: Scholastic Magazines, 1961. Pp. 112–19.

GRAY, WILLIAM S. (ed.). "Classroom Techniques in Improving Reading," *Supplementary Educational Monographs,* No. 69. Chicago: University of Chicago Press, 1952. Pp. 153–71.

Guiding Your Gifted: A Handbook for Teachers, Administrators and Parents. (Educational Service Bureau, School of Education, University of Pennsylvania.) Philadelphia: University of Pennsylvania, 1954. Selected pages.

HAVIGHURST, ROBERT, *et al.* "A Survey of the Education of Gifted Children," *Supplementary Educational Monographs,* No. 83. Chicago: University of Chicago Press, 1955. Selected pages.

HILDRETH, GERTRUDE. *Educating Gifted Children at Hunter College Elementary School.* New York: Harper and Bros., 1952. Chapter 4.

———. *Teaching Reading.* New York: Holt, Rinehart and Winston, 1958. Pp. 580–97.

NORTON, M. S. "Current Provisions for the Gifted," *Clearing House,* XXXIII (March, 1959), 425–28.

ROBINSON, HELEN M. (ed.). "Promoting Maximal Reading Growth among Able Learners," *Supplementary Educational Monograph,* No. 81. Chicago: University of Chicago Press, 1954. Selected pages.

RUSSELL, DAVID H. *Children Learn to Read.* 2nd ed. Boston: Ginn and Co., 1961. Pp. 489–523.

TINKER, MILES A., and MCCULLOUGH, CONSTANCE. *Teaching Elementary Reading.* New York: Appleton-Century-Crofts, Inc., 1962. Pp. 267–71.

Reading for Children of Low-Normal Ability

BIRCH, JACK W., and STEVENS, G. D. *Reaching the Mentally Retarded.* Bloomington, Ill.: Public School Publishing Co., 1955. Selected pages.

"Education of Exceptional Children, The," Forty-Ninth Yearbook, Part II, National Society for the Study of Education. Chicago: University of Chicago Press, 1950. Selected pages.

GRAY, WILLIAM S. (ed.). "Classroom Techniques in Improving Reading," *Supplementary Educational Monographs,* No. 69. Chicago: University of Chicago Press, 1952. Pp. 172–91.

———. (ed.). "Improving Reading in All Curriculum Areas,"

Supplementary Educational Monographs, No. 76. Chicago: University of Chicago Press, 1952. Pp. 104–9.

INGRAM, CHRISTINE. *The Education of the Slow-Learning Child.* New York: Ronald Press, 1960. Selected pages.

KEPHART, N. C. *Slow Learners in the Classroom.* Columbus, Ohio: Charles E. Merrill Books, Inc., 1960. Selected pages.

KIRK, SAMUEL, and JOHNSON, G. O. *Educating the Retarded Child.* Boston: Houghton Mifflin Co., 1951. Selected pages.

RUSSELL, DAVID H. *Children Learn to Read.* 2nd ed. Boston: Ginn and Co., 1961. Pp. 394–95.

SMITH, MARION F., and BURKS, A. J. *Teaching the Slow-Learning Child.* New York: Harper and Bros., 1954. Selected pages.

STRANG, RUTH, *et al. Problems in the Improvement of Reading.* New York: McGraw-Hill Book Co., 1952. Pp. 341–56.

WALLIN, J. E. *Education of Mentally Handicapped Children.* New York: Harper and Bros., 1955.

9

Organizing for Instruction

WHATEVER THE CHARACTERISTICS OF CHILDREN IN classrooms may be, the locale, the training and experience of teachers, or the administrative structure of the school, nothing is more controversial in the teaching of reading than the matter of organizing for instruction. No other phase of the reading program has received the benefit of more careful research; still, there is less conclusive evidence of the advantages of one system of organization over another.

Rationale for grouping. In order to meet the needs of individual children in classrooms, most teachers find it advisable to group children for instruction. Even experienced teachers in trying to group their pupils find it a difficult task; yet, with thirty-five children with diverse needs and interests, some grouping is always advisable.

1. No one way of grouping is better than another; local situations, individual strengths of teachers, and the range of abilities of the children will dictate the best system for a particular school.
2. Grouping should be flexible; groups should be changed as children give evidence of growth and as their interests develop.
3. The size of the group is not an absolute factor. Some groups, remedial in nature, should be small; others, in which children

can assume considerable responsibility for independent endeavor, may be composed of twenty children working on a common problem.

4. Children learn from each other; the opportunities to share common learnings within a group are basic to good education.
5. Groups should be established on the basis of many criteria: formal and informal testing, children's interests, specific goals of instruction, and the social needs of the children.
6. Children should be allowed to form their own groups occasionally, on the basis of interests, common research problems, or their abilities to help each other.
7. In terms of critical reading, group reaction is desirable in order to discuss and solve problems effectively.

Common fallacies. One of the basic assumptions which appears to dominate reading instruction is that there *must* be groups within the classroom or efficient learning cannot take place. Nothing is further from the truth, for it is possible that by sheer chance a teacher will have a fairly homogeneous group of children with respect to their reading needs. This would, of course, greatly simplify the problems of instruction. Because the possibility of such a phenomenon is a rare one, there will be many times when grouping can facilitate both informal activities and formal learning. Or it is possible that a particular teacher does not work efficiently with groups, but provides an excellent learning environment through working individually with her children.

Another common fallacy regarding grouping is that the act of placing children together somehow attains homogeneity. Obviously, any grouping merely *reduces the range* of individual differences; the children in any group are *not* homogeneous, but they may currently have a common need or interest. It is on the basis of common needs or mutual interests that the best grouping practices are effected, but the teacher can never assume that common needs indicate that the children in a group will progress at the same rate or learn the same amount.

One often hears the lament that, although careful testing of children was done before the organization of "homogeneous" classes was effected, there is still need for breaking the class into groups. To illustrate: the person offering such a remark is thinking of third grade as an absolute level of attainment and is assuming that all third-grade children should be alike. There is no more artificial type of grouping in existence in our schools than that of the grade level; it merely means that third-grade children have been in primary school three years. It does not mean that individual differences do not or should not exist. In the typical fourth-grade class, there will normally be children who are not reading above a first-reader level; in the same class, the possibilities are good that several children will be reading two or three reader levels above the grade designation. The tendency is to test children on an achievement test and to group them on the basis of the test results, assuming that the needs of all children who score 5.0 are alike and that those who score at 2.0 have similar needs. It is obvious that this practice merely reduces the range of achievement level, whatever that may mean, within a group. It says nothing about the actual reading needs of the children, nor does it tell us what the instructional goals should be.

Flexibility of grouping. Basic to effective grouping is flexibility, for several reasons. First, there are so many levels of achievement and so many activities in the day's span that to move a child from one group to another on the basis of his varying specific abilities in certain activities would seem sensible. The child who reads well in the literary-type materials of the basal readers may not do so well in reading in social science or science. It may become necessary to group him with other less fluent readers who also need specific instruction in reading in the content areas. In the middle grades, these differences in reading abilities of children become increasingly apparent.

Second, flexible grouping does not allow the child to feel that he belongs to a "dumbbell" group and cannot escape that stigma; he learns to accept his limitations for some activities, but he gains ego strength from being able to demonstrate his superior abilities in a certain activity with children who excel him in some other job. Nothing is more devastating than to remain a "sparrow" from September to June, with no hope of ever functioning as a "bluebird." It is deplorable that being a "sparrow" or a "bluebird" should determine where the child sits in the room, when and how he performs in all activities, and what the teacher expects in performance.

Finally, flexible grouping allows the teacher to provide for equal learning opportunities for the entire classroom of children. There may be occasions for total-group learning of certain skills, small-group instruction for specific skills, and frequent regrouping of children for activities which may or may not require reading. Thus, the goals of instruction are more likely to be met.

Systems of Organization

We frequently hear teachers or administrators refer to grouping or individualizing of instruction as "methods." It is probably preferable to refer to grouping as a technique or a system; grouping is not a method of instruction, but rather an administrative procedure which can facilitate effective teaching.

Total-group instruction. There are numerous times in each week when a class of children can be instructed as a total

GROUPING PLAN FOR SIXTH GRADE CLASS *

Day	GROUP I (High)	GROUP 2 (Average)	GROUP 3 (Low)
Monday	*Independent Reading.* Reading to answer questions related to social studies, science, or health, or to a previously read selection in *Arrivals and Departures.*	**Teacher Guidance.** Preparation of a new story. Discussion of old and new concepts pertaining to the story, review of familiar vocabulary, and introduction of new vocabulary. Presentation of guide questions for silent reading.	*Independent Reading*—or work on vocabulary and comprehension activities related to a previously read story.
Monday	*Recreational Reading.* Use of reading materials related to individual interests.	*Independent Reading.* Silent reading in the basic reader followed by accompanying Activity Book pages.	**Teacher Guidance.** Review of work done above. Oral reading. Plan an activity (perhaps a TV-Scroll) to be presented to the whole class on Friday.
Tuesday	**Teacher Guidance.** Preparation for reading a new story. Presentation of guide questions for silent reading.	*Independent Reading.* Assignment of teacher-made exercises to broaden new concepts or to develop word recognition skill, and independent reading of stories related to the story read silently on Monday.	*Independent Reading.* Assignment of Activity Book pages, and supplementary reading related to the story in the basic reader—or to social studies, science, or health.
Tuesday	*Independent Reading.* Silent reading of the new story. Previously developed teacher-made comprehension exercises could also be assigned.	**Teacher Guidance.** Discussion of the story read silently in the basic reader on the preceding day. Oral reading. Plan an activity to be presented to the whole class on Friday.	*Individual Activity.* Preparation of the reading activity to be presented on Friday.

Day			
Wednesday	**Teacher Guidance.** Discussion and review of common word analysis problems.		
	Teacher Guidance. Oral reading. Plan an activity to be presented to whole class on Friday. Discussion of a new story.	*Individual Activity.* Preparation of the reading activity to be presented on Friday.	*Independent Reading.* Silent reading of the new story.
	Independent Reading. Assignment of Activity Book pages. *Recreational Reading.* Use of reading materials related to individual interests.	*Independent Reading.* Assignment of Activity Book pages, or use of teacher-made materials to develop word analysis skill.	**Teacher Guidance.** Review of the assigned pages in the Activity Book. Preparation for reading a new story. Presentation of guide questions for silent reading.
Thursday	*Independent Reading.* Silent reading of the new story.	**Teacher Guidance.** Review of the assigned pages in the Activity Book, or the teacher-made exercises. Continue preparation of the reading activity to be presented on Friday.	*Independent Reading.* Assignment of Activity Book, or use of teacher-made materials to develop word recognition skill. Preparation of the reading activity to be presented on Friday.
	Independent Activity. Preparation of the reading activity to be presented on Friday.	*Independent Reading.* Reading to answer questions or problems related to social studies, science, or health. Continue preparation for Friday presentation.	**Teacher Guidance.** Review of assigned work. Oral reading for diagnosis. Continue preparation for Friday presentation.
Friday	**Teacher Guidance.** Discussion and review of common reading comprehension problems.		
	Whole-Class Activity. Presentation of the reading activities prepared during the week, such as story-telling, dramatization, brief reviews of library books, a puppet show, the showing of a TV-Scroll, or any other enrichment activity.		

* Reproduced from *Arrivals and Departures, Teachers' Manual,* "The Sheldon Basic Reading Series," by William D. Sheldon and Shirley Edwards. © Copyright 1957 by Allyn and Bacon, Inc. Used by permission of the publisher.

group. Skills of word attack, vocabulary, comprehension, and general study techniques can be introduced to the total group whenever a common need is apparent. For instance, in studying word meanings, all of the children in a particular class can be involved in searching for homonyms in a selection; subgrouping for antonyms, synonyms, words of multiple meanings, words with interesting origins, or words with particular connotations would be advisable, with subgroups reporting to the total group on their accomplishments.

Other possible total-group activities are choral reading of selections which are simple enough that all members can participate, dramatization of stories or historical events, reading and discussing articles in *My Weekly Reader* or a similar publication, listening as selected children read orally and then reacting to the reading, skimming for answers to questions in a particular selection, and reading to follow directions for a large group activity.

Ungraded primary. In many school systems in our nation, the traditional grade levels of the primary school have been set aside, and continuous levels of achievement have been substituted. Especially during the first three years of instruction, children are placed in achievement levels according to their accomplishments and their abilities; there is no end-of-year promotion or nonpromotion of children. Rather, as a child demonstrates his abilities to progress to the next level, he is moved upward at any time during the year. For less mature children the nine levels (the most common practice in existing ungraded systems) require four years of work; superior children may accomplish the levels in two years. Teachers, working cooperatively, determine the competencies or units of accomplishment which represent each successive level. Vital to the success of the ungraded primary is systematic and continuous evaluation, based on criteria concerned with the pupil's reading achievement, language facility, and emotional and social development.

Other important features of the ungraded system include:

1. The system is flexible and allows children to cover important phases of learning as rapidly as they are capable of moving; however, for those phases which require more time and deliberation, the child has an extended period of time.
2. Children do not fail or skip a grade; the slower child is paced according to his abilities, while the more able child can progress from level to level without skipping over essential skills.
3. Teachers often stay with a group of children for two years, thus providing essential continuity in their training.

Important to the success of the ungraded primary system are the understanding and support of the parents. Typical parents are accustomed to the traditional grade-level system, and their expectations of their children's accomplishments are geared to the year-by-year reporting and promotion policies which they themselves experienced. Certainly no school system should attempt to initiate an ungraded primary program without thorough planning with parents. Further, such a program should not be attempted without benefit of the experience of those school systems in our nation in which the ungraded primary is now well developed. Dearborn, Michigan, and Milwaukee, Wisconsin, are two examples of school systems in which the ungraded primary has been successfully administered for several years.

Staggered session. Many schools, especially for the primary grades, have adopted a staggered-session technique of grouping and have found it both practical and helpful in meeting the needs of the children in the reading program. On the basis of screening (check lists, teacher observations, and standardized tests), a class is divided into two groups. One group may come to school at nine o'clock in the morning and is handled alone for an hour of reading instruction. The second group then enters school at ten o'clock and is retained an hour later in the afternoon for reading instruction. Obviously, such grouping does not eliminate individual differences, but it does narrow the range of those differences, particularly if the groups are carefully selected.

In the staggered-session program, the teacher with thirty-five children in her classroom will have but seventeen or eighteen children at one time for reading instruction. It would seem practical to select for the morning group those children who are the slowest learners; brighter, more mature children have greater tolerance for the extended-day period. Children in both the morning and afternoon groups are further subgrouped for instruction in particular skills.

It is obvious that the staggered-session program demands an extra hour of the teacher's time in a particular day. However, in school systems where this program is in effect, teachers are the most enthusiastic supporters of the program. They feel that with the reduced number of children during the reading periods they can more nearly meet individual needs. Too, total-group instruction is easier, since the range of individual differences among the children has been reduced by the establishment of the two groups. Another advantage is that instructional materials, so often in scarce supply for thirty-five children, can be made available to each child in the smaller groups.

Achievement grouping. Many schools have experimented with grouping children for reading according to their reading levels as determined by tests, participation in reading activities, and teacher observations. All of the children in grades four, five, and six may be involved in this program. For instance, all of the children from each of the three grades who are reading at a second-reader level are grouped for one period each day and are given instruction at that level; all of the children in the three grades who are reading at an eighth-reader level are similarly grouped for one period of instruction at their level. Some schools arrange that achievement grouping be at each successive grade level so that there may be three or four groups at fourth-grade level, or at fifth, or at sixth.

This system of grouping has frequently been referred to as the "Joplin Plan," but it has been in effect for many years in other school systems in the nation, long before the publicity given to the Joplin, Missouri, program. There are sound arguments for and against the program.

On the positive side, it is obvious that children may gain status as a result of being able to read successfully at their independent reading level to which they have been assigned. Many teachers prefer this system of grouping since it allows them to concentrate on a particular level of instruction; one teacher may have all of the "remedial" children, while another teacher may have all of the advanced readers.

Disadvantages of such a grouping system appear to outweigh the advantages, unless the program is carefully coordinated.

1. The reading period is limited in time; children must move to other rooms for their instruction, and that instruction must be terminated at the end of the period. In the self-contained classroom, the teacher may prolong her reading period if she feels that extra time is needed for learning.
2. The individual classroom teacher for whom the children must read in the content subjects has little knowledge of the needs of her children in reading, since they are working with another teacher. Communication among teachers is difficult, when we consider the numbers of children we have in classrooms, the crowded daily schedule, and the extracurricular demands on the teachers' time.

3. There is little opportunity to carry over into the reading of content subjects the specific skills which are taught in a reading period; or, the reading teacher may completely ignore the skills demanded in teaching these subjects.
4. Grouping sixth-grade children with fourth-grade children for instruction in any subject has its problems. The differences in physical and social maturity and in intellectual interests may obviate any commonality in group enterprises.

In defense of achievement grouping, it is suggested that this program *does* have support in many schools, but it works best where grouping is done within a particular class level. For example, three sixth grades in a school are divided according to achievement levels and needs of the children, and an exchange of teachers is effected for the reading period. If close communication is maintained among the teachers, the children may benefit from this system of grouping.

Individualized reading. This is a term which has caused considerable controversy in recent years; proponents of the individualized, or "self-selection," system have made impassioned pleas for support of their opinions regarding the advantages of the system over traditional grouping systems.

Briefly, the individualized reading program calls for a wide variety of books on many subjects and at all levels of difficulty. Children are guided to select the book which they can read successfully and in which they are most interested. Reports are made to other class members and to the teacher. Each child is free to read any number of books he may choose to read. It is obvious that this program is not different from programs that have been in existence for several years, but for one factor. Many advocates of this system believe that basal readers have no place in the reading program; however, this would appear to be an extreme view. Any wise teacher of reading will provide a multitude of books for children to select on the basis of their interests and reading levels; but she also knows that provision must be made for sequential and continuous growth of skills under the careful guidance of the teacher and that there must be careful evaluation of the development of children's skills.

Successful administration of an individualized reading program depends on several factors:

1. The teacher *must* have a broad knowledge of children's literature; since children are selecting from various levels and areas of interest, and, since they report individually to the teacher on their reading, it is mandatory that the teacher *know* the literature in order to give proper guidance to the child's reading, to evaluate the accuracy and adequacy of the child's comprehension and interpretation, and to give suggestions for further reading.
2. Careful records must be kept on each child. To do this, the teacher must know good techniques of informal evaluation. The individual record should indicate where the child has been in reading, exactly where he is, and where he is expected to go. Only an experienced, broadly trained teacher of reading can make these decisions and record them so that they make sense to succeeding teachers of the child.
3. It is our experience that few schools have libraries adequate for a completely individualized program. It is recommended that a minimum of ten books for each child, at various levels of difficulty and dealing with several topics, is necessary for true self-selection.
4. Some grouping, for the teaching of basic skills, should be used for those children who indicate common needs.
5. Care must be taken to insure that the child is making selection of books commensurate with his skills; good readers often select books which are not challenging to them, while poor readers frequently select books which are much too difficult for them.

Individualizing a child's reading is the ultimate in any good reading program. However, teachers who deal with large groups of children should utilize a basal series of readers as a means of developing the hierarchy of skills called for in effective reading and then provide abundant opportunity for each child to read trade books of suitable level and topic.

Grouping in the self-contained classroom. It is still common practice in our schools for a particular teacher to group her children within her own classroom. She may have three or four groups in reading according to the range of abilities and the particular needs of the children. She plans her lessons daily, using basal readers and a wide selection of materials for free reading; she follows a pattern of continuous, sequential development of skills, attitudes, and interests. For the low group she may use basal readers at a lower grade level than she is teaching and will supplement with experience stories, wide reading of easy trade books and audio-visual aids. For the average group she will use basal readers at grade level and will lead from these readers to all types of materials in the content areas. For the advanced group, she may use basal readers which are designed for higher grades and will stimulate these children to read widely and in a variety of books, magazines, and other materials.

The self-contained classroom approach has many advantages, particularly in the primary and middle grades:

1. Flexible grouping is possible; a child may be moved frequently from group to group, according to current progress and needs.
2. Total-class instruction as needed can be given on particular skills, such as word-attack skills, word-meaning skills, oral reading skills, and others.
3. There is no time limit imposed upon instruction. The reading period may be extended if necessary to complete a good lesson.

4. The teacher has a better opportunity for applying reading skills throughout the day, in all content areas.

Summary

There is definitely no single way in which the reading program can provide for individual differences. Gifted children may have needs which are at a level far above the other children in a particular grade; on the other hand, the slow-learning child is incapable of participating at a level equivalent to his grade placement. Grouping, to be both practical and helpful, must be flexible. In the light of the needs which a particular class shows, groups should be organized; these groups should be disbanded as soon as needs have been met. The choice of a particlular system of grouping appears to be less important than the understanding which must precede any decision to use it. Experienced teachers may do an excellent job by using a basal series of readers and providing for individual differences through supplementary materials; they may find that it is possible to completely individualize instruction for one class, while the composition of another class makes individualization impossible. Any system of grouping is good if, through interaction in the groups, a child becomes an independent reader who is capable of understanding what he reads, reacting on the basis of his previous experience and knowledge, and communicating what he has read to others.

Selected References

AUSTIN, KENT C. "The Ungraded Primary School," *Childhood Education,* XXXIII (1957), 260–63.

"Classroom Organization: Differing Viewpoints," *The Reading Teacher,* II (1957), entire issue.

GOODLAD, JOHN I., and ANDERSON, ROBERT H. *The Non-graded Elementary School.* New York: Harcourt, Brace and World, Inc., 1959.

ROBINSON, HELEN M. (ed.). "Reading Instruction in Various Patterns of Grouping," *Supplementary Educational Monographs,* No. 89 (December, 1959). Chicago: University of Chicago Press, entire issue.

SARTAIN, HARRY W. "The Roseville Experiment with Individualized Reading," *The Reading Teacher,* XIII (1960), 277–81.

WHIPPLE, GERTRUDE. "Good Practices in Grouping," *The Reading Teacher,* VII (1953), 69–73.

WITTY, PAUL. "Individualized Reading–A Summary and Evaluation," *Elementary English,* XXXVI (October, 1959), 401–12.

10

Word-Attack Skills

PROBABLY NO AREA IN THE TEACHING OF READING has, over the years, been more controversial than the teaching of word-attack skills. The history of education reveals that there have been numerous "schools of thought" on this vital subject, and during the past one hundred years there has been a recurrence of one or more emphases in each decade. Educators have expounded numerous theories concerning the relative merits of such methods as "see-and-say" and phonetics until it is no wonder that teachers in our present-day schools are confused about what emphases, what values, are justified in the various methods or techniques.

Word-attack and recognition skills serve but one purpose in the total complex skill of reading: to aid the child in pronouncing the unknown word and associating it with the known word from his speaking and/or listening vocabulary. Today we are agreed that the teaching of word-attack skills is no longer a question of which method or how much of a procedure to use, but rather the appropriateness of the method for the particular child at the particular time in the particular context. If we believe that children learn at different rates, depending upon their capacities to learn, their experiences, and their desire to learn, then we must agree that no magic formula can be concocted which will serve the needs of all children in attacking new and unfamiliar words.

Word-attack and word-recognition skills are not solely the province of the teacher of the early primary grades. We may safely assume that the average child in today's modern classroom will have been *exposed* to most of the skills of attack and recognition by the end of the fourth grade, but it is likely that those skills have not yet been solidified and will not become solidified for many years. It is simply good learning theory to assume that repetition is necessary for the solidification of any skill, whether it is a matter of motor coordination or of the more abstract recognition of verbal symbols and their relationships to meaning.

It is well to remember that there are three distinct stages of the development of skills: the period of introduction, emphasis or reinforcement, and mastery. In a typical fifth grade, there may be children who need to be reintroduced to a skill, who for a variety of reasons both personal and school-centered, simply have not developed understanding of a skill. Having determined who these children are, through careful observation and informal diagnosis, the teacher will introduce the skill and give immediate exercise for the children. Others in the class are ready for emphasis of the skill, or reinforcement, through carefully prepared lessons which provide exercise. Still others will have mastered the skill and are ready for advanced skills. At each succeeding level, the teacher has the responsibility for assessing the skills of her students and for providing exercises for the maintenance of those skills.

Multiplicity of approaches to word attack. The child who approaches a new word may learn it in one of several ways. He may ask someone to pronounce it for him, take note of its use in that particular context, and remember it the next time he encounters the word in a similar context. He may figure out the word by himself by reading carefully all of the words around it and inferring the exact word needed to give meaning to the sentence or phrase. He may attempt to memorize, from the shape and general features of the words, all of the new words which are required for his daily reading; this child may soon reach a saturation point beyond which he can no longer depend on his memory. He may employ phonetic clues—the sounds of letters, combinations of letters, and known sounds of parts of words. He may depend on structural analysis—the roots, prefixes, suffixes, and inflectional endings which give clues to the pronunciation and the meaning of the word. Or he may become quite adept in the use of the dictionary, wherein he finds pronunciations, definitions, and examples of the use of the word in various contexts.

Obviously, the mature adult reader uses all of these techniques. Ask the average adult how he figures out new words and you will encounter confusion; the good reader employs several word-attack skills simultaneously, without thinking consciously just how he did attack the word. This multiple attack on words reflects long years of practice; it therefore makes sense to the teacher when she is told that children need direct instruction and support throughout their education in this matter of recognizing new words.

Certain dependable guidelines should be set up for the teaching of word-attack skills:

1. Never teach a word in isolation, unless you are sure that the repetition of known parts or elements of the word will lead to understanding of new words.
2. Always associate any word-attack skill with the meaning of the word under consideration.
3. Provide sequential training in all of the word-attack skills.

Your best guide is the teacher's manual for the basic reading books. Most of these manuals are carefully prepared on the basis of sound principles.

4. Do not assume that all children need the same amount or emphasis upon a particular skill. Some children appear to gain a thorough knowledge of word-attack skills without formal training; others will need constant guidance and repetition in order to see the reasonableness and application of the skill to actual reading.
5. Teach the skill as the need arises and it can be applied in the daily work of the children.

Dangers in the wrong approach to mastery of reading vocabulary. The controversy over the proper methods to be used in the teaching of word-attack skills is not a new one. Occasionally we experience a re-examination of methods, and someone is sure to advocate the return to "sure-fire" methodology. The result often leads to confusion for the inexperienced teacher. On the one hand, she depends upon her recent training to guide her in her work with children, but she may find that other teachers and administrators are making a frantic attempt to inject into the reading program many elements which they do not understand nor even recognize as unsound practice: a formal program of phonetics which includes daily drill periods for all children in the school; numerous games and puzzles, designed to aid the child in developing word-attack skills, but used instead as busywork with no relationship established to the reading program; "individualizing" instruction, on the basis of a belief that the child can work out his own needs for word-attack skills if his interests are met through a wide variety of materials. There are sound elements in each of these practices mentioned, but if one method is used to the exclusion of all others, real damage may be done to the child who really needs a sound foundation in *combined* skills. Some teachers will do a better job of teaching by one method and feel more secure in doing so; this is merely recognition of the fact that no two teachers are so constituted as to teach any subject exactly alike.

The problem of word-attack skills and recognition skills, then, is not a matter of how much or what kind of method is used, but its appropriateness as determined by the needs of the children in the individual classroom.

Word-attack and -recognition skills are of four closely related types: configuration clues, context clues, structural analysis, and phonetic analysis. We shall present each type separately with the understanding that they are interrelated, that the need for each will vary with the individual child or the particular problem presented by the reading selection, and that the teacher's competence and good judgment are paramount in the efficiency and appropriateness of the program.

Configuration Clues

When the child first encounters verbal symbols for the words which he already knows and uses as part of his listening and speaking vocabulary, he is learning to associate a particular symbol with a known word. He may notice that, when he says the word, it is a short one, and the symbol is also short, such as in the word *run:*

Run, Betty, run.
Run to Mother.

The teacher has provided training in visual and auditory discrimination before the child encounters reading of actual words, as we have discussed in previous chapters. The child has learned to listen for words that *sound* as if they were short or long. Now, when the verbal symbol is associated with the sound of the word, the symbol itself takes on meaning. When using this method, the child will usually learn many words from configuration clues and these words constitute the basic sight vocabulary.

Specialists differ rather radically on the number of words which a child will recognize from sight, and estimates have been made which vary from fifty to five hundred words. The assumption is, of course, that the child can employ configuration clues up to a certain point and then must depend upon other clues to discover the pronunciation of the word. It must be stated that we continue to build sight vocabulary for the remainder of our lives. It is impossible to determine the point at which a word moves from the level of analysis to the sight recognition level, but adults must recognize thousands of words from their peculiar characteristics or from constant repetition of widely used words in the language. In other words, there is no particular *time* to which we can point when configuration clues fail and other more analytical clues must be taught or used.

In the first stages of developing a sight vocabulary, the child will encounter little difficulty in determining differences between such words as *run* and *something*, since one is a very short word and the other is long. Difficulties arise, however, when he encounters words which look alike:

ran	on	these
run	an	those

and now he must fit the word into the sentence to see whether it makes sense or not. In this respect, he is beginning to use context clues.

Configuration clues depend upon the length, the height, and peculiar characteristics of words. The child will encounter less difficulty in determining the differences between *mother* and *Dick* then he will between *mother* and *father*, because of the different lengths of the words as well as their very different shapes. He may recall the word *fall* because of the height of the letters, as contrasted to such a word as *come*.

During the initial reading experiences, the teacher can provide aid in word recognition by calling to the child's attention the peculiar characteristics of the words: the length, the height, or an unusual over-all shape. It is not enough to demonstrate the visual elements of the word, however, since accurate memory of any word will depend upon its having meaning for the child. Auditory and visual discrimination are not complete until the child has spoken the word, heard himself say it, associated the symbol with the spoken word, and placed it in a meaningful context.

Context Clues

The goal of any word-attack skill is to enable the reader to gain meaning rapidly and efficiently; consequently, detailed word analysis can become a deterrent to fluency. When the child encounters a word that is unfamiliar, use of the context can be a valuable aid to him in inferring the meaning and pronunciation. Context clues depend largely upon *whole word* identification. Simply stated, use of the context means examining the known words around the unfamiliar word in order to get a hint that helps the reader discover what the unknown word is. If the context is a complete one and the unfamiliar word one which exists in the child's hearing or speaking vocabulary, the task may be a simple one. Take, for example, this sentence, in which the underlined word is unfamiliar to the reader:

Mother bought cookies and bread at the <u>bakery.</u>

The child, from his experience, knows that when Mother wants to buy cookies and bread, she usually goes to the bakery; hence, he can infer the word, and the sentence now gives complete meaning. What would happen, however, if Richard's mother always buys cookies and bread at the grocery store or supermarket and if Richard has no experience with a bakery? He could easily substitute *store* or *market* for the word bakery and still have the meaning of the sentence. This indicates that context clues are not infallible. The context clue gives a hint as to what the unfamiliar word might be, and the child is required to check the accuracy of his guess by other word-analysis skills. In this case, Richard might have initial training in the use of beginning consonants, and he would learn through careful checking that the unfamiliar word begins with the *b* sound. He would know, then, that *grocery store* or *store* or *market* is incorrect. He should have discovered, of course, that he needs only a single word, and he could have concluded that *grocery store* is two words. We cannot depend upon the child's perceptiveness, however, to that extent.

Many teachers make the mistake of launching children into the use of context clues too soon in the initial reading program. Seldom are the contents of the preprimers and primers complete enough for the employment of context clues. Let's look at this example:

Billy sees a little dog.
The dog is black and white.
Billy wants the dog.

Not one of these sentences is complete enough to furnish an accurate clue to the underlined words, unless we also use phonetic or structural clues to check the accuracy of the guess. On the other hand, the context can be very complete as in this example at a middle-grade level:

She painted a picture with oil colors and framed it for hanging in her room.

Context clues, just as any other word-attack skill used alone, have their limitations; yet we cannot overestimate the importance of this skill to the mature reader. As the child progresses into independent reading, he meets more and more words which are not a part of his listening or speaking vocabulary, and he must depend upon context to give the first clue to the pronunciation and meaning of the unfamiliar words. He learns, however, that the context clue must be checked by careful visual scrutiny, using phonetic or structural analysis or the memory of the shape of the word. In any case, the teacher can promote skill in the use of context clues if she (1) scrutinizes the material closely to determine whether the context *does* give a clue; (2) aids children in attaching appropriate meanings to the new words that are encountered; (3) provides many opportunities for children to extend their skill in the use of context clues.

Usually the child gets his first experience in the use of context clues when he scrutinizes a picture for a hint for what a word might be. Let's assume that we have a picture of a boy and a dog. The boy has thrown a stick across the lawn and the text beneath the picture reads:

Go, Spot, go!
Get the stick, Spot!
Go get the stick.

The child simply searches the picture for a clue to the word *stick*, which is the new word introduced in this particular section of the story. Beyond the stage of picture clues, however, many children are handicapped in their reading when they encounter unfamiliar words. Training in the use of context clues should accompany the training in inferring words from pictures. The teacher should occasionally cover a picture and allow the children to guess from the context, *if* the context is meaningful. In the example above, the children could be led to discuss just what a dog would get for the boy, and the chances are good that someone would guess the word *stick*. At this point, the accuracy of the guess could be checked against the picture; on the other hand, this is a perfect time for the introduction of initial consonant clues.

The social studies and science books which children read are rich with terms which are explained by the context. These are many times much more precise and meaningful than the context clue which is encountered in the simple narrative of a child's reader. At the upper-grade levels, the skill of inferring meanings and pronunciations of new words from materials in the content fields is vital to independence in reading.

Structural Analysis

Structural analysis is the careful visual scrutiny of a word to discover familiar elements which may lead to gaining both the pronunciation and the meaning of that word. After the child has gained a limited sight vocabulary and learned to use configuration and context clues, he must learn to attack new words systematically through careful visual scrutiny or analysis.

Structural analysis is generally divided into four types: inflected forms of known words, derived forms of known words, compound words, and syllabication. We shall consider each of these separately, although there are countless instances when they are encountered and used in combination.

The inflectional endings of our language are s, es, ed, ing, er, est, t, *and* en. We use inflected forms to indicate person, tense, number, the possessive case, comparison, and the present and past participle:

Person: I, me; he, him; she, her
Tense: want, wants, want*ed*, want*ing*
Number: girl, girl*s;* man, men
Possessive: Bob'*s,* your*s,* their*s*
Comparison: tall, tall*er,* tall*est*
Present Participle: runn*ing* water
Past Participle: bend, ben*t;* beat, beat*en*

Now these are all difficult concepts which are readily understood only by mature individuals, but the introduction of the concept cannot wait until adulthood. Very early in the first grade the child encounters his first inflected form: *run, runs.* He may not immediately recognize *runs* since, as we have indicated in the discussion of configuration clues, he has only a memory of the three-letter word *run.* But *runs* is in his everyday speaking and listening vocabulary; he uses it correctly as the occasion in language demands. Consequently, the teacher will point out the familiar element of the word and indicate the inflectional ending. From this one example she will go to several other words which are similarly inflected, and the groundwork is laid for careful visual scrutiny of new words.

Perhaps the simplest level at which to begin the training in inflectional endings is that of the singular and plural forms of nouns: boy, boy*s;* ball, ball*s.*

I see a boy.
I see two boy*s.*

Both the inflectional ending *s* and the *two* serve to indicate the plural factor, and the teacher should point to this fact in discussing the change which has occurred in the singular form. Of course, we cannot always depend upon both clues being present:

We saw elephant*s* and lion*s* in the zoo.

Some children will, because they are observant and bright, notice that adding *ing* to a known form often calls for the doubling of the final consonant. First-grade children frequently question why the word *walking* contains the familiar word *walk* and the inflectional ending *ing,* while *running* and *swimming* have added an additional final consonant to the root word before an inflectional ending. (See rule 3 below.) An understanding of this principle is essential to spelling and some children demand an explanation early; others are both unconcerned and unaware of the differences, but this gives no valid reason for denying an explanation to those who demand reasons. The teaching of spelling and grammar will be so much more meaningful to the child if his questions are answered when he demands the information from his initial reading experiences.

The root word in an inflected form is the meaning unit for the child, and care must be taken to provide many experiences for the careful scrutiny of both root words and inflectional endings. Pronunciation and auditory discrimination of these elements are, of course, vitally important. The skill of adding inflectional endings and recognizing familiar words in inflectional variants is based on a thorough understanding of these elements:

1. Many inflectional variants are formed by adding endings with no change in the root word: walk*ing,* match*es,* call*ed,* girl*s,* go*ing.*

2. If the root word ends in the final *e*, the *e* is dropped when an ending that begins with a vowel is added: tak*ing*, bak*ed* (the *e* is dropped; *ed* is added), din*ing*. (An exception to this rule will be learned later: the *e* is retained on root words which end in *ce* and *ge*, if the ending which is added begins with an *a* or an *o*; examples: courage*ous*, trace*able*.)
3. If a monosyllable or root word ends in a single consonant, preceded by a vowel (*tip*), the consonant may be doubled when an ending is added: tip*p*ed, swim*m*ing, fan*n*ed.
4. At the middle-grade level, the child will learn that the above rule applies in polysyllables *only* if the root word is accented on the last syllable; for example: prefer*r*ed′, but pref′erence, ben′efited.
5. If the root word ends in *f*, the *f* is usually changed to a *v* before adding an ending: cal*v*es, kni*v*es, hal*v*es.
6. If the root word ends in *y* preceded by a consonant (*cry, deny*), the *y* is usually changed to an *i* before adding an ending: cr*i*ed, cr*i*es; den*i*ed, den*i*es. Note that this does not apply when adding *-ing*, since this would cause an awkward combination of two *i*'s: cry*ing*, deny*ing*.
7. If the final *y* is preceded by a vowel (*buy, monkey*), the ending is added with no change in the root word: buy*s*, monkey*s*, play*ed*.

The argument may be advanced at this point that children do not need to know the reasons for the changes that occur in root words when inflectional endings are added, and that they seldom encounter these words in their initial reading experiences, particularly if they are reading from a carefully controlled basic reading series. This may be true for average and slow-learning children who may not be ready for such instruction until the higher grades; however, much of the reading which is done by precocious children is not that of the basic reader, but from a wide variety of books and children's magazines in which there is not the careful control and gradual introduction of the vocabulary. Questions will arise from the time children begin reading, and the good teacher is thoroughly prepared to give answers and reasons.

Derived forms are those words which are combined with prefixes and suffixes. The child will use the same techniques in attacking the derivatives that he used in the inflected forms: careful scrutiny of the word to discover the familiar root which conveys the meaning. He will learn that the prefix or suffix has a meaning of its own, and, when it is combined with a root word, the derived form may have a distinctly different meaning:

*un*happy, *un*attract*ive*, *un*law*ful*

Important, however, is the knowledge that the root word has *not* changed meaning. To aid the child in developing an awareness of the changes which occur when prefixes and suffixes are added to known words, the teacher should direct the careful scrutiny of the derived forms. *Unhappy,* for instance, occurs early in the reading experience of the child. He should be told that the *un* means *not; re*turn means to turn *back;* teach*er* is one who teaches, and so on.

As the result of working with children in the intermediate and upper grades, the teacher will discover that derived forms of words are the key to the extension of meaning vocabulary. A knowledge of the meanings of a minimum number of prefixes, suffixes, and roots can lead to the understanding of thousands of new words which have been derived from familiar words. They may be introduced as they are met in the daily lesson, or as the child expresses a desire to extend his meaning vocabulary. Here are lists of prefixes, suffixes, and roots which are most common in our language:

Common Prefixes

ab-	off from, away	absent, abscond
ad-	to, toward	admit

co-, con-, com-, col-, cor-	together, with	context, correlate
de-	away, down, out of	depart, demote
dis-	not, opposite	disclaim
ex-	out of, formerly	extend, ex-president
in-, im-, il-, ir-	in, not	inhuman
pre-	before	precede
pro-	forward	proceed
re-	back, again	return, rerun
un-	not, opposite	unhappy

Common Roots

dic, dict	to say, speak	predict
duc, duct,	to lead	conduct
fac, fec, fic, fect, fy	to make, do	factory, fortify
fer	to bring, carry	transfer
mit(t), miss	to send	transmit
pend	to hang	suspend
pos, pon	to put	deposit, expose
scrib, script	to write	prescription
spec(t), spic	to look	inspector
ven(t)	to go, come	convention
vert, vers	to turn	reverse

Common Suffixes

-able	capable of, worthy	lovable
-ance, -ence, -ancy, -ency	act or fact of doing, state, quality, condition	allowance
-er, -or	person or thing connected with, agent	teacher, auditor
-ful	full of, abounding in	thankful
-less	without, free from	worthless
-ly	like, characteristic of	queenly
-ment	state or quality of	amazement
-tion, -sion, -xion	action, state, result	tension, adoption

The teaching of prefixes and suffixes is not a simple matter, since some prefixes and many of the suffixes have multiple meanings; however, the bright child who becomes aware of the structural elements of the derived form will be intrigued with discovering the various meanings. Most important is aiding the child to develop an awareness of the structural elements in order that these may be recognized accurately and efficiently; in other words, the child must know what a prefix *is* before he can use the skill of dismembering the word to discover its meaning. At the primary level, these structural elements are taught incidentally, as the need arises and as the child demands understanding and clarification; at the intermediate and upper-grades levels, there can be direct teaching.

In teaching such structural elements, it is important that the teacher explain to the children the meaning of the words *prefix* (to fix before), *suffix* (to attach to), and *root* (the fundamental or essential part, the body). There is a tendency to describe these elements as "little parts" or "little words before and after," a practice which is totally unnecessary and which underestimates the intelligence of the child.

Syllabication is the dividing of words into their pronounceable units, or syllables. Beginning with the third-reader level, the child encounters an increasing number of polysyllabic words; many of these words cannot be analyzed either structurally or phonetically. To get to the meaning of the word, the child must pronounce it, and the need for understanding of syllabication has arisen. But the good teacher of reading does not wait until the need has arisen; in the readiness program she has given training in listening for word "parts" as she pronounces them for children. As words are added to the speaking and listening vocabularies of the children, training is given in detecting the accent in polysyllabic words.

This is best accomplished by slow and emphatic pronunciation of two-syllable words, pointing out that the accent sometimes falls on the first syllable, sometimes on the last syllable: *moth′er, re·turn′, ba′by, be·gin′*. A feeling for accent is further emphasized when children are allowed to tap or beat the accent with a finger or a pencil as the words are pronounced. In the initial training in phonetics, the child may become aware of the vowel sounds in words, and this presents another opportunity for pointing out that each vowel sound constitutes a pronunciation unit, or syllable.

An understanding of syllabication is vital to good spelling, speaking, and writing. Unless the child gains an appreciation for accurate pronunciation, each of these areas of the language arts may not be clearly developed.

Certain principles of syllabication should be taught as the need arises in the reading program:

1. Every syllable contains a *sounded* vowel: bē-gin′
2. Sometimes a vowel forms a syllable by itself: a-bout
3. When a single consonant appears between two vowels, the consonant is usually joined to the second vowel: ro-tate
4. When two consonants appear between two vowels, the syllable division is usually made between the consonants: num-ber
5. When the two consonants are either digraphs or blends, they often remain within the same syllable: se-cret moth-er tro-phy
6. When a double consonant (ll, pp, or the like) appears between two vowels, the second consonant is silent: happy—hap-i
7. When a word ends in *le* and the *le* is preceded by a consonant, that consonant is included in the last syllable: ta-ble (Note that when two consonants precede the *le*, as in pi*ck*le, the consonants remain with the first syllable: pick-le.)
8. In words that end in *tion, xion, sion,* the accent usually

comes on the next to the last syllable: re-jec′-tion con-cen-tra′-tion

9. The inflectional *ed,* when preceded by a *d* or *t,* forms a separate syllable: want-ed wound-ed
10. When *x* is preceded and followed by a vowel, it usually is in the same syllable as the first vowel: ex-it ex-ample tax-i
11. When a syllable ends in a vowel, the vowel is usually long: bā′con (this is called an open syllable); when the syllable ends in a consonant, the vowel is usually short: ăf-ter (this is called a closed syllable).

A well-developed skill in syllabication will give the child another important technique for attacking the many polysyllabic words which he will meet in his daily reading.

Compound words are those words which are composed of two or more known words, neither of which has changed form in the process. Each word forms not only a visual element, but a meaning unit as well, and the combined form contains meaning elements of each of the individual components: *basketball, roommate, applecart, snowman, playhouse.* When the child understands the composition of the compound word, he is ready to analyze new compounds as he meets them. He may find that he knows both words, and the pronunciation and meaning of the compound are clear; on the other hand, he may not know one part of the compound. If he knows the word *apple,* he is halfway toward understanding *applecart,* and inferring the second half is generally not difficult. Learning that neither word in the compound word changes form aids the child in his spelling and his writing. *Roommate,* commonly misspelled by adults, would not be a spelling demon if the individual understood the principle of compound words, and the teacher would not be constantly harassed by *roomate!*

An unfortunate trend has arisen from the practice of scrutinizing compound words: occasionally we find a teacher who encourages children to look for "little words in big words," with a total disregard for the distortion of the meaning units of the words. The child who is led to discover that *in* and *ink* are found in *think* is confronted with three separate words of different meanings. And those meanings are not a part of the word *think!* Even worse, they may find *at* and *hat* in *what* and know neither the meaning nor the pronunciation of the larger word. Such practices are more confusing than helpful; the goal of word analysis is to discover the meaning of the unfamiliar word and to pronounce it correctly. While the finding of little words in big words may be helpful in pronunciation occasionally, consider the confusion that arises when the child attempts to pronounce *was* by identifying the familiar element *as!* The analysis of words within words should be restricted to those root elements, inflectional endings, and prefixes and suffixes which in and of themselves convey direct meaning.

Phonetics: Analysis

Phonetic analysis is the process of associating appropriate sounds with printed words. To develop a knowledge of phonetic elements, a child must be able to identify sounds which are used in our language and, further, to identify the symbols which we use to represent those sounds. Despite the fact that some writers have contended that this is a simple matter, the understanding of phonetic principles is extremely complex. Taken individually, the sounds and symbols have no meaning. In combination, they may lead to the pronunciation of a word which is familiar, *if* the pronunciation is accurate. There are about forty-five sound units, or phonemes, in the English language as it is spoken by the American people; but we have only twenty-six letters in our alphabet to represent those sound units. Obviously, several of the letters of the alphabet have variant sounds, and it is because of this circumstance that phonetic analysis is a complex process. For example, consider the phoneme which is represented by the long *ā:*

b*ay*	w*eigh*	p*ai*d	g*au*ge
b*a*by	th*ey*	br*ea*k	g*ao*l

All of these letter combinations represent the sound of the long *ā,* and when we consider that each phoneme in our language may be represented by several symbols (letters or combinations of letters) we understand why phonetic analysis requires careful, sequential development.

The reason for teaching phonetic analysis is the same as that of other analysis skills: to aid in the perception of unfamiliar words. The child must be able to associate sounds with consonants and vowels and to blend these sounds into syllables—the units of pronunciation. Obviously, the goal is to discover what the word means in the particular context. Sometimes a single phonetic clue, along with context clues or structural clues, will be sufficient to discover what the unfamiliar word is. For example, "The mad dog *attacked* the little boy." Employing the context clue, the reader infers that the dog did something to the boy. The fact that the dog was mad is important in establishing an accurate clue. Now the reader knows the sound of the initial vowel and he may properly infer the word.

Another confusing element in phonetic analysis is demonstrated by the word which may be pronounced differently, though spelled the same, in different contexts. An example of this is found in—

He stood *close* to the tree.
Please *close* the door.

In this example, the meaning of the word is of paramount importance, and the pronunciation of the word depends upon a knowledge of the phonetic elements of the elusive *s*.

The kindergarten teacher may lay a foundation for phonetic analysis by calling attention to words that rhyme, words that begin with the same consonant, words that end with the same consonant, words that contain the same long or short vowel, words that begin and end with blends, and words that begin and end with digraphs. In the readiness stage for reading, it is important that auditory discrimination of these elements of phonetics be developed. Many children will develop discrimination quickly; others will not be able to make discriminations, but we have no evidence that such practices in the classroom are harmful to immature children. Rather, introduction of phonetics through carefully planned listening exercises lays a good foundation for eventual discrimination.

The wise teacher will introduce phonetic analysis when the child gives evidence of needing additional help in understanding and pronouncing new words which are encountered in his initial reading experiences. But she will introduce phonetic analysis in combination with structural analysis, context clues, configuration clues, and pronunciation units.

To learn to associate sounds with the symbols which are used to represent the words in our language, the child must be able to recognize and pronounce various types of vowel and consonant symbols. There are six distinct categories of these symbols, and we shall discuss each separately, although they do not appear separately in our language.

Single consonant letters are used to represent a single consonant sound. The child must be able to hear this sound distinctly and to reproduce it in his own speech before he can accurately associate the sound with the consonant. Primary children often have not learned to speak distinctly, and the teacher has the task of teaching them the proper vocal placement of the sounds which represent the consonants and other phonetic elements. The following chart represents some of the consonants and their association with the speech mechanism. It will be noted that the voiceless element is formed in the same position as the voiced element:

Voiceless	*Voiced*
f–fat	v–vine
k–kite	g–gate
p–pull	b–ball
s–some	z–zebra
	s–was
t–top	d–dog

It must be noted that a single consonant letter can represent several sounds. Take, for example, the letter *s* as it is pronounced in *s*ome, choo*s*e, and trea*s*ure; or the letter *g* as it appears in age and good. These elements give little trouble to the child if they occur in words with which he is familiar through his speaking and listening vocabulary; they are extremely tricky if he is attempting to attack a totally unfamiliar word.

Consonant blends are the combinations of two or three consonants which, when pronounced, blend into sounds which still retain elements of the individual consonants:

bl–blue	nd–kind
br–bright	nk–rank
cl–climb	nt–want
cr–crow	pl–play
dr–dry	pr–pretty
fl–fly	qu–quack
fr–free	rk–dark
gl–glow	rt–start
gr–grind	sc–scat

scr—scream	st—stamp
sm—smell	str—straw
sn—snow	sw—swim
sp—spot	tr—true
spl—splice	ts—cats
spr—spring	tw—twins
sq—squash	

The consonant blends occur in the above combinations so often in our language that they should be taught as blends and not as two single consonants. The child soon learns that *toy, tape,* and *tiger* do not have the same individual sounds as *train, twine,* and *try*. The blend becomes both a visual and an auditory element.

Consonant digraphs are two-letter symbols which represent a single consonant sound unlike the sound of either of the separate consonants which compose the element:

ch—choose	th—thing
gh—cough	th—this
ph—elephant	wh—what
sh—shoe	

The child cannot learn to pronounce the digraph by blending the two consonants. He must understand that the two letters represent a *single sound.*

Single vowels are the most flexible of our phonetic alphabet. Each vowel may represent several variant vowel sounds:

a—fat, fade, fare, far, ago, saw
e—we, get, father, weigh
i—it, nice, fir, machine
o—box, rope, for, dove, do
u—cup, use, fur

Some vowels as phonetic elements may be silent in a word: bo*a*t; others may be influenced by the consonant: f*i*r. Consequently, to teach the child to speak a particular sound for a particular vowel is at all times inadvisable. The child may have to try several sounds of a vowel in a particular word before the correct pronunciation is gained. A few phonetic principles, listed at the end of this section, may aid the child in the selection of the proper vowel sound.

Two vowel letters may be used to represent single vowel sounds. This principle is difficult for the child to understand, since there is so much variation encountered in simple words: *said, paid, again, leaf, bread, foot, fool, flood, floor.* However, it must be remembered that if the child gets the *meaning* of the word and has opportunities to use the word in his speech, it usually causes little difficulty after the initial encounter.

Diphthongs are combinations of two vowels closely blended into one phonetic element or sound:

oy–boy ew–few
oi–oil ou–house (but not a diphthong in *you* or *though*)
ey–they ow–cow (but not a diphthong in *blow*)

The diphthong may prove bothersome to the child, since it is in conflict with the commonly accepted principle that in the combination of two vowels the first is usually long and the second silent. Direct teaching, associating the meaning of the word with the sound, will overcome most of this difficulty.

Once the child has had practice in learning to hear accurately the sounds of single consonants, he then must have opportunities to associate the sound with the appropriate symbol. He has learned that *dog, day,* and *do* all begin with the same sound. Now, through visual scrutiny, he learns to associate the sound with the proper symbol: the initial consonant *d*.

In the same manner, experiences in the visual-auditory

perception of vowels must be provided before the child can associate the sound with the proper symbol. For example, he learns that *fat, as, has,* and *tap* have similar sounds. Now through careful visual scrutiny, he discovers the symbol which stands for that sound.

An accepted technique for teaching consonants is that of initial- or final-consonant substitution:

hat, fat, rat, sat, mat, pat, bat
rat, ran, ram, rag, tap, tan, task

In such an exercise, the child uses configuration clues, or memory of a sight word, plus the substituted consonant. In a similar fashion, vowel substitution may be used:

tin, ten, tan

No exercise of this type is advisable unless it is used to generalize from particular instances in which the need has arisen to explain phonetic principles. For example, the child has encountered difficulty with the word *hat,* and in helping him with an understanding of the pronunciation of the word, the teacher may list similar words, using vowel or consonant substitution.

Phonetics: Principles

Certain principles may be used in aiding children to learn the complex phonetic elements which they encounter in their daily reading and for which they have need in gaining skill in pronunciation and meaning of unfamiliar words. There are exceptions to each principle, since our English language is a complex language, derived from several sources; however, the exceptions are few and can be explained as the need arises.

1. When a double consonant appears in a word, one of the consonants is silent:

   willow: *wĭl′-ō*

   If the double consonant is followed by a vowel, the word usually has two syllables.

2. In certain combinations of consonants, one of them is typically silent:

   g*n*aw *k*nee *p*neumatic hal*f* wa*t*ch

   In some cases, both consonants may be silent:

   thou*gh* throu*gh*

3. The sounds of single consonant symbols may vary:

   c (when followed by *e* or *i*) has the sound of *s:* *c*ent, *c*igar

   c (when followed by *a, o,* or *u*) has the sound of *k:* *c*an, *c*ome, *c*ut

4. In certain cases, the same sound is represented by different symbols:

   *j*oy *g*em ma*g*ic e*dg*e gra*du*ation

5. Some vowel symbols are silent:

   a. A final *e* on most words is silent, and usually serves to prolong the sound of the preceding vowel:

      hom*e* cam*e* tim*e* tun*e*

   b. When two vowels come together in a word or syllable, the first vowel usually is pronounced with its long sound and the second is silent:

      bo*a*t ra*i*n be*a*t dre*a*m fe*e*t

      (Beware of the diphthongs in applying this principle!)

6. If there is but one vowel in a syllable or a word which ends with a consonant, that vowel usually is short:

   m*a*n r*u*n w*i*th g*i*v*e*n *u*nd*e*rst*a*nd*i*ng

   If the vowel comes at the *end* of the syllable or word, it is usually long:

   b*e*-gin *a*-ble tr*y*-ing

7. If there is a single vowel in a word or syllable, followed by *r*, the sound of the vowel is usually affected by the sound of the *r:*

   f*ar* f*ur* di*r*t wo*r*k h*er*

8. When the only vowel in a word or syllable is *a,* followed by *l* or *w,* the *a* usually has neither its long nor short sound:
   r*a*w, b*a*ll, fin*a*l

Summary

The question of when and how to teach word-attack skills appears to be foremost in the minds of most teachers. The inexperienced teacher will profit from following closely the manual which is provided with the basic readers, but she must also be prepared to answer the need when it arises and is expressed by the more precocious children in the classroom.

Usually, the first-reader level introduces the use of initial consonants, short and long vowels in monosyllables, and simple inflectional endings: *s, es, ed,* and *ing.* The second-reader level demands a knowledge of consonant blends, digraphs, diphthongs, compound words, and the shifting sounds of certain vowels and consonants. At the third-reader level, we introduce syllabication, prefixes, and suffixes. Obviously, the reader levels indicate that level at which the average child is expected to be able to grasp the concept of the word-attack skill. Many children will learn word-attack skills far ahead of the expected level, and these children will have questions which must be answered with specific information.

There is no quantity or combination of word-attack skills which is known to be sufficient for all children. Each child will have specific needs for the different types of skills, at different stages of their development. The good teacher is one who anticipates the needs of children and is ready, through her own thorough preparation and knowledge, to satisfy those needs.

Selected References

ARTLEY, A. STERL, *et al.* "Controversial Issues Related to Word Perception," *Reading Teacher*, VIII (April, 1955), 196–201.

DURKIN, DOLORES. *Phonics and the Teaching of Reading.* New York: Bureau of Publications, Teachers College, Columbia University, 1962.

GRAY, WILLIAM S. *On Their Own in Reading.* Chicago: Scott, Foresman and Co., 1960.

SLOOP, CORNELIA B.; GARRISON, HARRELL E.; and CREEKMORE, MILDRED. *Phonetic Keys to Reading.* Oklahoma City: Economy Company, 1952.

SMITH, NILA B. "What Research Says about Phonics Instruction," *Journal of Educational Research*, LI (September, 1957), 1–9.

11

Developing Word-Comprehension Skills

RECENTLY, A YOUNG MAN NAMED RICHARD, AT the age of five, came to his father and said, "Dad, Molly called me stupid. She doesn't know much, does she?" After a few careful questions, Father learned that his son was not objecting so much to having been insulted as he was to the misuse of the word, because Richard added, "Besides, I couldn't be stupid. That's not what it means."

"Just what does stupid mean, Richard?"

"Well, dad, you know. Stupid is a woman driving a car!"

Father was impressed. It was brought home to him, in that moment, that a child's concept of a word or an idea depends much upon the experience that child has brought to the word or idea.

In the preceding chapter, we examined the means by which children learn to recognize and attack words in order that they might be able to pronounce the words and learn the meaning. It was stated that the new word means nothing to the child, unless he has had some experience to which he can relate it. The acquisition of word meanings is a complex process, one which must wait upon such developmental skills as these: the ability to listen and speak; the ability to reason; the ability to infer from gestures, facial expressions, and sense impressions; and the ability to gain ideas from an experience. In short, the acquisition of word meanings depends upon the child's gradual awareness of the need for language and communication.

Role of Experience in Developing Word Meanings

Types of vocabularies. There are four distinct vocabularies which develop through the child's experiences. His first vocabulary develops through his listening; he hears words as he observes that his parents and brothers and sisters are attempting to communicate with him. Very soon he begins to associate certain words with certain acts or gestures or objects. He responds appropriately, because he finds that his responses bring pleasure to other people and to himself. Soon he attempts to approximate the sounds or words which he has often heard repeated. His needs widen in scope, and he has found that there is magic in being able to communicate those needs. As his speaking vocabulary develops, he may learn that there are some expressions which are more effective than others; some may bring the disfavor of his parents or little friends, and he learns not to use those words except in a very special sense. Perhaps he has learned that there are some words, effective though they be, which are reserved for adults only!

The child's introduction to school develops the third vocabulary: reading. Here he learns that there are symbols, or printed words, for the words and expressions which he has heard and spoken, and he wants to broaden his experiences by interpreting what those symbols say. Soon he becomes involved in writing those same words, in an attempt to communicate ideas to others, and his fourth vocabulary is beginning to develop.

The breadth and depth of the vocabularies which the individual child will use in his everyday experiences and the rate at which those vocabularies will develop as he grows older will depend upon several factors: his capacity to learn from experiences, the opportunities to hear and practice the use of words, the stimulation he will receive from home and community and school, and his natural curiosity about language itself.

Preschool experiences. The child's preschool experiences will have a marked effect upon the development of his meaning vocabulary. Certainly there is no clear-cut beginning point for reading, since reading is the gaining of meaning from the printed page, and those meanings are based upon the child's ability to bring experience to the printed page. Surely those experiences begin long before the child enters school. They begin with the conversation of parents, the level of the language which is spoken in the home and the community, the stimulation of the child through reading which is done by parents and older brothers and sisters, the opportunities for him to use language and to experiment with expression as it is received and given by peers and adults, and the opportunities to gain wide experiences through other media of communication: the movies, radio, and television. Let us examine each of these briefly.

It has often been stated that the child who speaks a foreign language in the home and community is at a distinct disadvantage when he enters school and must learn to read and to speak English. It is both easy and dangerous to generalize from this statement. Obviously, the child is at a disadvantage when he is compared to children who have spoken English and have known no other language. But the greatest handicap which the child faces is not the foreign language itself, but the *level* of that language as it is spoken in the home. If the parents are educated and communicative, the foreign language may give the child a distinct advantage in learning to acquire word meanings in English. In fact, this child may experience less difficulty than the English-speaking child who comes from a language-impoverished home and community.

The kindergarten teacher can generally identify the children who have come from homes where reading is a part of each day's activities. These children have learned that pleasure and information can be gained from books; they have learned the care and respect for books, and they do not have to be told that the symbols on the page represent the words and ideas which they speak and hear.

Unfortunately, many children from good homes have never had opportunities to develop their natural desire to express themselves and to communicate freely with others. All of their needs have been met by older members of the family, and there has been little opportunity to express needs. Or these children may be the victims of parents who feel that children should not be free to express themselves as children; living in a world of adults, their natural exuberance has been stifled, and they have found it is wise not to attempt to measure up to the unrealistic adult standards. We would like to feel that these children are in the minority in any classroom. On the other hand, there is the child who has been given every opportunity to express himself freely and naturally; his adults and peers have seized every opportunity to aid him in his development of language. They have furnished him with answers when he inquired or demanded explanations for the things that he observed in his rapidly changing and expanding environment.

Today, as never before in the history of education, our children are coming to school with wide listening and speaking vocabularies which have been augmented through television and radio. Television, through its audio-visual presentation, has developed rich concepts, or understandings, of a wide world and a variety of experiences which young children a few years ago knew nothing about until several years after they entered school.

Coupled with the vicarious experiences which our children are gaining through television and similar media are the direct experiences which many of our children are gaining through travel and outings with families and friends. A great number of children in our schools have lived in other sections of the country; our population today is a mobile one, and the experiences of moving into and settling in new communities are valuable in terms of broadening horizons of understanding of other lands and other peoples. The average family enjoys numerous vacation journeys, as well as trips to accessible zoos and places of historic and natural interest. Even the families who live in isolated farming and industrial areas are provided with greater opportunities for travel to the city, the park, or places of general interest.

Children in today's classrooms bring to the initial reading experiences broader concepts than many of the authors of basic materials have anticipated; thus, the teacher and the school have added responsibilities for evaluating accurately the needs of children for the development of further word meanings and subsequently meeting each such need.

School experiences. The child's experiences in the school have a marked effect upon the development of his meaning vocabulary. Beginning with the first day in kindergarten, the child is directed toward a richer development of concepts which will prepare him for reading. In Chapter 4 we have discussed the readiness program and its contribution to the child's language skills. From this stage on, the richness of the child's experiences in the classroom will have a marked effect upon the development of his meaning vocabulary. There are definite procedures through which all teachers can contribute to this development: they can encourage the child to use and to discuss new and interesting words; they can encourage him to demand meaning from what he reads and to inquire further into related meanings of the word, the phrase, or the sentence; they can demonstrate and give the child opportunities to learn that the content of textbooks is related to life itself; and they can provide appropriate audio-visual aids to supplement and give meaning to the text book or the activity.

The teacher is the most important force in the classroom for the stimulation of interest in word meanings. The language she uses along with the carefully planned repetition of any new words which she provides through her conversation with children, through reading aloud to children, or through her written communication to them, will have effect upon each child in the room. The manner with which she presents new words to be learned, the enthusiasm she shows as she aids children in seeking meaning, and the opportunities which she provides for the children to discuss and use words will determine the breadth of meanings which the children gain.

Children must learn that meaning is demanded when they read. If they are allowed to say words glibly, with no attention given to their very special meanings, they are expending fruitless energies. Consequently, in the initial experiences which the child has with reading, he should be guided to discover the *what, why, when, where,* and *how* that are conveyed by the words on the page. He should be encouraged to inquire into meanings of the words which he reads and to use those words in his speaking and his writing. The very young child is often content to relate the meaning of a word with a particular context or incident, and to him the meaning is limited. Each time he meets the word in a new context, however, his concept can and should broaden.

Children are reasonable creatures, but we often forget that they do not see the reasons for so many of our activities in the classroom. As adults, the reasons for learning history, science, and mathematics are perfectly obvious: they are a part of life itself and a knowledge of each content field has aided us in understanding ourselves and the world around us. They have given us vocational respectability; they have added to our leisure-time pleasures and our avocational satisfactions. Few children are prepared to handle the complex vocabulary of the content fields when they first encounter such areas as mathematics and science; even if they learn to pronounce the words and read the sentences, they may have no understanding of the ideas which are to be communicated. As we shall see later, the development of meaning in technical vocabulary is complex but vital to the growth of concepts.

The most carefully precise description of a pyramid may fail to impress the child unless he has a chance to see a model or picture of the thing which is described. Without the visual aid, he may fail to develop understanding, or he may gain a quite distorted picture of the thing described. One of your authors carried with him for years such a distorted concept of a camel. Attending a one-room rural school in an isolated farming community, he, as a first-grader, was told of the camel and its function as "a ship of the desert." Having no library facilities to which he could turn to seek further clarification of this figurative language, and fearing the ridicule of other students and the teacher if he asked the obvious question, he puzzled for several years, each time he encountered in his reading any mention of a camel, why it was necessary to fit sails on an animal. His active imagination had even led him to liken the sand dunes, which had been glowingly represented in that original discussion of the camel, to the waves of the ocean! Audio-visual aids are our richest resource materials in developing complex meanings which otherwise are too abstract or too far removed from the child's actual experiences.

Difficulties of Word Meanings

The meanings of new words may present many difficulties. When we consider meaning, we are thinking either generally or specifically. Even the simplest word in our vocabulary may have both general and specific significance to us, depending upon our experiences. For example, consider the word *train.* This is a word with variant meanings:

> I rode the train to the city. (transportation)
> Santa brought me a train for Christmas. (toy)
> Her lace train billowed behind her. (clothing)
> We must train each man for the job. (give instructions and experience)
> I always train my roses on trellises. (bring into shape or position)
> A train of red ants crossed our path. (line or succession)
> Train your eye on the front sight. (bring to bear)

To the small child, the word *train* denotes either the means of transportation or a toy representing it. This is a general meaning of the term for most children. As the child's concept of the word expands, however, he will demand a context in which he can discover the specific meaning which was intended.

Another example of the general and specific meanings of words is the word *dog*. Generally, this word means a four-legged animal with which we are all familiar. But specifically this word may have widely variant connotations for each child in the classroom. David may think of a dog as a small black spaniel that nervously chases him as he plays in the back yard; to Susan a dog is a huge, smooth animal of mixed origin that lumbers after her and tenderly protects her as she walks to school each day. Thus do we encounter difficulties through specific and general meanings of words.

Word meanings which may be perceived through the senses are the easiest for us. If we can see the object, smell it, feel it, hear the sound it makes, or taste it, it immediately has meaning for us; we have had direct experience with it. Knowing this fact, we can provide experiences and activities for children through which they may develop clear concepts of the words which are encountered in reading. But some words can not be objectively experienced for a variety of reasons:

1. They may be outside our everyday experience in the way of activity or discussion. This is true of many literary terms which are discovered by boys and girls in the upper grades. Notice these words of Longfellow:

   > Silently, one by one, in the infinite meadows
   > of heaven
   > Blossomed the lovely stars, the forget-me-nots
   > of the angels.

   The poet has used figurative language, and the inexperienced reader may fail to get the meaning, particularly if he has never seen a forget-me-not.

2. Many words which the child encounters are remote from his experience, and it is difficult except through visual aids to provide an association: *pyramid, penguin, ambergris, chariot, mesa.*
3. Many words represent abstractions, and the development of a clear concept for such words is gradual as examples and explanations can be given. The child may have a vague idea of the word *love,* and it is quite certain that his concept of this word will expand; consider, however, the difficulty he will encounter when he must deal with *democracy, justice, sportsmanship,* and *guilt.*
4. Many words have meaning in a local sense. The city child will readily understand *subway, escalator,* and *square;* what difficulties will he have with *harrow, registered,* and *stanchion?*
5. Many words serve to show relationships between words, phrases, or sentences. Among these are the conjunctive adverbs, such as *moreover, consequently, therefore, thus, however,* and *meanwhile.* Each of these words establishes a definite relationship which must be readily understood if clear meaning is to be gained. Also, the relationships which are established by the simple conjunctions *and* and *but* are so vital to meaning that these words must be taught not merely as sight words but for their function in particularizing meaning in the sentence.
7. Many meanings are implied, and the reader must infer from the context what the author meant to convey:

> First there came the faint rumble as if thunder had sounded, but in the next moment a mighty roar of falling trees, splintering timbers, cascading boulders, and grinding sheets of heavy glacial ice deafened us, as we stood rooted to the path, too frightened and shocked to move.

Experience would tell the reader that this is a description of an avalanche, a landslide, or perhaps the aftermath of dynamiting. The meaning is implied, but it cannot be exactly defined without further context or a descriptive term.

It is apparent from the foregoing discussion of the difficulties in word meanings that the teacher cannot assume that the child will gain breadth and depth of word meanings unless careful teaching is directed toward that end. Discussion helps. So do audio-visual aids.

Teaching Word Meanings

Incidental teaching. Incidental teaching of word meanings is helpful but limited. As the child develops habits of wide reading, he encounters the same word in different contexts. His limited and specific understanding of words expands as he learns that *bank* may be a mound of earth, the edge of a river or a creek, or a depository for money, depending upon its use in a particular context. The alert teacher will look for examples of expanded meanings of words and, as they appear in the daily lesson, she will call them to the attention of the children. We cannot assume that the child will, unaided, gain wide meanings from wide reading; often the context is either inadequate or ambiguous, and the child infers a different meaning than that intended by the author.

Incidental teaching may involve waiting until the child expresses need for the meaning of a word encountered in his assigned reading and then taking time to explain the word and its use in the particular passage. The evidence of investigations dealing with the teaching of word meanings appears to support the practice of having the teacher anticipate the needs of the group and teach directly the meanings which are essential for complete understanding of the selection.

Direct teaching. Direct teaching of word meanings implies that the word is taken out of the context and studied, again placed in suitable contexts, and used in speaking, listening, and writing activities which will support the development of a concept. If the child is encouraged to demand meaning from what he reads, he will become involved in unlocking meanings of individual words. It is helpful for the teacher to train the child who wants to add new words to use these three steps: (1) learn how to pronounce the word by breaking it into syllables, noting the accent and pronouncing the word several times aloud; (2) learn the meaning by examining the context in which the word appears, examining the word for structural clues (prefix, suffix, root, or compound elements) or consulting the dictionary; (3) make the word a part of the speaking and writing vocabulary by using it often and placing it in several sentences which will illustrate any different meanings which the word might have. If the teacher aids the child in the primary grades in following such procedures, and encourages him often as he shows evidence of vocabulary growth, her efforts will be richly rewarded as the child moves upward into higher grades.

There are innumerable activities which the teacher may provide in order to help children develop their power of word meanings. These are all *direct* teaching activities, and we shall discuss several of them briefly.

1. *Firsthand experiences:* As we have indicated in earlier chapters, many of the activities in the primary grades are centered around direct experiences of the child with his immediate environment. A natural starting point for the teaching of word meanings is provided for the teacher through these experiences. Before a trip to the museum, the fire department, or the bakery, she should anticipate the new words which might be encountered, list these for study and discussion, and then make certain that the words are introduced throughout the activity. After the group has returned to the classroom, the words again should be discussed and perhaps used in preparing the group experience

chart or report. In the upper grades, anticipating vocabulary which will be essential for understanding the experiences of a science or social studies field trip is particularly effective. At any level, children may be encouraged to consult the dictionary to discover variant meanings of the new words and to write sentences or stories which illustrate those meanings. Again, there should be many opportunities for discussion of the new words.

2. *Games and puzzles:* Occasionally, the teacher may mimeograph word puzzles for each child or make puzzles out of cardboard and place them on the table in the library corner, thus providing a means of repeating and using new words. Here are samples of games which the children themselves might want to construct and present to their classmates:

a. Each of our new words will fit one of the definitions given below. Write the word in the spaces on the left. The word will not be opposite its definition.

c	o	n	s	u	l	t	To develop gradually
e	v	o	l	v	e		Invented stories
m	y	t	h	s			To seek advice of

b. Here is a list of words which may be arranged under the titles in the boxes. Write each word under the title with which it belongs.

raincoat
squash
tent
apartment
macaroni
trousers

Food	Clothing	Shelter

The teacher will use her ingenuity in devising puzzles and games to fit the occasion. Two excellent sources of games,

Reading Aids through the Grades and *Let's Play a Game,* are listed at the end of this chapter.

3. *Exhibits:* In the early primary grades, emphasis is placed upon labels which are appended to classroom equipment, objects which are brought to the classroom by the children, and special exhibits of materials. This practice of labeling is not limited to the primary grades, however, as there is no better way of learning technical vocabulary for collections of butterflies, insects, rocks, or native woods than to label each object and perhaps write a short sentence of identification on each label.

4. *Experiments and construction activities:* A splendid technique for teaching the meaning of terms which pertain to a particular experiment or activity is to prepare labels for each piece of apparatus or material used and to place a master list of these words either on a chart or the blackboard for future reference. A preview of these words before the experiment or activity to determine the children's previous experiences with the terms, and frequent reference to the terms during the activity and at the end of the activity, will aid the children in expanding their meaning vocabulary.

5. *Dramatics:* There are many words which cannot be illustrated by pictures or demonstrated by concrete objects. Such words are action words and abstractions. Through dramatics, children may act out words of feeling (sorrow, disgust, happiness, elation), words of movement (clumsily, trippingly, snail-like), or the more difficult abstractions (sportsmanship, cooperation, rejection). At the upper-grade levels, children enjoy writing short plays to illustrate a single word or a series of words. Pantomime and charades are often effective too. A single dramatic presentation of a word may be much more effective than a lengthy explanation or definition.

6. *Use of the dictionary:* From the third-reader level onward, children are encouraged to use the dictionary to find meanings and pronunciations which they need for their reading and writing. In another chapter we shall discuss the use of the dictionary at all grade levels; there is no better independent aid to the child than the dictionary, but he cannot be expected to use it efficiently without directed practice.

7. *Skimming for new words:* Practice exercises in identifying and studying unfamiliar words are helpful. For example, at the direction of the teacher children may often be asked to skim a new story or selection for words which they do not immediately recognize. They are encouraged to "read around" these words, or use the context, to attempt to get the meaning. They are encouraged to use pronunciation skills to determine whether they have heard the word before. A short period for discussion of new words should precede much of the reading which children are asked to do in the content fields.

Many children like to keep a notebook in which they list the words which give them the most trouble; another section could contain words which they particularly like and would like to use again and again. Illustrations, either cutouts which are pasted in the notebook or the child's own drawings, are an excellent means of enriching the meaning of the words.

8. *Typographical aids:* Children who are doing research reading encounter italics, footnotes, and transitional words which are especially helpful in giving meaning to the selection. They should be taught to observe italics and footnotes closely; transitional words or phrases, such as *on the other hand, in summary,* and *the second point,* are meaningful in and of themselves, in that they direct the attention of the

reader to a shift in mood, a contrast or comparison, a beginning, or a conclusion; the conjunctive adverbs (*consequently, moreover, however*) serve the same purpose.

9. *Relationships among words:* Many word meanings are learned as the child becomes aware of the relationships which exist among them, such as words of similar meanings, words of opposite meanings, words pronounced alike but of dissimilar meanings, and words with common origins.

The teacher should be aware at all times of the opportunities for direct teaching of—

a. Homonyms: words which are pronounced alike, but are unlike in both spelling and meaning

   wait, weight   rap, wrap   bowl, bole, boll

   These words often cause difficulty in spelling; only if the child has an opportunity to hear or read the word in a definitive context will he be able to use the proper form. Children of low ability, however, work well with homonyms.

b. Antonyms: words that are opposite in meaning

   warm, cool   capture, release

   It is often easier to give an antonym for a word than it is to give a synonym. For example, an antonym for *happy* would be *sad;* a synonym for *happy* is more difficult to determine.

c. Synonyms: words that are similar in meaning

   often, frequently   brave, courageous

   The child who has developed skills in the use of the dictionary has learned to depend upon synonyms, since so many definitions in beginning dictionaries are given in the form of synonyms. We must remember, however, that many times the synonym is no clearer in meaning to the child than was the word for which he was seeking a definition. Teachers too often use synonyms in giving definitions to children in the classroom.

d. Words of multiple meanings

bear watch right

Since so many of the words in our language do have multiple meanings, meanings which in some cases are widely dissimilar, the teacher should frequently check to see that appropriate meanings are understood by the children.

e. Prefixes, suffixes, roots: structural elements which give definite clues to meaning of derived words. The simple forms may be understood by primary children, but analysis of words through these forms may be too difficult for the slow-learning child. At the middle- and upper-grades levels, children find the use of prefixes, suffixes, and roots a fascinating technique for adding to their meaning vocabulary. These elements may be taught in several ways. One is by introducing and examining root families such as this one:

tract: to draw, extend, stretch
tractor
distract
extraction
subtract
tractable

Literally dozens of words in our language may be analyzed for meaning through knowledge of the meaning of a single root.

Another good technique is to begin with a known word and to analyze its parts; then encourage the child to think of another word which contains one of the parts which you have just examined. List that word and see if the children can add more words.

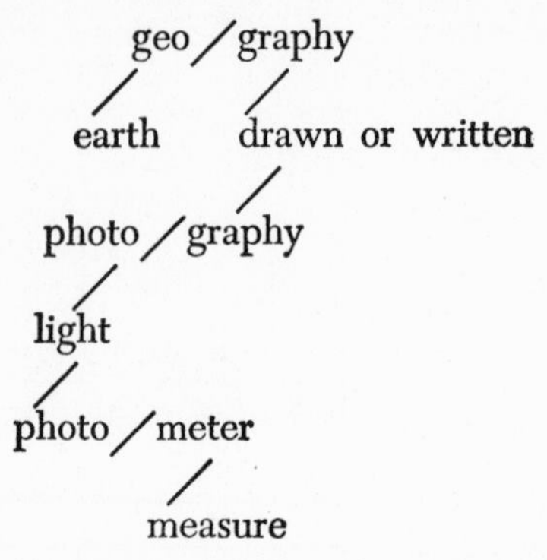

Children will learn that there are endless possibilities for adding to their knowledge of words if they are sensitive to these structural elements and the meanings which they convey.

f. Origins of words: When the child first develops curiosity about language, he wants to know how words originated. We have an excellent opportunity at this time to help children develop an appreciation for the richness of our English language. At the end of this chapter are listed some books which will be helpful to the teacher who is interested in improving her own knowledge of the origins of our language; as children express a desire to know about the beginnings of words, she should be prepared to help them. Many words which children use daily in their speaking and writing have fascinating histories, and a part of good dictionary study is the examination of that portion of the entry which gives the origin of the word. For example, the word *bonfire* originally meant the *bone fire* in which were heaped the bones from a feast.

Working with a heterogeneous group of children in a classroom, it is possible for the teacher to assign to small groups the task of determining the meanings of words at different levels. As an example, consider this paragraph:

> The old grizzly bear crouched in a patch of wild daisies while her cubs lay basking in the sun. Now and then she peered over the bank of the creek, attracted by ripples in the water below. A fat perch was wriggling his way up the stream, and the mother bear was thinking what a good meal he would be!

Group I – Homonyms (Locate words and write their homonyms.)

bear, bare   in, inn   lay, lei   sun, son
way, weigh   be, bee   would, wood

Group II – Antonyms (Teacher selects the words and children give antonyms.)

old   good   below   fat   wild

Group III – Synonyms (Teacher selects the words and children give synonyms.)

crouched   basked   peered   creek   wriggling

Group IV – Multiple Meanings (Children locate words that have multiple meanings.)

bear   bank   perch   patch   peer   meal

Group V – Interesting Origins (A superior group of children may select words to be studied.)

grizzly   bask   daisies

Other groups, or individual children, may be assigned the task of working with words which contain prefixes, suffixes, or roots (*attracted* is an example); still others may wish to discuss the connotations of such words as *crouched* and *peered.* What do these two words tell us about the grizzly bear's actions that a definition of the words would not tell us?

Summary

The acquisition of word meanings is a complex process. At any grade level the range of vocabulary is great, and there is considerable overlap with other grades both below and above the particular grade level with which the teacher works. Vocabulary development is definitely related to the maturation of the child, but it also depends upon the home and school environments and the richness of words which they have provided. Children should be given careful guidance in gaining precise word meanings and using those words in their speaking and writing until they have become an integral part of their meaning vocabulary. Comprehension of what is read is dependent upon the child's ability to recognize and get meaning from the individual words and the word groups; speed of reading depends so much upon the ease and confidence with which the child gains meaning from the printed page. The teacher should be prepared to do much incidental teaching of word meanings, and she should be ready at all times to do direct teaching of meaning as the need arises among the children who are seeking pleasure and information from their daily reading.

Selected References

BETTS, EMMETT A. *Foundations of Reading Instruction.* New York: American Book Co., 1957. Chapter 24.

HART, ARCHIBALD, and LEJEUNE, ARNOLD F. *The Growing Vocabulary.* New York: E. P. Dutton and Co., 1956.

Let's Play A Game. Boston: Ginn and Co., 1956.

MCCULLOUGH, CONSTANCE M. "Implications of Research on Children's Concepts," *The Reading Teacher,* XIII (1959), 100–107.

RUSSELL, DAVID H. *Children Learn to Read.* 2nd ed. Boston: Ginn and Co., 1961. Chapter 9.

12

Oral Reading as Interpretation

ORAL READING IS AN IMPORTANT PART OF THE total reading program. When properly taught, it contributes significantly to children's enjoyment of, and appreciation for, well-written prose and poetry. On the other hand, oral reading activities can be made a matter of dull routine and purposeless stumbling—and all too often it is. Chapter 12 presents a defensible and fruitful program for teaching children to read aloud effectively and enjoyably.

Place of Oral Reading in the Curriculum

The social significance of oral reading. Because it has true social significance, oral reading deserves a major place in the curriculum. In the first place, the printed page is the writer's vehicle for conveying his ideas to a wide audience; and the oral reader can so interpret the printed message that it takes on an impact that silent reading cannot convey. The reader is here an intermediary who highlights for his listeners the information, expresses the emotions, and carries the convictions that the writer has tried to express. The interpretative oral reader is a powerful agent in helping an author to get his message across.

In the second place, pupils in our schools profit from oral reading. When the oral reader actually senses his mission of conveying a message to his listeners, he can read with conviction and authority. He may have located information for which his classmates have sought in vain and may read from the original source or from a report summarized in his own words. If he has found literary passages of genuine appeal, he not only brings enjoyment and appreciation to his listeners but adds to his own pleasure through his efforts to bring out the beauty of the passages he is reading. Oral reading can and should be a major means of building tastes and developing interest in good literature.

For adults, also, oral reading is a socially useful activity. There are minutes and reports for club meetings, responsive readings in religious services, papers to read before civic and social organizations, and—in the home—comics to read to young children, anecdotes and news stories to share with the family, or a book of bedtime stories to read to the wee ones. Even though the bulk of adult reading is silent, there is still enough occasion for oral reading to justify considerable school time in teaching pupils to read orally in a smooth and meaningful way.

The proportion of oral reading. Despite its importance, teachers should at no level of instruction emphasize oral reading as much as they stress silent reading. In the early primary grades, where pupils read everything silently before attempting to read orally, oral reading can at the most receive equal emphasis with silent. However, after the pupils have mastered a fair-sized sight vocabulary, children should do much silent reading and they should do considerable selective oral reading where only part of a story is read aloud. Consequently, silent reading is consistently receiving more stress than in the introductory phases of reading.

In general, pupils in the middle grades should have a greatly reduced schedule of oral reading. At this level children should be perfecting lifetime mechanical skills that determine their rate of silent reading and, because oral reading is so much slower than silent, they should establish these skills through the more rapid silent-reading activities. (A child can read aloud only as fast as he can articulate the words. He can learn to read silently several times as fast.) Still there should be a certain amount of oral reading experience in grades four to six because (1) pupils who do no oral reading begin to lose the skills they have acquired in earlier years, and (2) the children find enjoyable and informative passages that they wish to share through oral reading. Slow-learning pupils, who may still be reading at the primary level, need considerable oral reading as they continue to work on a basic sight vocabulary and the earlier skills of word recognition.

At the upper-grade levels, pupils may frequently read aloud as they share their own creative stories and written reports, as well as literary passages that appeal to them. Also, when a point is under dispute, they may wish to settle the issue by reading authoritative passages aloud. Since these pupils have become quite mature in the skills that determine their rate of reading, they can engage in slow-paced oral reading without injury to the speed of their silent reading. Even so, silent reading is much more used than oral reading because of the demands of study and especially the opportunities to enjoy individually selected library books.

Types of oral reading. The elementary school curriculum involves several types of oral reading. In the first place, there is the kind of oral reading that accompanies silent reading in the primary grades. Whether reading a sentence, a paragraph, a half page, a whole page, a half story, or an entire story, the pupils in grades one to three read "with their eyes" before they read orally. Thus prepared, they are more likely to read fluently in a natural, conversational tone; word-calling in a monotonous, high-pitched voice is discouraged. Through listening to her pupils read, the teacher can determine whether pupils are really comprehending, mastering a basic sight vocabulary, and learning to figure out words for themselves. Too, through oral reading pupils get a sense of accomplishment and note their progress toward true fluency. Often the oral reading is done in response to a question that calls for selective thinking: Who can find the part which shows that there were bears on Hemlock Mountain? or, What did Jimmy say when he saw his birthday present? or, Find the part that tells about the picture on page 57.

After pupils have become quite proficient in both silent and oral reading, they may occasionally do sight reading, that is, oral reading of materials without first reading them through silently. A skillful reader may read at sight an easy storybook or reference; he may read the funnies to a younger brother or the instructions on a new mechanical toy to his father. When sight reading is permitted, the materials should be at least two grade levels below those which a pupil is using in his reading class; for instance, a child reading in a sixth reader should do sight reading at the fourth-reader level or below. Actually, schools do not stress sight reading much because so many elementary school pupils read poorly at sight—they need more maturity and more advanced skills than can normally be expected at this level. Most of the oral reading should be of the audience-situation type. Here children read orally to entertain or inform an audience, preferably something no one else has read. Each pupil may select a choice part from his library book, a juvenile magazine, or a single copy of a supplementary reader; or he may read something he himself has written. It is possible, however, to have an audience situation when an entire pupil group has already read a selection silently as, for instance, reading an excerpt for a classmate to act out. Essential to the audience situation is an *interested* listener or group of listeners.

A fourth type of oral reading consists of lessons for improving skills such as enunciation, adaptation of rate and voice quality to mood or action, emphasis through inflections of the voice, and proper phrasing of sentences. In the middle grades, there is special need for such training lessons.

Oral Reading in the Primary Grades

In the primary grades, most children progress from no reading ability at all to a level of considerable skill in the third grade. In the beginning stages, the teacher gives much guidance through a preparatory discussion and a carefully worded question that leads into each sentence of the story. The pupil first reads silently, then orally. The silent reading reveals the answer to the teacher's questions and prepares for any follow-up discussion or oral reading.

Avoidance of word calling. From the very first day of reading instruction, the teacher should encourage the pupils to use a natural, conversational tone in their oral reading. If a child does read word by word, she repeats the question, asks the pupil to *tell* her the answer, and then requests him to read the answer as if he were telling it. Sometimes she may demonstrate fluent performance by reading the sentence herself; the pupil can then almost surely "get the feel" of smooth reading as he reads again after noting her performance.

It is important that a pupil should acquire a growing sight vocabulary so that he will be master of the words that he meets on each page. Through using parallel charts, sentence strips and word cards in matching exercises, and other types of informal reading, the teacher must make sure that each pupil is thoroughly mastering the words which he is meeting in each book story or that, in the upper primary grades, he is learning to figure out new words for himself. It is disastrous for a child to progress so rapidly through a book that he is amassing a constantly increasing stock of words he does not know. Word calling is inevitable when a child reads laboriously passages full of words he does not recognize. How soon a pupil completes his reading book is not important; what does matter is that he be reading well any stories he does read.

Oral reading of informal materials. A review of the chapters dealing with primary reading instruction will reveal the mention of many situations that involve the oral reading of informal materials. In teaching children to read a news story or an experience chart which they originally dictated for the teacher to record on the chalkboard or a chart, she uses some of the following procedures:

Letting each child read the sentences he has contributed
Asking a pupil to read the sentence that answers a specific question (1) in sequential order (2) in miscellaneous order
Playing a game with sentence strips, such as Postman or Spider and Fly (See page 202.)
Matching sentence strips to corresponding sentences on a chart
Having a story party on Friday to review chart stories

Other types of informal oral reading arise as pupils do some of the following:

Reading a label on a child's picture
Clarifying a misunderstood direction for an activity by having some pupil read it aloud
Reading a child's original ending to an unfinished story
Reading an entirely original story

Oral reading from books. In the earliest stages of book reading, the children progress down the page a sentence at a time, with silent reading before oral. Later a group of sentences can be handled in the same way. As sight vocabulary increases, the length of the reading passages gradually increases and, more and more, the oral reading becomes selective. Some of the selective oral reading procedures are as follows:

After silent reading of an entire page, locating and reading orally a passage that explicitly answers a specific question
After silent reading and discussion of a large part of a story or of an entire story, reading of selected parts orally, such as—
- Conversation between characters (Stories abound in conversation, and each child can assume the dialogue of a particular character and read it orally.)
- Locating and reading aloud the paragraph or part paragraph in a story that relates to a specific illustration
- Selecting and reading orally the sentence or sentences that afford the answer to each of several questions that have been raised
- Choosing and reading aloud the sentences or paragraphs that suggest action to be pantomimed or "cartooned" after these parts have been read orally

Reading of an entire familiar story orally, each child handling an installment, for the following purposes:
- Enjoyment of a favorite tale; or
- Preparation for an assembly or a sharing period with another class

As with informal reading, oral reading from books should be fluent and natural-sounding. This means that materials should be sufficiently simple and the vocabulary familiar enough to enable smooth and expressive reading, and the children should definitely prepare for their oral reading. (Even at the second- and third-reader level, many pupils need much supplementary informal reading to guarantee thorough mastery of a sight vocabulary and ability to figure out new words.)

Illustrative games. When certain sight words prove to be difficult for pupils to master, the teacher may find it advisable to supplement readers with parallel charts and sentence strips that may be matched with corresponding portions of the charts. Games such as the following help to maintain interest. Many more games are contained in the manuals that accompany the various basal reading series.

The Whisper Game: Sentence strips are distributed to the members of a group. These match the sentences in the reading chart. A pupil looks over the chart and silently selects a sentence from it, then whispers the sentence to the teacher. Each pupil takes his turn reading the strip he holds, after asking: "Was it this sentence?" As soon as the correct one is read, another pupil selects from the chart, and the game proceeds as before.

The Postman: After a group has read through the sentence strips which the teacher holds, she starts the game by holding up a sentence strip for all to read silently. She chooses one child to be postman. He carries the strip to another child. If the latter reads it aloud correctly, he receives the letter (sentence strip). The postman must, of course, know how to read the letter if he is to deliver it correctly.

Spider and Fly: After the group has gone through the sentence strips which the teacher holds, every child but one receives a strip. This one child is the spider. He tries to catch some flies by reading as many of the strips as he can. Each fly will deliver his strip only if the reading by the spider is correct.

Is It Mine?: Two sets of sentence strips are needed. One set is delivered to the children, face down. The teacher holds up one of the strips in her set. Each child then looks at his sentence and, if it matches that of the teacher, he reads his aloud after asking, "Is it mine?" If correct, he wins a point. After a few sentences have been thus matched, the strips are shuffled, and redistributed among the children. The game starts again.

Illustrative lessons. There follow descriptions of parts of several oral reading lessons. *T* stands for *teacher; P* for *pupil.*

Lesson 1

T: You read the story very well today. You seemed to understand everything in it. Now we will read out loud. Turn to page 42 and find the sentence that tells how Fido helped Jimmy. Look up at me as soon as you are ready to read the sentence. (*And so on*)

Lesson 2

T: Look through the story we have just read. Find a part that you would like to act out. Plan what you will do. Remember you will not say anything. When you are ready to act, sit up straight. (*After several are ready*)

Jack will act out his part first. (*Pause while he acts*) Now look through the story and find the part that Jack acted out. (*Pause*) Kathy, read the part that you think Jack acted out.

Lesson 3

On separate strips of paper, the teacher has written questions on a story for each pupil in the group. Each reads through his question silently. When called up, he reads it aloud.

P: Where did Peter Rabbit go early in the morning?

T: Each of you open your book to page 75 and find the answer to Jane's question. Be ready to read it to Jane. She will tell you whether you have found the right part. (*And so on*)

Lesson 4

T: Yesterday each of you drew a picture about the story of the unhappy kitten. I am going to let you show your pictures, one at a time. Be sure not to tell what your picture is about, because we want the others to guess what your picture shows. They will open their books to the story and find the part you have drawn. Then one of them will read the part he has chosen.

P: This is my picture. Here is the unhappy kitten. (*Pupils skim; one of them reads aloud.*) Yes, that is the right part, Mary.

Poetry in the primary grades. Since young children have a natural love for the rhythm and melody of poetry and since poetry should always be given aloud, the teacher should provide frequent experiences with verse. She should do most of the oral reading herself as she reads or recites one or more poems with her pupils whenever a good opportunity arises. On her desk will be suitable collections and anthologies, entire volumes devoted to the verse of a single poet, such as Robert Louis Stevenson or A. A. Milne, and a notebook or file with her own favorite poems. Then she will have ready upon a moment's notice just the right bit of verse to suit any occasion; for example, Vachel Lindsay's "The Turtle" when a child brings his miniature painted pet to school for a show and tell period, or "Moving," by Eunice Tietjens, for the little boy who has just moved into the community. Poetry should definitely be included in her bibliographies for the social studies units which she teaches.

In order to present the poems well, the teacher will, at the very least, rehearse her oral reading so that she can read smoothly, with voice modulated to suit the mood and action of the poem and with due emphasis on the leading ideas and subordination of lesser phrases. She will read as if she were talking while actually experiencing the situation portrayed by the poet. Better still, she will memorize many of her own favorite juvenile poems—those most likely to please the children.

Children tend to ask again and again for the poems that have special appeal because of contagious humor, vividly portrayed action, graphic phrasing, or catchy rhythm. As the teacher reads these poems from day to day, the girls and boys are likely to chime in on the lines they have effortlessly learned; and thus they are led into simple phases of choral speaking.

Once the children have enjoyed the experience of joining the teacher in repeating verse, they will get much pleasure out of the simple types of real choral speaking. For instance, the teacher may read the rhyme about the gray billy goat and they may repeat together: "Dinkums, dinkums, little gray billy boat" at the end of each stanza; or one group in the class may ask, "What does little birdie say in the morn at break of day?" and the remaining pupils may give the answer in unison; or the entire class may repeat softly, in nicely blended voices, the various nursery rhymes they like particularly well. Here the teacher may make large charts of the favorite nursery rhymes, let the pupils illustrate them with crayons, then "read" them in choral reading style. Such activities enhance children's enjoyment and appreciation of poetry and give them the socializing benefits of doing things cooperatively.

Oral Reading in the Middle Grades

There are two major types of oral reading in the intermediate grades: *audience situations* and *training lessons.*

The former will often be part of a silent reading lesson; the latter will usually be a lesson in itself as the pupils work to improve their enunciation, voice quality, phrasing, ability to emphasize key ideas, and the like.

Audience situations. Many of the reading periods in the middle grades will include only silent reading accompanied by clarifying, orderly discussion. Some selections, however, contain passages that are excellent for oral reading and, by wise planning, the teacher can provide a genuine audience situation where the pupil group is interested in listening to a classmate read orally although its members have already read the selection silently. Some of the possible audience situations are suggested in the list below. Any resourceful teacher can devise others.

Materials Familiar to the Audience

I. Dramatic reading (conversation; passages full of action)
   A. Each pupil takes the part of one of the characters in the story, and reads what this character says in a running conversation (trying for a vivid, lifelike quality).
   B. He pantomimes a bit of brisk action in the story; his classmates skim to find that part and try to read the exact portion aloud.
   C. He reads a portion full of brisk action, then asks a classmate to act out what he has read.
   D. An able reader reads all of a dramatic story while classmates pantomime it in parallel action. (This is an opportunity to listen to high-quality reading as a demonstration of superior reading; the teacher does not indicate that she has this purpose.)

II. Selective thinking and reading
   A. A pupil finds the part that answers a specific question and reads it aloud.
      1. A series of questions is written on the chalkboard or worksheet (skimming practice as well).

2. A series of questions is asked orally by the teacher (or a pupil).
3. A question per pupil is written on slips of paper.
   a. Pupil reads his question, locating the answer in the story and reading the exact portion aloud.
   b. Pupil reads his question aloud and surprises his classmates by asking them to locate the answer and be prepared to read the answer from the book.

B. A pupil reads individually chosen parts, such as—
   1. The part he likes best.
   2. The part that interested him most.
   3. The most exciting part; the most "scarey" part.
   4. The funniest episode.
   5. A word picture he likes.

C. A pupil locates specific passages and reads them aloud, such as—
   1. The climax; the three or four main steps in the plot.
   2. The part shown in each illustration.
   3. The part that explains the title.
   4. The part that describes a character, place, or incident.
   5. Parts that show the contrast in persons, behavior, places, or incidents.
   6. The passage that proves a point under dispute in class discussion.

III. Holding of a rehearsal as a tryout to see who will read a story to another class or to guests. (Usually several pupils to take the parts of the characters in the story or to read the story by sections.)

As often as possible, audience situations in reading should utilize materials that are new to the audience. Library books and stories that have been clipped from a child's magazine should often be used. Some schools follow the practice of ordering one to four copies of various supplementary readers and collections of stories to be used exclusively for oral reading. Some of these books should be quite simple (yet not babyish) for the use of the less proficient readers; other more advanced. Usually a story will be divided into several parts (for instance, three parts if there are three copies of the book) and each pupil who has that book will prepare only the part he is assigned, and will subsequently read aloud. Only he knows the portion of the plot contained in the part of the story which he is reading to his classmates. Pupils' own original stories and reports provide another source for audience situations.

There follows a list of audience situations in which each pupil reads something that no one (or very few) in his audience may have read for himself.

Materials New to the Audience

I. Sharing of some favorite literature
   A. The pupil reads an entire selection in a single-copy reader.
   B. He reads part of a well-liked book so as to persuade others to read it for themselves.
   C. He displays self-made illustrations or the illustrations in the book, and reads the part that has been illustrated.
   D. He pantomimes action, letting the audience try to interpret it, and then reading the actual account from the book or story.

II. Sight reading of simple materials, using either a periodical or a book.

III. Reading of cut up stories. (These are clipped from a magazine, then cut into sections to distribute among a number of pupils who prepare to read the parts in sequence.)
   A. The parts are numbered to help each reader to know his turn.
   B. The parts are unnumbered so that each reader is "on his guard" to recognize his turn.
   C. The title is omitted so that the main part of the story will suggest an original title to the pupils; there is later comparison with the actual title.
   D. The last section is retained by the teacher so that the

listeners have an opportunity to make up original endings before the ending is read.

IV. Sharing of individually volunteered materials
   A. Jokes are clipped from a paper. (Teacher-approved, just to make sure!)
   B. Anecdotes about famous people may be read.
   C. Supplementary information that will help a class project is used.
   D. Materials are screened and selected for an assembly.

Training lessons. Even the most fluent, expressive readers in the middle grades will profit from lessons that show them how to improve and that give subsequent practice on a specific skill. Enunciation, a flexible and pleasantly modulated voice, fluency, phrasing, and emphasis on key ideas are elements to be trained.

In *enunciation*, a common difficulty is carelessness in pronouncing the endings of words; for example, saying *in'* for *ing* endings, or failing to sound a terminal *d, t, k, p,* or hard *g* sound clearly. Here the teacher may find or devise sentences that feature such sounds and let the pupils who really need the practice read these sentences aloud while a "critic" sits at the back of the room to report on how clearly the terminal sounds come through; or he may later listen to a tape recording for purposes of self-appraisal. The following sentences illustrate the kind of practice exercises the teacher may devise and use for such practice.

> Harold should find a kind word to say. (*d* ending)
> The baby sheep jump up, skip, and leap. (*p* ending)
> The big stag stood on the jagged crag. (*g* ending)

Reading lines from a poem like Eugene Field's "The Duel" gives good mixed practice on terminal sounds in words; for instance—

> The gingham dog and the calico ca*t*
> Si*d*e by si*d*e on the table sa*t*;
> Twas half-pas*t* twelve an*d* wha*t* do you thin*k*?
> Neither one nor 'tother ha*d* slep*t* a win*k*.

Sometimes, too, initial sounds give trouble, especially *w* and *wh*. Exercises similar to those above can be used for practice. Tongue twisters like "Peter Piper picked a peck of pickled peppers" are helpful and amusing.

To cultivate a *flexible and pleasing voice,* there should be much reading or conversation that reflects strong emotions, such as fear or great joy. Many selections in readers and library books contain such conversation. In almost any silent reading lesson, the teacher can find time for two or three pupils to read any emotion-freighted passages that call for expressive reading where a flexible voice is demanded. Hearing the teacher read well and listening to classmates who read fluently and expressively have an indirect, beneficial effect.

The need for *proper phrasing* can be shown by demonstrating the humorous or tragic effect of inaccurate phrasing; for example, a pastor is said to have read the following announcement incorrectly:

> A man going to sea, his wife asks the prayers of the congregation.

He read it to sound as follows:

> A man going to see his wife asks the prayers of the congregation.

In the reading of poetry, skillful and accurate phrasing is especially important because pupils tend to let the rhythm dominate their reading and may not keep the continuity of thought implicit in the integrated idea that runs past the end of one line into the next. Note how necessary it is for a reader to tie two lines together without pause in the following sonnet:

Oh! I have slipped the surly bonds of Earth
  And danced the skies on laughter-silvered wings:
Sunward I've climbed, and joined the tumbling mirth
  Of sun-split clouds—and done a hundred things
You have not dreamed of—wheeled and soared and swung
  High in the sunlit silence. Hov'ring there
I've chased the shouting wind along, and flung
  My eager craft through footless halls of air.

Oh, oh, the long, delirious, burning blue!
  I've topped the wind-swift heights with easy grace
Where never a lark, or ever eagle flew—
  And, while with silent lifting mind I've trod
The high untrespassed sanctity of space,
  Put out my hand and touched the face of God.

—From "High Flight" by JOHN G. MCGEE, JR., RAF,
in *Forth* (World War II)

The mood and meaning of passages determine the *rate* at which they should be read orally. Despondency or hesitancy may be reflected by a somewhat slower articulation of the words, as well as an occasional slight pause to add emphasis to the mood, while excitement calls for some speeding up of articulation and fewer pauses. Compare these passages. Note especially how the punctuation helps to indicate mood and to show where pauses should occur.

Janet hesitated, paused, then strolled along slowly.
Jimmy's fingers raced over the keyboard in a frenzy of action.
George lingeringly fingered the keyboard of the piano he loved.
"Quick! Quick!" cried Kathy. "You'll get hit!"
"Well, I'm not sure," drawled Sam. "I'll have to think it over."

Note how poets use long vowels to show unhappy feelings so that the reader *must* slow down:

Break, break, break,
On thy cold gray stones, O Sea!
—TENNYSON

How different is this verse of Browning's that shows happiness and a light heart:

The year's at the spring,
And day's at the morn;
Morning's at seven;
The hill-side's dew-pearled;
The lark's on the wing;
The snail's on the thorn:
God's in his heaven—
All's right with the world!

Fluency is the outgrowth of considerable experience in oral reading—if the materials are sufficiently simple, if the child knows his vocabulary, if he has prepared his materials by reading them to himself several times. In fact, middle-grade children should be taught that it is discourteous to read haltingly, mumblingly, inaccurately. Their listeners have the right to expect to enjoy and understand what is being read. Pupils should come to feel a real responsibility for selecting materials of appropriate difficulty and for preparing thoroughly all passages they are to read orally.

One good way to check comprehension and to determine whether a pupil really understands and appreciates the situations in reading materials is to have him read aloud. The way he emphasizes critical ideas determines how well he is thinking. Emphasis is indicated by the way the voice is inflected, by the pauses that give time for an idea to sink in, and sometimes through stress on a particular word through changing the volume of the voice. A single sentence can be read as many ways as there are situations which this situation may reflect. There follows a list of situations that govern the sentence below the list. Try reading this sentence (in bold type) to reflect each of the situations (wherein a child listener has been careless and is emphatically told the correct thing to do).

1. The child put the *new* hat on the shelf.
2. He put an old *brown* hat on the shelf.
3. He put his father's *cap* on the shelf.
4. He put the hat on the *lower* shelf.
5. He put it in the top *drawer.*
6. He took a hat *off* the shelf.

Put the old black hat on the top shelf.

Pupils will profit from reading a single sentence in various ways. Once or twice a week the teacher should think up a sentence (with several adjectives or adverbs to give flexibility) and spend five minutes in practicing emphasis to reflect varying situations. She can also select passages from a reading selection where there is a question of proper emphasis. This, too, can be done frequently. Choral speaking is another experience that calls for proper emphasis on words.

Poetry in the middle grades. As in the primary grades, children at the intermediate-grade level should hear much poetry. In connection with holidays, weather, and the seasons, community happenings such as a county fair or parade, interesting events in the life of the pupils, national and world happenings, and on-going units in the classroom itself, the teacher will find countless occasions for bringing in one or more relevant poems. These she herself will read with genuine enjoyment and subtly apparent appreciation. The pupils, too, may volunteer to read poems they have found and liked; but each such reader should hold himself responsible for thorough preparation and vivid portrayal so that his listeners can get the utmost in understanding and pleasure from his reading.

Even more than in the earlier school years, children of the middle grades profit from choral reading. They are now old enough to grasp meanings and sense the moods that the poet has tried to convey and can join with the teacher in planning the most effective way to arrange the lines for choral rendition: a solo by a rich voice to be interspersed among the lines spoken by groups (Beatrice Curtis Brown's "Jonathan Bing" is a good example); alternate lines or stanzas by two groups in a question-answer type of poem; a refrain spoken by a small group after each of several stanzas which are recited by solo voices; an entire short poem given in unison.

If the pupils are inexperienced in choral speaking, they should begin much as primary children would. The teacher should speak many of the lines and take much responsibility for suggesting the more effective ways of arranging the poems until the children are familiar enough with the different forms of choral rendition to take an intelligent part in the planning. (The simple introductory ways are *refrain*, *line-a-child* in which each child says a line or two in a poem that naturally divides in that way, and *antiphonal* or two-group arrangement with alternating participation by the two groups.) The chapter's bibliography suggests various sources of poems suitable for use in the intermediate grades.

Oral Reading in the Upper Grades

In the upper grades, oral reading continues to be a form of communication in which the reader conveys to his listeners fresh information, convincing evidence on a disputed point, or a striking illustration of a moral-ethical principle. For the better readers at this level, however, oral reading should become much more than a useful form of communication because they can make of it a fine art—complete response to an author's intended meaning and mood through proper emphasis on main ideas, subordination of minor details, and voice inflections to express the doubt or conviction, joy or sadness, scorn or admiration, surprise or boredom that the situation warrants.

Audience situations. As has been indicated, oral reading can and should serve a useful purpose. This is true when the reader is presenting materials that supplement the facts and evidence already available to his group so that his listeners have good reason for listening and he himself feels a true responsibility for making himself clearly understood by reading *well.* To be effective, he must have made careful preparation by thoughtful silent reading that has brought him full understanding—sometimes by going to the dictionary or encyclopedia to reinforce and clarify his ideas—and he even feels a need for preliminary rehearsal so that he can be sure of his ability to pronounce the hard words, to emphasize the main ideas, and to suit the volume of his voice and his rate of reading to the ability of his audience to take in what he is reading.

Much of the audience reading, however, should be designed to bring pleasure to an audience. The reader may have written his own amusing or adventurous story, an original riddle, or a bit of graphic verse. Even more often he will be sharing some favorite passages from literature—stories, library books, verse that he has discovered and enjoyed. In such reading, he is responsible not only for the ideas but the mood which the author has wanted to convey; and this is where the artistry comes in.

Effective oral reading of literature. Materials that are well written should be well portrayed. In the first place, the oral reader-to-be must assure himself that he has an over-all grasp of the situation pictured in the complete literary selection. Only then can he decide on the main points to be stressed, the details to be subordinated, and the mood he should try to induce in his listeners. Sometimes thoughtful silent reading may be sufficient to accomplish these points; sometimes he may have to paraphrase certain passages to make sure of their significance. At times, a paragraph may require additional thoughtful study to decide whether certain points are coordinate with neighboring passages or whether they are subordinate.

To carry over the proper emotional tone, the prospective reader must really get himself into the situation and spirit of the selection. Only then can his voice be modulated and keyed to the emotions to be reflected in his oral reading. Sometimes a teacher may find it helpful to have pupils work with short passages that express very different strong emotions as she asks them to interpret each passage with slightly exaggerated pitch, loudness, rate of articulation, and inflections. They will find it great fun to see how many ways that a single word can be spoken to convey different emotions; for instance, saying "Oh" to express (1) being startled, (2) feeling extreme doubt, (3) being suddenly convinced of something that you have been doubting, (4) experiencing a shock just as an accident is happening, and so on. Too, they will enjoy making a tape recording of their various endeavors to read a tricky passage so as to stress main ideas, subordinate details, convey a subtle mood, or articulate clearly. Discussion of such efforts can be very fruitful in building up high standards for reading fine literary passages. Another helpful procedure is having the pupils listen to recordings, radio and television programs, or face-to-face reading by an expert and then deliberately try to emulate these excellent productions.

Most of all, it is important that the pupils have many opportunities to read aloud worth-while materials. The skills of oral reading are learned "through doing." One interesting way for pupils who are interested in becoming accomplished oral readers is the organization of a club or "readers' bureau" whose members will make themselves available for assemblies, appearances in other classrooms, and out-of-school clubs for oral reading of literary selections.

Poetry in the upper grades. Many longer narrative poems are appropriate at the upper-grade level; for instance, Longfellow's *Evangeline* or Noyes' "The Highwayman." These the teacher should read to the pupils—usually as a whole first so as to give an over-all impression and to play up the story and action that are basic to each poem. Later she and the pupils may select particularly vivid or beautiful passages and endeavor to read these orally in the most expressive way. More than in the earlier years, the pupils themselves can read to their classmates—but only after careful preparation so that continuity of ideas, emphasis on main ideas, subordination of minor ones, and expressive voice inflections will be achieved. Some pupils may have original verse to present.

Of course, choral reading is even more important than in the middle grades because a class may now be divided into several groups, each of which will work out an arrangement for a poem which it prefers. This is possible after the teacher has helped the pupils understand the workings of a verse choir in which low, high, and possibly medium voices are grouped separately and in which they blend their combined voices to attain an anthemlike effect. (Arbuthnot explains verse choirs very well.)

Summary

While silent reading should, throughout the elementary school period, receive more time and attention than oral reading, the latter still has a significant role to play in the curriculum. Pupils read aloud as they bring to their listeners information, evidence, and enjoyment in such a way as to convey the author's intended meaning and mood. In practically all cases, materials must be read silently before oral reading takes place in order to enable the pupil to read smoothly with proper emphasis, subordination, rate, continuity, and voice quality. In the middle grades, there should be less oral reading than at any other level since children are then acquiring lifetime reading skills that determine their rate.

Nearly all the oral reading should be in an audience situation where the reader is conveying something new, fresh, and interesting to his listeners. In the middle and upper grades, there is also need for some training lessons that will develop and improve proficiency in conveying meanings and moods through oral reading.

Selected References

(* recommended)

Broom, M. E., *et al. Effective Reading Instruction.* New York: McGraw-Hill Book Co., 1951. Pp. 216–34.

Durrell, Donald. *Improving Reading Instruction.* Yonkers, N.Y.: World Book Co., 1957. Pp. 149–71.

Farris, Herbert J. "Let's Read to the Children," *NEA Journal,* LXII (December, 1953), 545.

Gray, William S. (ed.). "Basic Instruction in Reading in Elementary and High Schools," *Supplementary Educational*

Monographs, No. 65. Chicago: University of Chicago Press, 1949. Pp. 179–200.

HARRIS, ALBERT. *How to Increase Reading Ability.* New York: David McKay Co., Inc., 1961. Pp. 185–219.

HESTER, KATHLEEN. *Teaching Every Child to Read.* New York: Harper and Bros., 1955. Pp. 262–78.

MCKEE, PAUL. *The Teaching of Reading in the Elementary School.* Boston: Houghton Mifflin Co., 1948. Pp. 596–608.

MCKIM, MARGARET. *Guiding Growth in Reading.* New York: The Macmillan Co., 1955. Pp. 410–19.

*ROBINSON, HELEN M. "Oral Aspects of Reading," *Supplementary Reading Monographs,* No. 82. Chicago: University of Chicago Press, 1955. Selected pages.

TINKER, MILES A., and MCCULLOUGH, CONSTANCE. *Teaching Elementary Reading.* New York: Appleton-Century-Crofts, Inc., 1962. Pp. 203–12.

On Choral Reading

ABNEY, LOUISE. *Choral Speaking Arrangements for the Lower Grades.* Magnolia, Mass.: Expression Co., 1952.

———. *Choral Speaking Arrangements for the Upper Grades.* Magnolia, Mass.: Expression Co., 1953.

ARBUTHNOT, MAY HILL. *Children and Books.* Chicago: Scott, Foresman and Co., 1961.

RASMUSSEN, CARRIE. *Speech Methods in the Elementary School.* New York: Ronald Press, 1949. Pp. 90–92; 234–39.

WERNER, LORNA S. *Speech in the Elementary School.* Evanston, Ill.: Row, Peterson and Co., 1947. Pp. 75–122; 205–7.

13

Developing Comprehension Skills

CERTAINLY THE END PRODUCT TO BE DESIRED IN our teaching the proper word-attack and word-meaning skills is comprehension of what has been read. Most people will agree that comprehension is a complex thing, including all that the child learns about words, phrases, sentences, and paragraphs; differing from day to day in terms of the quantity to be learned, the quality of what is learned, and the purpose for learning; and developing gradually just as other reading skills are developed in the maturing child. It is complex because it includes all that we know of vocabulary skills, of the rate of perception, and of the accuracy of recognition.

In this chapter we shall discuss the comprehension skills: the factors which influence the development of those skills, the various types of skills (comprehension, organization, rate, and critical evaluation) which are important for the child's success in the classroom and life activities, and many techniques which may contribute to the refinement of those skills.

Factors Influencing Comprehension

When the child comes to school, he has already developed some skills of comprehension. As he has listened to others talk or read, he has learned to give attention, to react to what he has heard on the basis of his own experiences, and to come to conclusions about what he has heard. At this stage of his development, he is dependent upon his listening comprehension. His safety, his comfort, and his pleasures are often related to his ability to respond to what other people communicate to him.

Most teachers make use of the child's listening comprehension in developing readiness for reading and eventual comprehension of the printed page. They know that there is a wide variance in the children's ability to listen carefully and accurately, depending upon the same factors which influence reading comprehension. The child in kindergarten is totally dependent upon his visual and auditory skills for gaining understanding of the world around him. Later, as he moves into the stage of independence in reading, his reading comprehension approximates his listening comprehension. At a later date, as he matures and learns adult skills of reading for meaning, his listening comprehension may be at a lower level than his reading comprehension.

Intelligence. The quality and quantity of comprehension will often be determined by the purpose which the child has for reading; it is possible for him to read the same selection at different times, with different goals in mind, and comprehend the ideas quite differently. Even though we aid the child in defining his purpose for reading and guide him throughout the selection, the *number* of ideas that he understands and the *depth* of his understanding will be largely dependent upon his general capacity to learn. Too, the rate at which he associates what he reads with previous knowledge or experience will be influenced by this thing which we commonly call intelligence. The slow-learning or dull-normal child cannot be expected to show the same reactions nor gain the same appreciation as the bright child when they read together for pleasure or to gain information.

Experience. As we have indicated in each chapter, children differ greatly in the depth and breadth of their experiences; much of the teaching of comprehension skills is concerned with providing experiences for children through which they may respond to books. The boy or girl with limited experiences may have difficulty in comprehending many of the ideas and activities with which other children are familiar before they come to school. While slum or isolated areas typically are deficient in providing experiential background, the socioeconomic level of the home and community is never an absolute determinant of the extent of children's experiences. From some of our "best" homes come children who have been denied opportunities for normal experiences.

Mechanics of reading. If our children have all mastered the skills of word attack and word meaning, if they have learned to handle books properly, if they have learned to read from left to right on a line of print, and if all of these skills are performed smoothly, then comprehension should be easier for them. On the other hand, if the child must pause frequently to figure out words, pronounce them and stumble ahead to the next words; if he has not developed the visual skill of following a line of print without hesitation and frequent regression, then his chances are poor for comprehension of the sentence or the paragraph. The smooth flow of words into phrases, phrases into sentences, and sentences into paragraphs is an essential in comprehension. Occasionally we encounter a child who has developed such a compulsion for correctness in word-calling that he has become a "mouther of words" rather than a reader who perceives and reacts to and integrates the meaning which was intended on the page. Obviously, there must be a fine balance somewhat in each child between careful attention to word attack skills and to comprehension skills.

Interests and interest span. It is a truism that we all respond quickly to what we read if we are interested in the topic or are at least familiar with it. The depth of comprehension which a child will gain from a story or discussion of a science topic will be in direct proportion to the amount of interest he already has in the selection or the interest we, as teachers, can awaken in him. The average person is interested in those things which are related to his best aptitudes; however, one of the most fascinating tasks in teaching is aiding children and young adults to develop new and broad interests.

Very often the interest span is related to personality factors; a disturbed child who has encountered many unfortunate experiences at home or in the school may be unable to persevere when required to read for comprehension of ideas. But interest span in the child is also most directly related to the purposes he has for reading; at the early stages of reading, the teacher will establish those purposes carefully, through discussion of children's experiences, visual aids, and relating to immediate needs.

Skills of comprehending. Another obvious factor which influences the depth and amount of comprehension is the skills which the child has developed for that purpose. Like all reading skills, the ability to comprehend what we read develops gradually from the simple to the complex skills. The balanced program should include direct teaching of techniques which will aid the child in developing attitudes and skills of thoughtful, purposeful reading.

The Comprehension Skills

Basic to good comprehension is an understanding of the manner in which words are fused into meaningful phrases, phrases into sentences, and sentences into paragraphs. These are the structural elements of written communication. Early in his primary training, the child becomes aware of the respective functions of periods, commas, quotation marks, and question marks—each a grammatical element which aids the writer in conveying meaning to the reader. He may also learn, when he begins to write simple sentences, that the addition of descriptive words or phrases adds color and zest to what he has to say. The concept of the phrase, sentence, and paragraph is not an easy one, but it is vital to the teaching of comprehension skills. The child may learn that full meaning is not conveyed by a single word; rather, the combinations of words into phrases and sentences carry the complete meaning. As the teacher aids the child in comprehending his reading materials, she is also directing his attention to the groups of words which best convey the meaning. Thus, gradually the child gains a concept of grammatical structure. He gradually becomes aware of the fact that the meaning he seeks is embodied in different combinations of words, throughout the paragraph or the selection.

Getting the main idea. In her very first oral discussions with groups of children in the classroom, the teacher is laying a foundation for comprehension skills in reading. Each time she tells a story and asks such questions as, What was this story about? What was it that taught Sally always to tell the truth? she is directing attention to main ideas or general impressions of the story as a whole. It is essential that the child gain the meaning of the passage as a whole before he can be expected to react to subordinate details. Since the teacher is usually in the role of interrogator, she should take care that her questions actually lead the child to think in terms of general impressions. For instance, if the child has been told the story of Little Red Riding Hood and is asked, "What is this story about?" a satisfactory answer is not "Little Red Riding Hood." Rather, this is a story of a little girl who visits her grandmother and encounters the dangers of a wolf. Now the details of her experiences can be elicited by careful questioning, because the group has a main idea with which the details can be easily associated. Other questions, which require the children to react to or interpret parts of the story, may follow.

Here are some suggestions for guiding children in finding the main idea or gaining a general impression. The suggestions are listed in order of their difficulty for the child.

1. Read a short selection and select the best title, from several listed, for the selection.
2. Read a short selection and give it a title, in the child's own words.
3. Read the title of a chapter and attempt to predict what the author is going to say.
4. Read the introduction of a chapter and note carefully just what the author has outlined.
5. Read the summary of a chapter and tell, in a simple sentence, what the chapter covered.
6. Read a paragraph and reduce it to a simple sentence, by paraphrasing the author.
7. Rapidly skim the titles and subheads of a selection and attempt to list details which will give a general impression of the entire selection.
8. Read the first and last sentences of an entire selection.
9. Turn each subhead or subtitle into a question. The answer to that question will be the main idea of the paragraph or paragraphs.

10. Give the children a newspaper and present them with a clearly stated problem. Ask them to skim rapidly for a solution to that problem. In the beginning, it is best to confine the exercise to a single selection from the newspaper.

Reading to note relevant details. When the child has had considerable experience in finding main ideas, details are needed for a complete understanding of that idea. Reading for relevant details is demanded in certain content areas: science, geography, arithmetic, home economics, and history. It is much slower reading than the reading for general impressions or main ideas, directly related to the reader's purpose. If he is seeking dates or pertinent data for an experiment or construction activity, he must read carefully and relate the details to each other and the main idea. It is possible that much of our classroom testing encourages children to read for details, which are often really unimportant. This is not intended to discount the necessity of reading for details, but many details are useless to the child unless he sees them in relation to main ideas. The teacher may find these activities helpful in teaching children to read for relevant details.

1. Select a paragraph which contains a clearly stated main idea and several supporting details. Read the main idea and identify it as such for the children. Now ask them to write down the details which they hear as you read the remainder of the paragraph. Allow the children to compare the details which they have selected.
2. State a main idea and encourage the children to read a selection for details which will explain or support that idea.
3. At upper-grade levels, have the children list all of the details which have been given in a particular paragraph or selection. Then classify the details, as to their contribution to the main idea, as important, as merely informative, or as actually unnecessary. This may aid the child in seeing that he must be

prepared at all times to "let words go" when they are not essential to his purpose for reading the selection.

4. Select a problem for discussion, perhaps from social studies. Discuss the problem carefully and list the information which the children already have on the problem from their previous experiences. Through discussion, decide what information is needed to solve the problem and elicit opinions as to where the information might be found. After the children have gathered the information, discuss the relevancy of each child's contributions. Now it is time to organize the details which have been gathered, and this may be done by listing all of the relevant details on the blackboard and then numbering them in the order in which they should appear for giving the best solution to the problem. Although this would appear to be a technique which one might use with upper-grade children, it is nicely adaptable to middle grades, if care is taken to limit the problem.

Reading to predict outcomes or solutions. A technique which is often used by the kindergarten teacher is the telling of a story up to a critical point and asking children to predict the ending. The mature reader is one who has fully developed this skill; given a few essential points, he may draw on his rich background of experiences and be able to anticipate a solution to a problem, or a climax to a story. As soon as he has checked the accuracy of his prediction, he may find that further reading is unnecessary. Or he may find this such an excellent concentration device that he becomes more and more involved with the details of the solution which the author proposes. When children become adept at predicting outcomes, drawing conclusions, or proposing solutions, we have good evidence of their growth in comprehension skills. Obviously, to be able to draw conclusions or to predict outcomes or solutions requires careful reading of the problem or the story.

In a day's activities in the average classroom, generalizations are stated time and again; but often these generalizations are not founded on sound information or facts. It is a dangerous practice to allow children to make generalizations without truly adequate information for doing so. On the other hand, many children never learn to draw the definite or sound conclusions which are actually warranted. The teacher should be very alert to the possibility that children are often inaccurate in such matters. Frequent discussions, when children make errors in conclusions and generalizations, may help the children to see the importance of getting facts. Encouraging wide reading to find definite information and to get at facts is always helpful, but this would be worthless unless the children were given opportunities to use the teacher and each other as sounding boards to test the accuracy of their information.

Reading to follow directions. Many adults do not follow directions accurately; as a result, literally thousands of hours are wasted in a single day. Perhaps this is because each of us is required to follow so many directions in a single day that we either become totally confused or choose to ignore them. The boy or girl in the classroom is exposed to directions many times in a day's activities, and there is good evidence that the reason this boy or girl never learns to follow directions is that he or she has never had systematic training in doing so. The teacher gives directions for play activities, she makes assignments, she outlines field trips and excursions, she aids an individual child in solving a problem; each of these is one aspect of giving directions.

To follow directions accurately, the child must listen carefully. He must either establish a mental picture or write down the sequence of the directions and then attempt to see the reason for participating in the activity. Consequently, the wise teacher will relate directions to activities which children are really interested in or are so stimulated by that they feel a need for following through the activity: taking a trip to the museum, making a breadboard for Mother's birthday, or planning a program to be presented to another class. The individual child's failure to follow directions will result in his being unable to participate fully in the activity. It is perfectly reasonable that we teach children to give full attention when directions are being given by another person; it is also perfectly reasonable to deny the privilege of participation, occasionally, to the child who persists in his inattention. At a later date, faced with critical specifications or confronted with a test which requires careful attention to the details of directions, this same child will profit from the training he has received.

Teaching children to take directions can be both pleasurable and profitable. There are two prerequisites: full attention and expectation of a definite sequence of data. And this is one activity which can be easily checked for accuracy; either the child has followed directions and accomplished the task, or he has failed.

There are numerous activities which might be associated with learning to take directions. Here are a few suggestions:

1. Encourage children to play games in which directions are given on how to make something, how to reach the children's library, how to play a game. Allow the leader to choose one child who will either execute the directions or will repeat them for the group.
2. Occasionally give the responsibility of assignments to one of the children, who will command the attention of his classmates and check to see that each child has accurately recorded the directions given.
3. Provide opportunities for children to give and read announcements, both to their classmates and to other classes. Point out

that these activities require careful, sequential statement of facts and directions.

4. Make it a practice to precede each activity in the classroom by giving explicit but simple directions for that activity. Occasionally call on individual children to review those directions before the activity is actually begun.
5. Encourage each child to be responsible for the printed directions at the beginning of units in workbooks, tests, or project sheets.
6. Discuss with the children how they may become accurate guides for such events as Parents' Day, giving directions to the grown-ups who visit the school.

Reading to establish sequence. When the child first faces the task of reading arithmetic problems, he may have difficulty if he has not learned to organize facts in sequential order. Problem solving, experiments, directions—each of these requires that there be a definite order of the facts presented. Developing a sense of sequence has other advantages, too, in addition to being able to follow facts. At any point, it is often important to stop to consider what has come before a fact and to be able to predict what will follow. Cause and effect relationships cannot be clearly established unless there is a fairly definite picture in the reader's mind of the order of events.

In the primary grades, children may learn to listen carefully to a story in order that they might be able to tell it accurately to others. The teacher can easily identify the child who consistently fails to establish proper sequence of ideas or events and will want to point out to the child that the effect of a story is often lost if the proper sequence is not followed.

When children have learned to read sentences with ease and accuracy, they may engage in activities which require their arranging sentences in proper order; older children may do the same with paragraphs. Very often the skill learned in establishing such a sequence will be very useful in the child's creative writing. The outline is also an excellent illustration of the sequence of ideas and relevant details. Comic strips, date lines, chronological events in the life of a great man, and the developmental stages of an insect or animal are other examples of the necessity for sequential order of facts or ideas in order that there may be accurate comprehension.

Reading to gain visual images. So much of the reading which is done in content areas demands that the child be able to visualize from a word description. We know that some children are better endowed than others in this ability of visualization, yet activities which are designed to aid the child in developing the skill may also contribute to his comprehension of the selection as a whole. In the primary grades, opportunities are provided for giving descriptions of what children hear, see, or otherwise receive through the senses. Most of the books which the primary child reads are illustrated, and he has a chance to compare his own word picture with the illustration. As the number of illustrations is reduced in each succeeding textbook, however, the child must depend more and more upon his ability to visualize from word pictures alone; the accuracy with which he comprehends a selection may fail because of his inability to visualize the thing described.

Consider the difficulty the child of limited experience and knowledge might have when he reads—

> Life was rugged on the wild frontier of the West.

What mental pictures does the average child have of *rugged? wild?* Is *frontier* a line which can be drawn, a place? In the limited experience of the child, is the *West* a rugged chain of mountains, rolling plains, a wide ocean, or hills forested with redwoods? Obviously, the example is a limited one, but not an improbable one. Unless very detailed description of the Western frontier follows, the child may fail in comprehension. Very often our social studies and science texts assume that the child has a background of experiences which he does not have; in this case, the good teacher should be ready to supplement the text with vivid word pictures and audio-visual materials. She should be ready to compare the concept to a well-known one, to contrast today's Oklahoma with yesterday's Indian territory. She should give opportunities for discussion of individual children's visual images of what they read, encouraging them to tell others what they hear, see, smell, or feel as they read a description. She will call attention to figurative language and the manner in which it gives added imagery to the sentence; she will encourage children to use figures of speech as they describe and discuss what they have read. Occasionally, a child will be asked to place himself in the role of a character of history or fiction and describe how he feels, what he thinks.

Reading to discover the author's organization. When the child becomes sensitive to main ideas and relevant details, sees the sequence in which ideas are presented, and gains an understanding of the general outline of the selection he is learning to discover the author's organization. For boys and girls in the upper grades, this is an important skill. No longer do their textbooks follow the narrative form of the simple stories in the readers; now the plot may not be discovered until the last paragraph of the story! It is essential that these youngsters be aware of the manner in which the author of the textbook presents his information. If he opens each chapter with a carefully constructed introduction, develops point sequentially under explanatory subtitles, and summarizes all points at the end of the chapter, the reader should be acutely aware of this. In research-type reading which is required of the pupil in the upper grades, the variance of authors' organization is extreme, and careful reading of a selection should be preceded by skimming to discover the plan of organization. The reader may ask himself such questions as these:

1. Does the author state his topic clearly? Do I really know what he is talking about?
2. Does he provide any study questions which might guide my reading?
3. Are there illustrations which might help me understand the points he presents?
4. Does he give warning of points to be made, such as "There are four reasons why the South was not concerned about Lincoln's statement . . ."?
5. Does he use occasional transitional words or phrases which might help me, such as, "In the first place," "Contrary to what we had expected . . ."?
5. Do there appear to be sufficient details to give understanding of the main ideas?

We shall discuss the use of a textbook in another chapter, but an understanding of how the author organizes his points is vital to comprehension.

All of the comprehension skills we have discussed here will profit from direct teaching. Factors which will enhance comprehension in any classroom are the type of questions which the teacher asks, the use of discussion as an aid to understanding what is read, the use of all types of audio-visual materials, and activities which give children practice in the refinement of the skills.

Rate of Comprehension

So much has been written about the speed of reading, both in popular and professional journals, that children and adults everywhere are very conscious of this factor in reading. Many ridiculous claims have been made for phenomenal rates of reading, and innumerable gadgets have been devised which are reported to increase both the rate of reading and comprehension. It is sufficient to state that sound research studies refute most of these claims, since there is virtually no transfer of the skill learned on a reading gadget to the actual reading of the printed page.

Rate of reading does not exist in and of itself; if this were so, we would have to select a new definition for reading. The rate at which an individual receives ideas from a page, selects the relevant and discards the irrelevant, reacts to the ideas expressed, and finally integrates the ideas into his own experiences depends upon several factors. The goal of instruction in reading is not rapid, superficial reading, but the thoughtful, purposeful reaction to ideas expressed by someone else. Obviously, if the child is reading at the rate of 150 words per minute in all materials and getting nothing from his reading, it might make sense to teach him to read at 400 words per minute in order that he might do nothing in less time. There is no evidence that increasing the rate of reading increases comprehension; on the other hand, there is sufficient evidence that increasing the skill and ease of comprehension will result in a greater flexibility of the rate.

Purpose in reading. A child asked his teacher, following an assignment to read Longfellow's *Evangeline,* "How long should it take me to read this?" And the teacher's reply was,

"Why do you want to read this poem? What do you expect to learn from reading it?"

Let us ponder for a moment the purposes the child might have for reading *Evangeline:*

1. He loves the language of poetry, and this selection appeals to him. It is filled with figurative expressions, to be digested thoughtfully and deliberately.
2. He is involved in a project concerning Nova Scotia and has learned that this poem gives a picture of early life in that land.
3. He is interested in characterization and wants to write a play which will use the characters and events of *Evangeline.*
4. He has studied other poems written by Longfellow and is seeking a general impression of this poem as compared to others he has read.
5. He has been directed to read it and wants to finish as quickly as possible.

These are not all of the purposes which an individual child might have for reading a poem. The teacher or his classmates might have provided motivation for reading the poem in an entirely different manner from any of those listed. It is apparent that for each specific purpose he will read the poem in a different manner. He may skim through it; he may read selectivity, skipping long descriptive passages and carefully perusing others; he may become so interested that he wants to taste, hear, feel every word and every line. Thus, the purpose which an individual child has for reading a selection will determine the rate at which he will read it; inherent in the purpose is what he expects to get from the selection—or the comprehension intended.

Content and rate. It makes little sense to direct children to read their arithmetic problems as rapidly as they would read a familiar narrative. Some materials, because of the compactness and sequence of their ideas, simply cannot be read rapidly if the individual expects to comprehend what he is reading. Most of the materials of science, mathematics, industrial arts, home economics, and social studies must be read thoughtfully and carefully. The simple narrative may be read rapidly and with little attention to details; if a detail is missed, it might not be important. However, a detail missed in mathematics may be critical to the solution of a problem; hence, the rate at which one reads the various materials in the classroom will depend upon the content itself.

Familiarity and rate. If the child is familiar with the author's organization of the textbook and has learned how to find main ideas and relevant details without reading every sentence, it is conceivable that he may learn to read new materials in the book at a very rapid rate. He will skim for the main ideas, select relevant details, read introductions and summaries carefully, and be satisfied that he has comprehended the selection. A second reading of a much loved story or poem may proceed at a much faster rate than the first reading. On the other hand, if material is unfamiliar, if the author uses unusual word order in his sentences, if there is an abundance of details and subordinate ideas, the child is required to pace his reading at a much slower rate.

Flexibility of rate. It is often wise to remind children that their main concern is not so much the number of words per minute or per page, but the number of *ideas* to be gained per minute or per page. The rate at which an individual reads will vary from sentence to sentence, from paragraph to paragraph, depending upon the importance of the ideas presented, the complexity of the ideas, and the order in which they are presented. The mature reader is one who can virtually "shift gears" as he assesses the reading task and knows the demands of the page; he will *not* read at a consistent rate on a single selection, nor from one selection to another. He adjusts his rate of reading according to his ability to receive and react to the ideas which are presented and always in relation to the purpose for which he is reading.

Skills and rate. Can children actually be taught to read faster? The answer is affirmative, but only in relation to the high degree of skill which the child has in word recognition, word meanings, and the various comprehension skills. It is evident that there is a positive relationship between the ease of reading and the grasping of concepts. If the child's reading is belabored by insecurity in word-attack and -recognition skills, if he lacks a clear purpose for reading, or if he has not developed skills in comprehending what he reads, then his rate of comprehension will obviously be slow. But, as he learns to attack words efficiently, to fuse words into the meaning units of phrases and sentences, to see the relationships between the various ideas presented, to integrate those ideas into his own experiences and develop new concepts, to read always with a clear purpose in mind, and to adjust his rate of reading to his purpose and the content of the selection, his rate of comprehension will increase.

Although good vision and accurate perception are vitally necessary to reading, visual gymnastics definitely are not the essence of the rate of comprehension.

Critical Reading

Critical reading is not a technique which can be neatly categorized or classed as a particular skill. It is all of the skills of word meanings and comprehension, but it goes beyond these in demanding that the reader *react* to the ideas which he has comprehended. When the reader becomes aware that the ideas which he is receiving are awakening emotional responses and arousing feelings of approval or disapproval, he is beginning to read critically. The child is reading critically when he begins to weigh and to judge the ideas which he encounters in books and newspapers; and to test their reasonableness, probability, and possibility.

Critical attitudes toward what is read are often shockingly lacking in people who otherwise give evidence of reading widely and well. There is a tendency among most people to accept as infallible and incontrovertible what they read in print; it is often surprising to find that these same people would doubt the authenticity of the same statements if they were offered orally. Surely in a world which each day becomes smaller and in which people are more interdependent, there is a great need for our schools to produce readers who regard the printed page with healthy skepticism.

The beginnings of critical reading are found in primary instruction, as children are asked to react to simple stories which are designed to arouse their pleasure, their dislikes, and even their prejudices. Small children often candidly express opinions concerning the authenticity of statements which they find in stories, and these reactions should be encouraged. The distinction between opinions and facts cannot wait until the upper grades; the first-grade child is accustomed to distinguishing between reality and fantasy; he accepts the unreasonable, the impossible, or the improbable *if* he knows that the author intended to create fantasy. The roots of critical reading are established at this stage.

There are many ways in which we can encourage critical reactions to reading, and we shall list a few suggestions which may be applied to any level of instruction.

1. Be alert for contradictions that appear in selections which the children read. Discuss them frankly and help the children to accept the reason for such contradictions.
2. Encourage children to read with these questions in mind:

a. Who is the author? Is he an established authority? What is his reputation? Does he often write on this topic?
b. Exactly what is he attempting to say? What does he infer that he does not state directly?
c. What is his purpose in writing the selection? Is he informing or attempting to arouse feelings and emotional responses? Is he merely being entertaining?
d. When did he write it? What difference would this make?
e. Where did he write it? For what type of an audience? Could it be possible that it was not intended to influence the present reader?
f. What language does he use? Does he use techniques of propaganda (name calling, glittering generalities, testimonials, plain folks, band wagon, identification with well known figures)?
g. Is his statement reasonable? Possible?
h. Just what is the balance between opinion and fact?

3. Encourage children to discuss their reactions to what they read. Help them understand that we react on the basis of biases, prejudices, attitudes, ideals, and value systems which are all related to our personal experiences.
4. Examine newspapers, magazines, and billboards to discover the techniques which are used by advertisers to appeal to people's needs.
5. Select editorials, from different newspapers, and attempt to reconcile the differences of opinions.

Summary

Reading without comprehension is mere word-calling, and the skills of word recognition and perception are but a part of the complex process of reading which leads to the comprehension of ideas. Intelligence, experience, mastery of mechanics, interests, span of attention, and the actual skills of comprehension are all factors which determine the depth and ease of comprehending the ideas on a page or in an entire selection. Like any other skill, comprehension skills must be taught, and adequate opportunities must be provided in the classroom to ensure children's getting constant practice in the development of those skills.

Selected References

DeBoer, John J., and Dallman, Martha. *The Teaching of Reading.* New York: Henry Holt and Co., 1960. Pp. 117–51.

McCullough, Constance. "Teaching Creative Reading," *Journal of Education*, CXXXVI (April, 1954), 200–203.

Russell, David H. *Children Learn to Read.* 2nd ed. Boston: Ginn and Co., 1961. Pp. 106–12.

Serra, Mary C. "How to Develop Concepts and Their Verbal Representations," *Elementary School Journal*, LIII (January, 1953), 275–85.

Tinker, Miles A., and McCullough, Constance M. *Teaching Elementary Reading.* New York: Appleton-Century-Crofts, Inc., 1962. Chapter 9.

14

Study Skills

THE TEACHER OF ELEMENTARY CHILDREN IS OFTEN faced, at the middle-grades level, with a host of children who do a good job of reading with accuracy and adequate comprehension so long as they are confronted with the basic reader; yet these same children may not have developed the study skills which are so vital to the reading of textbooks. And reading in the basic reader is not the same as reading a textbook in science, arithmetic, and the social studies!

There is a tendency in the primary grades to place emphasis upon word-attack skills and word-meaning skills to aid children in learning to read fluently; these fundamental skills are carefully outlined, in sequential form, in the teacher's handbook which accompanies basic readers. The child learns to attack words, get their meanings, and follow a plot of an interesting story. Suddenly, at the middle-grades level, he is confronted with arithmetic problems which require organization and retention of ideas, social studies assignments which demand that research-type work to be done in locating information, and lessons in science and language which require that he select and evaluate items of information with reference to a particular narrow topic. If his previous reading experience has been limited to reading stories, he is poorly prepared to meet the challenge of the reading study job.

There are five kinds of study skills in which every student, from the primary grades through college, must become proficient. These are not initiated at the middle-grades level nor at the high school level; but, like all skills of reading, they are introduced at the primary level. Growth in the study skills is sequential and continuous. The skills which students should develop are:

1. Selecting and evaluating information with reference to a particular problem or purpose
2. Organizing what is read according to the task at hand
3. Remembering what is read, after a decision has been made regarding those parts which should be retained
4. Following directions
5. Locating information

In providing opportunities for children to have experiences in the reading-study tasks, the teacher must keep in mind that there is neither a clear-cut starting point nor a definite stopping place. There is no level at which we can assume that complete mastery of a study skill has been attained, nor is there a level at which a particular skill is most needed. Planned, sequential teaching is necessary at all levels in the curriculum if students are to become independent in the use of all of the study skills.

Selecting and evaluating information. At first glance, the primary teacher is likely to state that this skill is too complex for her students and to feel that it is most applicable to those tasks which are undertaken by students in the upper grades. But selecting and evaluating at a simple level include such activities as collecting pictures for a bakery unit, locating parts of a story which illustrate a point, or determining which steps should be taken in a construction activity. The first-grade child may select words or phrases in a story to answer a question or complete a sentence; with the purpose in mind, he must skim for the appropriate word or phrase, judge its accuracy, and then check it against the question or sentence to see if it fulfills the purpose.

Some of the activities which may be provided to teach the skill of selecting and evaluating information are:

1. Selecting words, phrases, sentences, paragraphs, and stories to illustrate a point or give information
2. Selecting the part of the story which expresses joy, sadness, excitement
3. Finding the part of a story which describes a character
4. Finding answers to specific questions which have been raised by the teacher or through the discussion
5. Finding the main idea of a paragraph
6. Finding those details which support the main idea
7. Finding those details which are informative in nature but not necessary to the understanding of the main idea
8. Selecting and evaluating information which supports a generalization or a conclusion
9. Selecting and evaluating information which proves a point
10. Examining statements to determine whether they represent fact or opinion
11. Locating and evaluating statements which are used as propaganda devices to inform, convince, dissuade, or appeal to a need
12. Noting inconsistencies, anachronisms, or faulty reasoning

Organizing what is read. As the child learns to locate and evaluate information, he also becomes aware of the fact that certain ideas appear to belong together, while other ideas do not relate to the problem at hand. He may learn that there is a sequence of events which is important to understanding a problem, either in terms of step-by-step procedures or events that occur one after the other in terms of time. At the primary level, children learn to group together those pictures which pertain to a particular story or idea; they may develop a scrapbook, which is organized in terms of units or stories. They often are required to arrange in a sequence sentences which have been printed on tagboard for a chart story. Sometimes it is good practice to ask children to classify the names of birds, animals, toys, articles of clothing and furniture, and other items under the proper category. Eventually, they will learn to classify ideas; for example, a story has been developed following a trip to the dairy. The teacher will print a group of sentences which describe activities and observations which pertain to the dairy. She will insert several sentences which do not relate to the dairy. The children are then asked to select those sentences which actually relate to their experience in the dairy and to set aside those sentences which are not relevant. Other primary activities which develop this study skill of organization are the planning of a story for dramatization, organizing episodes from a story in a logical sequence for pantomime, and planning a program for their parents. In each case, it will be necessary for the teacher to act as the scribe to indicate to the children that both planning and recording of ideas in an organized pattern are important.

Activities which may be considered to develop organization skills in the middle and upper grades are:

1. Selecting bits of information from several sources in order to solve a problem or answer a question
2. Classifying, under appropriate headings, the steps required for a construction activity
3. Placing in chronological order several events from history
4. Listing events which pertain to a particular occurrence in history
5. Recalling and mentally assigning to a particular locale the products, industries, animal and plant life, and topographical features mentioned in the study of a particular geographical area

6. Visiting the library and locating in several sources the information which is needed to solve a problem or prove a point
7. Summarizing paragraphs in a single sentence and combining sentences to illustrate the organization of a chapter or selection
8. Gathering facts and figures and making charts, graphs, or maps which illustrate the ideas learned in a unit

Remembering what is read. When the primary teacher asks the children in her class to draw a picture which will illustrate a story which she has just finished telling, she is laying the foundation for skills of remembering, since the child will attempt to recall as many details as possible in order to draw an accurate picture. Many activities call for oral recall of events which children have experienced in a trip or classroom activity; to aid the children in "fixing" those events in their memory the teacher often records them as they are given to her by the group. At a later date, she may ask the children to recall the events again; this time she has the chart against which they may check their memory. Through such simple activities children learn that recalling information is important.

Certainly the skill of remembering is an important one, particularly as the child progresses through the various grades and is required to select and evaluate, organize *and* remember masses of information which are necessary for tackling a new problem. Both arithmetic and the social studies curricula are arranged sequentially, and the child is required to remember facts, figures, places, names, events, and processes which will aid him in understanding the next process or event. A consideration of learning theories points to the fact that ideas are most easily recalled if they are associated in some way with a known key idea or fact; consequently, the teacher should continuously aid her students in recognizing associations which are helpful in learning new material. These activities may aid children in remembering information:

1. Reading with intention of remembering ideas relevant to a specific problem
2. Recalling the speeches of characters in a story and dramatizing the story
3. Recalling the sequence of events in a story and recording them in a chart story
4. Filling in blanks in a sentence to complete the meaning
5. Establishing cause and effecting relationships whenever possible
6. Reading for main ideas and attempting to write them down in simple terms
7. Recalling relevant details to support a main idea
8. Taking notes; examining these notes and striking out those points which are not necessary. Underlining the most important points
9. Reviewing the underlined items
10. Each time a date is encountered in history, attempting to establish a mental time-line which includes other events that occurred on the same date
11. Preparing a brief outline of a chapter; reviewing the chapter by filling in the details under each part of the outline

No one can actually tell a student *how* he should remember the many bits of information which he will need in subsequent learning situations; a study of memory skills reveals that each person develops his own peculiar techniques. However, each child will gain skill from activities which are designed not only to give practice in the skill but also to impress him with the importance of remembering information.

Following directions. It has often been said that more time is wasted in the typical classroom in giving directions than in any other activity. Sometimes the teacher's directions are neither clear nor complete. As a final result, many adults cannot and do not follow directions accurately and consequently they are often lost, confused, and uninformed.

From the first day in school, the child is required to follow directions; activities which are directed for a group demand that some directions be given which all will follow or which individual members may be required to follow. The child who has not learned to listen, or who apparently is tuned in on another frequency, is either a laggard in the group activity or he is engaged in doing things which have no relevancy to the activity. From the very beginning activity in the kindergarten, the teacher should impress upon the children the importance of listening carefully as directions are given for simple activities; those children who do not listen are often denied the privilege of participating, or they may be embarrassed by having done the wrong thing. For older pupils, care should be taken to record directions on the blackboard or on a chart—directions to which the child with short attention span may refer when he becomes confused. The teacher may wish to create activities in which children take the responsibility for giving directions to the rest of the group or the class; practice in *giving* directions is as important as *receiving* them.

At the level of the upper grades, the student is more and more dependent upon memory of directions to indicate the assignment, the source of information, or the course of an activity. Again, if the teacher is content with giving directions several times for each activity, she may learn that children depend upon second and third presentations and disregard directions the first time they are given. Eventually, they may learn to disregard directions altogether. Remembering directions should be as important to the child as retaining information. Frequent checks should be made to ascertain that the child has received directions accurately, just as frequent tests are given to determine what facts and figures have been remembered. These suggestions may help the teacher who wishes to develop in her students the skill of remembering directions:

1. Give directions simply and clearly, in proper sequence.
2. Occasionally ask a child to repeat the directions, while the other children listen to check the accuracy.
3. Write directions on the blackboard and suggest that children write them in their notebooks.
4. In the middle and upper grades, insist that students keep an assignment sheet on which they record their daily assignments and any particular directions for that assignment.
5. Give students practice in taking directions by listening carefully and recording what they have heard. For example: "I heard the fire whistle and rushed out the front door of the house. Turning left, I ran two blocks straight ahead and then turned one block to the right. There I found the fire engines, and saw that a big, dilapidated house was slowly crumpling under the raging fire. Now draw a diagram of how I reached the fire."
6. Outline carefully the steps to be taken in a simple experiment or construction activity. Test the students in their ability to follow those directions without further prompting.
7. In language activities and science experiments, occasionally read the directions aloud, or ask a student to read them aloud, as others read silently or listen. Close the book and discuss what has been read, giving particular attention to exact details and sequence.

Locating information. At the beginning of his school experiences, the child is required to locate information in sources other than his textbook. For instance, in the kindergarten a story may be developed around kittens. Each child is asked to look through magazines and books to find as many pictures as he can of kittens. As the pictures are brought back to the group, much information is shared, and a research project has been completed. The fifth-grade boy, while reading his geography book, finds a statement which reads: "Turn to page 140 and locate on the map all of the food products which are raised in this valley." In his English class, the eighth-grader is told: "Find interesting details in the life of the author which seem to have influenced his writing." Each of these activities calls for skills of locating information, and, as we have indicated, skill-building activities are initiated at the very beginning of the school experiences.

In the primary grades, children are asked to consult the table of contents for determining page numbers in their books, to gather further information by consulting the titles of books, to collect and organize series of pictures, and to find exercises in a workbook which correlate with the story in a basic text. They will have practice in locating phrases, sentences, and paragraphs which give pertinent information; in referring to the table of contents; in occasionally referring to a glossary or a beginner's dictionary for the meaning of a word; and in locating stories which may be related to a class activity.

There is certainly no means of determining *when* a child should be given instruction in the use of the dictionary; the experienced teacher knows that occasionally a child in the second grade becomes quite proficient in referring to the dictionary for the meaning and pronunciation of words. However, formal instruction in the glossary and dictionary should be given to all children by the time they have reached the fourth grade. Planned instruction in the use of the dictionary is far more effective than teaching the skills incidentally. At every level of the reading program, the child will have need for the information which is contained in the dictionary, and, if he has learned to demand meaning from what he reads, he may come to regard the dictionary as an indispensable aid to learning.

In the primary grades, children are often introduced to the dictionary through the picture dictionary which each child develops; pictures are pasted in a scrapbook to illustrate the meanings of new words. Soon some children will wish to consult a junior dictionary to find meanings for words which are in their speaking-listening vocabulary but for which they have hazy meanings; they will hesitate to use these words unless they can find exact meanings. Other uses of the dictionary are soon learned: (1) as a guide to the meaning of words which are unfamiliar and cannot be unlocked by use of the context; (2) as a guide to pronunciation of unfamiliar words; (3) and as a source of correct spelling of words which are difficult.

Certain minimum skills are required for efficient use of the dictionary, and for each one the teacher must plan careful and stimulating instruction. These skills are of three types: (1) locating words, (2) pronouncing words, and (3) determining the appropriate meanings of words.

Location skills require the child to know the sequence of the alphabet. Thousands of words have been written about the advantages and disadvantages of teaching the alphabet to children in the primary grades, but there is no evidence available that points to the fact that a child has been hurt by the knowledge of the alphabet. It is true that not much is gained by teaching the alphabet as a rote exercise in the first grade, as was once the practice in primary education; but surely there is much to be gained in dictionary and other location skills by the child who knows his alphabet and is confident of the relative positions of the individual letters. Such knowledge is easily mastered as the child develops his own picture dictionary or makes his personal spelling list in alphabetically arranged sheets. Knowing that the *m* entries are found in approximately the middle of the dictionary and that the *b* and *x* entries are near the beginning and end of the dictionary is necessary for efficient location of words needed.

Another location skill is knowing how to use the guide words at the top of columns and pages. Much time can be wasted in thumbing through pages without using guide words efficiently, so it is necessary that children be given practice in locating words through the use of guide words. Certain skills of alphabetizing must precede efficient use of guide words, however. These may be developed by asking the children to alphabetize words which begin with different consonants or vowels:

apple
ball
mother
toy

The next step in alphabetizing is developed through words which begin with the same letter but must be arranged according to the remainder of the word:

baby
boat
boot
bread

A knowledge of structural analysis is necessary in locating inflected forms of words. If the child is seeking a meaning for the word "casting," he should know that the root form is "cast" and seek the root form; difficulties arise when the child does not recognize the root form of such a word as "biting." He must recall that the final *e* has been dropped from the root form of "bite" and seek that root.

Pronunciation skills require a knowledge of variant vowel and consonant sounds, as indicated by diacritical markings, key words, accents, and phonetic spellings. If the child knows the long, short, and unstressed vowel sounds and the variant sounds of the *c*, *s*, and *g*, he is well on his way to understanding the pronunciations of most words. The teacher will be wise to consult the teaching instructions which are included at the beginning of any reputable dictionary; these should provide a key to the symbols used. For example, a common practice in many dictionaries which have been published recently is the use of the *schwa*, a phonetic symbol which represents many indeterminate vowel sounds which are very common in pronunciations of common words. This symbol may be substituted for any of the vowels, as, for example:

camera — kăm′ ərə
colon — kō′ lən
teacher — tē′ chər
habitat — hăb′ ə tăt

Many excellent guides to the teaching of the dictionary are available; some of these are listed in the Appendix.

Determining the meaning of a word from a dictionary entry can be very confusing to the child if he has not learned to differentiate among the various meanings listed and to select the most appropriate meaning for the context in which the word appeared. In the middle and upper grades, he will learn that many words which are spelled alike are used as different parts of speech and consequently may have different meanings, as in—

Close the door. (verb, meaning "to shut")
He stood *close* to the door. (adverb, meaning "near")

Direct teaching will be necessary to be certain that the child learns to select the meaning which is most appropriate and useful.

The student in the upper grades can be expected to understand and apply all of the symbols used in the dictionary, to be able to locate quickly and accurately any word, to select appropriate meaning with reference to the original context in which the word appeared, and to use the dictionary whenever he needs to verify spelling and syllabication of words which are needed for his written work.

In addition to the dictionary, there are many other valuable sources in which the student is expected to seek information, including encyclopedias, the card catalog of the library, the *Reader's Guide to Periodical Literature,* the World Almanac, and other standard reference works.

Practice in the use of encyclopedias is most effective when information is sought to solve a problem or answer a question. Children in the middle grades may learn to use encyclopedias effectively. They must know how to use the guide letters or words on each volume and the index (if available) in order to locate information. They should also learn the value of cross references which are listed for most entries; certainly they should be aware of the accuracy of most encyclopedia entries, since individual entries have been verified by our leading scholars. If encyclopedias are available to the children, there is seldom a motivation problem in getting children to use them, if such use is directed and purposeful.

Acquaintance with the library should be encouraged among primary children. A trip to the library and a guided tour by an efficient librarian often are the beginnings of pleasant, lifelong associations between a child and this treasure-trove of knowledge and satisfactions. Children

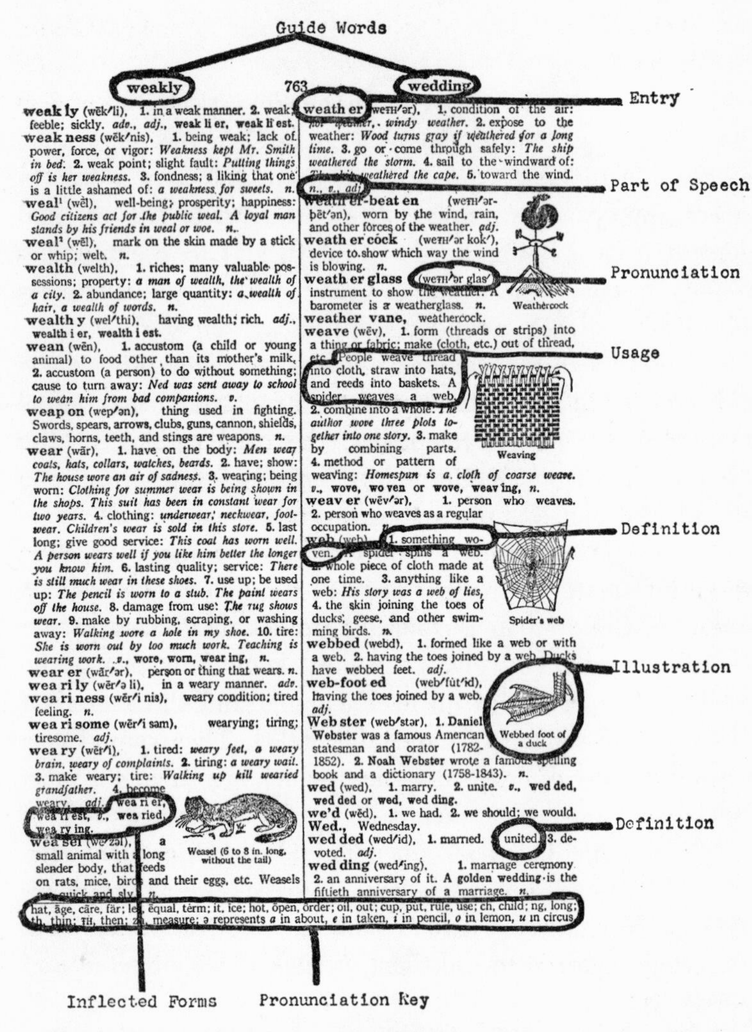

weakly 763 wedding

weak ly (wēk′li), 1. in a weak manner. 2. weak; feeble; sickly. *adv., adj.,* **weak li er, weak li est.**

weak ness (wēk′nis), 1. being weak; lack of power, force, or vigor: *Weakness kept Mr. Smith in bed.* 2. weak point; slight fault: *Putting things off is her weakness.* 3. fondness; a liking that one is a little ashamed of: *a weakness for sweets. n.*

weal¹ (wēl), well-being; prosperity; happiness: *Good citizens act for the public weal. A loyal man stands by his friends in weal or woe. n.*

weal² (wēl), mark on the skin made by a stick or whip; welt. *n.*

wealth (welth), 1. riches; many valuable possessions; property: *a man of wealth, the wealth of a city.* 2. abundance; large quantity: *a wealth of hair, a wealth of words. n.*

wealth y (wel′thi), having wealth; rich. *adj.,* **wealth i er, wealth i est.**

wean (wēn), 1. accustom (a child or young animal) to food other than its mother's milk. 2. accustom (a person) to do without something; cause to turn away: *Ned was sent away to school to wean him from bad companions. v.*

weap on (wep′ən), thing used in fighting. Swords, spears, arrows, clubs, guns, cannon, shields, claws, horns, teeth, and stings are weapons. *n.*

wear (wãr), 1. have on the body: *Men wear coats, hats, collars, watches, beards.* 2. have; show: *The house wore an air of sadness.* 3. wearing; being worn: *Clothing for summer wear is being shown in the shops. This suit has been in constant wear for two years.* 4. clothing: *underwear, neckwear, footwear. Children's wear is sold in this store.* 5. last long; give good service: *This coat has worn well. A person wears well if you like him better the longer you know him.* 6. lasting quality; service: *There is still much wear in these shoes.* 7. use up; be used up: *The pencil is worn to a stub. The paint wears off the house.* 8. damage from use: *The rug shows wear.* 9. make by rubbing, scraping, or washing away: *Walking wore a hole in my shoe.* 10. tire: *She is worn out by too much work. Teaching is wearing work. v.,* **wore, worn, wear ing,** *n.*

wear er (wãr′ər), person or thing that wears. *n.*

wea ri ly (wēr′ə li), in a weary manner. *adv.*

wea ri ness (wēr′i nis), weary condition; tired feeling. *n.*

wea ri some (wēr′i səm), wearying; tiring; tiresome. *adj.*

wea ry (wēr′i), 1. tired: *weary feet, a weary brain, weary of complaints.* 2. tiring: *a weary wail.* 3. make weary; tire: *Walking up hill wearied grandfather.* 4. become weary. *adj.,* **wea ri er, wea ri est,** *v.,* **wea ried, wea ry ing.**

wea sel (wē′zəl), a small animal with a long slender body, that feeds on rats, mice, birds and their eggs, etc. Weasels are quick and sly. *n.*

Weasel (6 to 8 in. long, without the tail)

weath er (weᴛʜ′ər), 1. condition of the air: *hot weather, windy weather.* 2. expose to the weather: *Wood turns gray if weathered for a long time.* 3. go or come through safely: *The ship weathered the storm.* 4. sail to the windward of: *The ship weathered the cape.* 5. toward the wind. *n., v., adj.*

weath er-beat en (weᴛʜ′ər bēt′ən), worn by the wind, rain, and other forces of the weather. *adj.*

weath er cock (weᴛʜ′ər kok′), device to show which way the wind is blowing. *n.*

weath er glass (weᴛʜ′ər glas′), instrument to show the weather. A barometer is a weatherglass. *n.*

Weathercock

weather vane, weathercock.

weave (wēv), 1. form (threads or strips) into a thing or fabric; make (cloth, etc.) out of thread, etc.: People weave thread into cloth, straw into hats, and reeds into baskets. A spider weaves a web. 2. combine into a whole: *The author wove three plots together into one story.* 3. make by combining parts. 4. method or pattern of weaving: *Homespun is a cloth of coarse weave. v.,* **wove, wo ven** or **wove, weav ing,** *n.*

Weaving

weav er (wēv′ər), 1. person who weaves. 2. person who weaves as a regular occupation. *n.*

web (web), 1. something woven. A spider spins a web. 2. whole piece of cloth made at one time. 3. anything like a web: *His story was a web of lies.* 4. the skin joining the toes of ducks, geese, and other swimming birds. *n.*

Spider's web

webbed (webd), 1. formed like a web or with a web. 2. having the toes joined by a web. Ducks have webbed feet. *adj.*

web-foot ed (web′fu̇t′id), having the toes joined by a web. *adj.*

Web ster (web′stər), 1. Daniel Webster was a famous American statesman and orator (1782-1852). 2. Noah Webster wrote a famous spelling book and a dictionary (1758-1843). *n.*

Webbed foot of a duck

wed (wed), 1. marry. 2. unite. *v.,* **wed ded, wed ded** or **wed, wed ding.**

we'd (wēd), 1. we had. 2. we should; we would.

Wed., Wednesday.

wed ded (wed′id), 1. married. 2. united. 3. devoted. *adj.*

wed ding (wed′ing), 1. marriage ceremony. 2. an anniversary of it. A golden wedding is the fiftieth anniversary of a marriage. *n.*

hat, āge, cãre, fär; let, ēqual, tėrm; it, īce; hot, ōpen, ôrder; oil, out; cup, put, rüle, ūse; ch, child; ng, long; th, thin; ᴛʜ, then; zh, measure; ə represents *a* in about, *e* in taken, *i* in pencil, *o* in lemon, *u* in circus.

A TYPICAL PAGE FROM A DICTIONARY. (From E. L. Thorndike and Clarence L. Barnhart, *Thorndike-Barnhart Advanced Junior Dictionary*. Copyright, 1952, by Scott, Foresman and Company, Chicago).

should receive instructions in the use of the card catalog, the locations of the various types of books in the library (atlases, encyclopedias, general reference works, periodicals), and the procedures for checking a book out of the library. If there is a children's librarian, she is often available to visit rooms and share interesting books with children; she may invite a class to the library for a story hour or a directed browsing hour among children's books. She usually has a supply of intriguing book jackets which she may loan to the teacher for display on the bulletin board.

Instruction in the use of the card catalog may include references to three types of entries: author card, subject card, and title card. In the upper grades, a knowledge of the Dewey Decimal System and all of the entries on the catalog card is essential.

The *Reader's Guide to Periodical Literature* and other important sources should be taught as the child has need to seek information from a wide variety of sources. A library unit in the English program is a desirable means of introducing most of the information needed by the student, but the teacher must not overlook the value of incidental teaching as the need for the use of the library arises in each day's activities.

Studying a textbook. Getting acquainted with a textbook, or any book, can be fascinating and rewarding. Books become personalities to children, particularly if they realize that someone—another person—is speaking to them through the print in the book. Then reading becomes a two-way conversation between the reader and the author. Children who develop skills of critical reading are accustomed to "talking back" to an author, challenging ideas or becoming an ally to the ideas presented. Obviously, stimulating and interest-provoking writing is the first prerequisite to such a relationship between the reader and the book, but acquaintance with the book—its purposes, organization, and content—is also helpful in involving students in the pleasures of reading and study.

Too often teachers in the middle and upper grades are so anxious to get to the contents of a textbook that they forget that the child has really not been introduced properly to the book. An orientation period, or perhaps two or three periods, may help the child to feel that the book is a treasured possession—one from which he can anticipate many hours and weeks and months of pleasurable association. We would not consider taking a long-awaited trip without first consulting a map and perhaps gathering information about the points of interest which we hope to experience. Thus it is with introducing a new book to a group of older children; they need to know where they're going, what signposts to observe along the line, and what pleasures they might anticipate as the book unfolds. What, then, are the parts of a book which we should teach?

Obviously, we would first consider the *cover*. With children of any age, it is important to consider the binding, the colors, the print, and the title itself. Perhaps this would be a good point to demonstrate to the group just how a book is put together; a trip to a bindery or a print shop is invariably rewarding!

The next important part of the book is the *title page*. Here are found several entries which should be discussed:

1. Title: What does it promise or state?
2. Author's name or editor's name: At the upper-grades level, consider this person's reputation. What other books has he written? What do we know about him? Is he an authority?
3. Illustrator: In the primary grades, children are very aware of illustrations. Do they recognize illustrations which are done

How Do I Find A Book In The Catalog?*

For every book in the library there is usually an author card, a title card, and one or more subject cards.

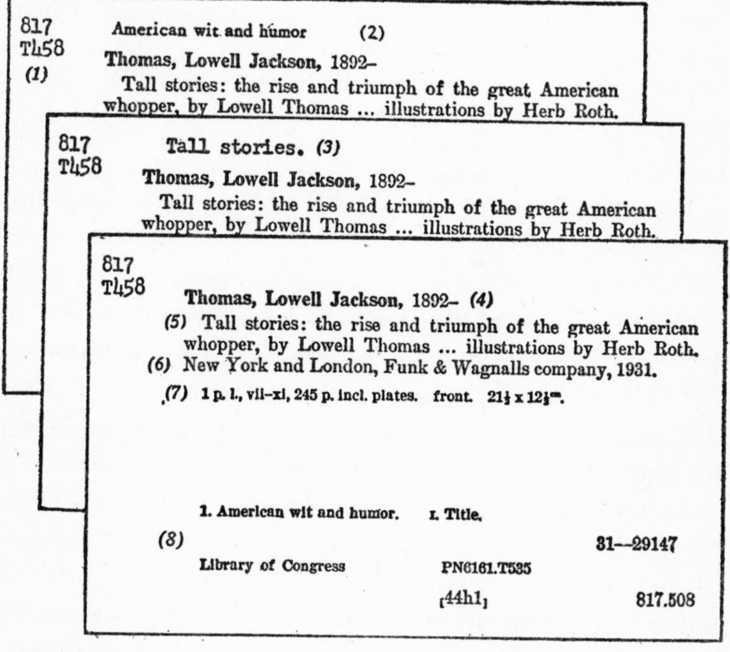
817 American wit and humor (2)
T458 Thomas, Lowell Jackson, 1892–
(1) Tall stories: the rise and triumph of the great American whopper, by Lowell Thomas ... illustrations by Herb Roth.

817 Tall stories. (3)
T458 Thomas, Lowell Jackson, 1892–
Tall stories: the rise and triumph of the great American whopper, by Lowell Thomas ... illustrations by Herb Roth.

817
T458 Thomas, Lowell Jackson, 1892– (4)
(5) Tall stories: the rise and triumph of the great American whopper, by Lowell Thomas ... illustrations by Herb Roth.
(6) New York and London, Funk & Wagnalls company, 1931.
(7) 1 p. l., vii–xi, 245 p. incl. plates. front. 21½ x 12½ᶜᵐ.

1. American wit and humor. I. Title.
(8) 31—29147
Library of Congress PN6161.T535
[44h1] 817.508

* Reprinted by permission of Sacramento State College Libraries.

(1) Call number
(2) Subject entry
(3) Title entry
(4) Author's name and birth date
(5) Title
(6) Place, publisher, and date
(7) Pages, illustrations, size
(8) Technical notes

by a person who perhaps illustrated another book which they cherish?

4. Publisher and place of publication: Was it written in this country? What difference would this make if the textbook had been written in England or Japan?
5. Date of publication: How recent is this material? Is recency important in this particular subject?
6. Copyright: On the back of the title page, usually, is a statement of the date of copyright. This term means the right to print, copy, and sell any literary or artistic material; it protects the author and indicates the date on which the material was produced. Two copies of the copyrighted book have been placed on file in the United States Copyright Office. The copyright is issued for a period of twenty-eight years, with a privilege of renewal for another twenty-eight-year period.

The third part of the book to be examined is that of the *preface*, or *introduction*, or *foreword*. Here is stated, in the words of the author or someone selected to write for the author, the purposes of the book and perhaps suggestions for using the book.

Now we turn to the *table of contents,* which lists the chapter titles or stories which appear in the book. It is particularly important that the children be given an opportunity to discuss the contents of the book, as indicated by the table of contents. In many ways it sets the path which the reader will follow; it defines limits of the subject. It may indicate, in the case of a reference book, that an inappropriate choice has been made and the reader must seek further for information. Anticipating the contents of a book is like looking forward to a clearly defined journey, where the signposts are all visible and indicate the route over the next hill.

The *list of illustrations or tables and maps* is found next in a book, particularly in social studies and science texts.

Now comes the contents of the book itself, with its chapter divisions. In introducing a book, the teacher should allow time for the children to examine the contents carefully. It is fun to anticipate what a chapter might present.

Three major parts of a book are found at the back: the *bibliography,* which lists books and materials for further study or those books and materials which were consulted in writing the book; the *appendix,* which usually gives additional information relating to many ideas presented in the body of the book; and the *index,* which is an expansion of the table of contents, with an alphabetical listing of all of the topics found in the book and the exact pages on which those topics may be found. Some indexes list authors, subject, and first lines (particularly those which refer to poetry).

Each new book should be introduced with care. Children need practice in the use of the table of contents, the appendix (or glossary), and the index. Locating information can be rewarding if the child has the tools for handling a text or reference book efficiently.

Summary

To read accurately and with adequate comprehension in all subjects, the elementary school child must develop study skills which will aid him in selecting and evaluating information, organizing what is read, remembering what is read, following directions, locating information, and using a textbook. Instruction in the study skills should be an integral part of any subject area, since all study skills are reading skills. Development of these skills is sequential and continuous, beginning at the time of the child's first school experiences and reaching no known limit of proficiency.

Selected References

GRAY, WILLIAM S. *On Their Own in Reading.* Chicago: Scott, Foresman and Co., 1960.

HEILMAN, ARTHUR W. *Principles and Practices of Teaching Reading.* Columbus, Ohio: Charles E. Merrill Books, Inc., 1961. Pp. 286–94.

RUSSELL, DAVID H. *Children Learn to Read.* 2nd ed. Boston: Ginn and Co., 1961. Chapter 11.

WALRAVEN, MARGARET K., and HALL-QUEST, ALFRED L. *Teaching through the Elementary School Library.* New York: H. W. Wilson Co., 1948.

15

Reading in the Content Fields

IF ONE WERE TO ASSESS THE MANY TYPES OF reading which are demanded by the adult reader in any period of a week, or even of a single day, he would be impressed by the fact that what we so often regard as "reading" in the lower grades of the elementary school is but a preliminary step toward the complex skills demanded of the upper-grade student, the high school student, and the adult. The reading program prior to the fourth grade is centered mainly in the basic reader and the beginnings of wide reading in supplementary books. It is often true that a student may read very well in the narrative "story-book" type of material and suddenly give evidence of reading disability when he encounters arithmetic, science, and social studies. A sound program at the lower-grade levels will provide experiences in which the child encounters many types of reading material—experiences which constitute a readiness program for the compact, concept-loaded reading that lies ahead in the upper grades.

There are several reasons why reading in the content fields—science, social studies, English, mathematics, homemaking, industrial arts—is more difficult than reading narrative materials which so often are stressed in beginning reading experiences:

1. Ideas are more complex, and there is no control over the number of ideas introduced in a particular selection.
2. Vocabulary is introduced more rapidly; often technical terms are encountered in a particular context and not experienced again by the child for several pages, if at all.
3. A greater demand is made on the reader to relate his previous knowledge to the reading task at hand; science, arithmetic, and the social studies develop on an ascending scale of concepts.
4. Wide reading is often demanded in a variety of sources, and the student encounters large amounts of supplementary materials in each of the content fields.
5. Very often the student is faced with a mass of unrelated facts which he is supposed to retain and organize, sift for relevance or significance, and relate to a particular purpose in one of the content areas.
6. Vital interrelationships must be established by the reader if understanding is to be gained; geography and history are inextricably related, as are mathematics and science.
7. The student is required to read critically—to judge the pertinence, authenticity, and value of much that he reads.
8. The student must learn that mastery of maps, tables, and graphs is an integral part of reading a particular textbook or reference.

Fortunately, today's curriculum is organized in such a way that many essential relationships are established for the student. History, geography, sociology, civics, and family and community problems are woven into one mass of the social studies. But the teacher must never assume that essential relationships are inherent in the material which the student reads. Out of her own experience and wide knowledge of the various areas of the social studies, she must be prepared at all times to interpret, to establish relationships for young people, and to aid in the organization of many of the ideas encountered. She must never be satisfied with the teaching of content; she must constantly point to the *how* of mastering the content. Each of the areas of the social studies is written in a different way; geography is *not* written in the same manner that history is written; the studies of city and state and national governments are in a different language. Experience has taught us that these subjects are best presented in their own language, and the term "social studies" does not describe all of the tasks which are required of the student who must read in each of the areas which are included in that term.

The content of each of the areas of the curriculum is vitally important, but it is also vitally important that we teach each area in such a way that habits of clear thinking, as well as desirable attitudes and interests, are developed in our students; that students give evidence of having grasped concepts and made them a part of their experience; and that boys and girls develop into students who are capable of judging the relative importance of ideas which are presented in each of the content areas.

There certainly is no less need for reading in any content area than there was in our curriculum of many years ago, yet many of our teachers are poorly prepared to teach reading skills which are peculiar to a given content area. Many times we encounter young teachers who are master teachers in such areas as literature, poetry, and the developmental reading program, but who may never have mastered the techniques for teaching the child to read in science and mathematics. The daily assignment in a textbook, which has formed the traditional basis of most content areas, is today supplemented by a host of other aids to learning; the teacher of reading in these areas must choose appropriate aids to learning and combine them with techniques which are perhaps peculiar to a given content.

Social Studies

No other area of the curriculum of the elementary school receives so much time and attention as the social studies. It has been estimated that one third of all the time spent in reading in the middle and upper grades is devoted to the social studies; it is through reading that students experience vicariously the wonderfully rich development of mankind, since direct experiences are obviously limited. Each good teacher of the social studies recognizes the need for instruction in both the extensive and intensive reading of materials which relate to daily assignments or units. The content of the typical social studies book is condensed, and, to grasp the significance of many of the ideas presented, the student must depend upon previous knowledge or experience with associated ideas. For example, examine this paragraph from a sixth-grade social studies text:

> An accident brought the Portuguese sea captain, Pedro Cabral, to Brazil in 1500. He was trying to reach India by following the known route around the southern tip of Africa. But strong winds drove his fleet westward to the coast of Brazil. He claimed the land for the King of Portugal. According to the Pope's Line of Demarcation, this land did belong to Portugal.[1]

The assumption is made that the student has previous knowledge of these place names: Portugal, Brazil, Africa, and India. He must recall that the trade route around the tip of Africa was established earlier than 1500; he is required to relate the date 1500 to a mental time-line of events which

[1] William L. Gray, *et al., Exploring American Neighbors,* California State Series, California State Department of Education, 1956, p. 222.

led European sea captains to seek India and to establish reasons for these voyages; he obviously must recall the meaning and importance of the Line of Demarcation. All of this in one short paragraph! Yet this is the language of the social studies.

Teaching in the social studies certainly demands more than relating facts and figures; the basic skills of reading for good comprehension of history, geography, and other areas of the social studies should be an integral part of the teaching. Just what are these skills, and what can the teacher do to assure her students' development of skills?

Vocabulary. The vocabulary of the social studies is complex; hence, we must seize every opportunity to teach directly these words which are new, rare because of rather restricted usage, or abstract.

(*a*) *Technical terms.* Any given content area has its own body of terms which are the language of that area. Understanding technical terms depends upon the student's ability to recognize and pronounce words, and his ability to use the dictionary. Many of the terms of the social studies appear nowhere else in the student's reading. For example, the words *headwaters, plateau, latitude, manioc, latex,* and *fazenda* appear in a discussion of Brazil. Students must be guided in pronouncing the words, fitting them into a proper context and attempting to understand their meanings. If the meaning is not clear in the context, perhaps the glossary of the text (how few reference works provide glossaries!) may be used; if this fails to clarify the meaning, the dictionary must be consulted. A good unit in dictionary study may be developed around a social studies unit rather than in the basic reading program, where the need is seldom so great as in social studies, arithmetic, and science.

(*b*) *Abstract words. Freedom, peace, democracy, friendship*—these are words whose meanings develop gradually as the student matures and sees their application to everyday experiences or as he reads of examples in history. Since each such word in and of itself is virtually meaningless, it must be applied to experience or previous knowledge if it is to become meaningful to the student. Many of our abstract words develop meaning on a continuum and *exact* definitions are difficult, unless the word can be related to situations and experiences. Requiring students to write definitions of such words is seldom desirable; asking them to relate *examples* of the words is most helpful.

(*c*) *Multisyllabic words.* Since there is little control over the introduction of vocabulary in the social studies, students often encounter words which present a formidable appearance. Perhaps the student has not learned to look for familiar elements, or he may not have developed skills of pronunciation. The pronunciation of root elements or derived forms may be enhanced if the student learns to scrutinize word forms carefully: *immigrant* and *emigrant* are easy if the meanings of *im* and *e* are known. Many of the students in a classroom will not realize that *migrate* and *migrant* are root forms in *immigrate* and *emigrate* unless the teacher takes care to point out these relationships.

(*d*) *Concepts.* The development of concepts in the social studies is so very important that entire chapters have been devoted to this aspect of teaching and learning. The concept is composed of more than words or groups of words; it is a mental image or an abstraction which results as the individual generalizes from particulars. The richness of a concept depends not only upon a student's experience, but also upon his maturity and his intelligence. As his experiences, both direct and vicarious, broaden, the child develops concepts which he uses in reacting to, and judging the value of, ideas in drawing conclusions and generalizations and in determining what action to take. For instance, respect for the rights of the individual is a concept which develops from early childhood as he is taught and experiences the limits of his own demands upon other people and the demands of others upon him. As he matures, his concept of these rights may broaden and become much more complex, particularly with reference to religion, race, and political affiliation. On the other hand, broad experience may serve to simplify the concept. The teacher can never assume that stating concepts in simple language is sufficient for children, even though the concepts may be immediately understandable to the adult. Broad reading, simple explanations, and wide experiences are necessary for the development of concepts which are so numerous in the social studies.

Reading important ideas and separating main ideas from details. The student of the social studies is often dependent upon a dozen source readings for information pertinent to a particular unit. From these he must select those bits of information which are necessary to understanding of the unit or parts of the unit. He must learn to discard nonpertinent details and to retain others which are necessary for understanding main ideas. There is a real danger that much of our teaching in the social studies might develop "place-and-date-locators" or "bit-pickers" among our students who fail to see essential relationships because the assignment or the teacher's questions were directed toward nonessential details.

Small fruits and berries grow especially well in this region. Most of the berries ripen late and therefore bring high prices in the nearby New England markets.[2]

[2] *Ibid.*, p. 298.

In this paragraph it would be important that the statement regarding the late ripening of the berries be explored further, since a relationship to high prices has been established. Here the student would want to explore the reasons for late ripening of berries: climate, length of season, special conditions pertaining to berry culture. Also, he should establish *why* late-ripening berries bring high prices in New England markets. To the good student these facts may be obvious; to the average or poor student who has not been taught to inquire into the *why* of things, the facts may be meaningless.

Reading in the social studies requires a constant vigilance on the part of the reader with regard to *important* facts and details. So many details are introduced in a single chapter of geography that young students must learn to differentiate between those which are important to remember and those which are necessary only to understand the main ideas. Place names, products, distances, conditions of climate, topography, industries, and the lives of the people are inextricably woven into any discussion of a nation, a country, or a continent. The student cannot and will not remember all of the details nor all of the main ideas, but he may retain essential relationships which give understandings of how men live and work together throughout the world.

Locating and evaluating materials. One of the critical skills demanded of the student of the social studies is the selection of materials which will aid him in developing understanding of a particular unit. No textbook is sufficient for the types of understandings which we wish our youth to develop. Possible solutions, insight into problems, or added information must be sought in reference materials.

(*a*) *Gathering, organizing, and interpreting data* from the mass media of communication (charts, magazines, newspapers, movies, television programs, books, and lectures) require directed activities which include careful reading, listening, and writing.

(*b*) *Defining and analyzing the problem* often requires that some research be done. Finding out whether a problem actually exists in the unit, determining the limits of research required to satisfy the purposes for which the unit is being pursued, and determining the relevancy of other areas of the curriculum to this particular problem, are steps which must be taken in the development of good study skills. Students cannot follow these steps alone; the teacher is responsible for helping her students to define a problem clearly and locating information which might suggest possible solutions or further knowledge. (It is not inconceivable that the teacher of the social studies class may have to teach children the use of the library facilities. In what more favorable setting could the library be better introduced?)

Reading maps, tables, and graphs to relate history and current issues and developments to locations, sizes of cities, industries, ways of living, climate, races, religions, and other pertinent facts. Essential to the student of the social studies is the *reason* for maps, charts, graphs, and the like, in the textbook or reference book; many students never see the relationships which are intended by the author between the written text and illustration. They have never learned to "read" maps and graphs and other types of graphic materials in the same way that they read ordinary text. It is not uncommon to meet a high school or college student who habitually ignores the graphic materials in his textbook or reference materials; this student has not developed an essential study skill.

Maps are of several types: thermal, typographical, cultural, global, and magnetic. Each may use a different scale and different symbols (colors, letters, numbers, figures). The reading of maps requires not only a knowledge of scale and symbol, but also an understanding of terms such as longitude, latitude, temperature, current, altitude, region, equator, hemisphere, and others; hence, it appears to be a sensible approach to teach these terms as students encounter maps and written text which are essential to the development of concepts. Charts and graphs are often taught as a part of the arithmetic curriculum, but no graphic presentation is meaningful unless it is related to a particular problem. The teacher should begin her instruction in graphic materials with the use of simple data and progress to more complex data; she should constantly refer to graphic materials as sources of information and time should be allowed in any period for the "reading" of these materials.

Developing a sense of sequence of events and cause and effect relationships. It is certainly possible for a group of students to learn everything about the cliffdwellers and never see the relationship of the lives and times of these people to events in history which occurred simultaneously or realize the effect of this particular culture upon subsequent cultures. It is possible to teach the geography of a particular area in such a way that each student may have a detailed knowledge of products, climate, peoples, and industries, and fail to see the relationships which exist among these factors. We have created the term "social studies" with the belief that relationships *do* exist among the various subjects which are included in this broad term and that understanding of man and his physical world is best attained when these relationships are established in the mind of the student.

Relationships among events in history are most easily established through a chronological table or time-line. For instance, it is important for the student of United States history to realize that, at the same time that Americans were struggling for their independence, there were two other great revolutions against authority taking place in the world: the French Revolution and the Industrial Revolution. Lives of free men throughout the world were influenced simultaneously by these movements toward freedom from oppression of politics and ideas. Relationships of this sort are possible in all areas of the social studies, whether they be of persons, places, times, or events. For example, in the paragraph quoted earlier with reference to Pedro Cabral and his reaching Brazil, the date 1500 alone could be used for essential relationships. It is closely related to the events of Columbus' voyages, Ponce de Leon and Puerto Rico, Balboa and the discovery of Central America and the Pacific Ocean.

The *what, where, when,* and *who* factors of any event or situation are generally easy to establish, but the *why* and *how* factors are more difficult. Cause and effect relationships cannot be established until the *why* and *how* factors have been determined in addition to the *what, where, when,* and *who.* The type of question which the teacher asks so often determines which of these factors the student will consider.

Discriminating between fact and opinion. At the early stages of the elementary school, children learn to distinguish between the "real" and the "fanciful," the "true" and the "false," the "likely" and the "unlikely," as they read of and experience events in the lives of other people. They may become quite critical of what they read, particularly in terms of materials which they encounter in basic readers and supplementary reading books. Inconsistent with their attitudes toward reading materials, however, is the attitude which they so often develop when they read the social studies. Here they tend to regard the written word as infallible and to accept it without question. The ability to think for oneself, to accept or reject ideas or theories, develops slowly in the average student. Critical reading ability *can* be developed, however, in the social studies program through careful guidance by the teacher.

(*a*) *Comparing sources of information.* The nature of the social studies demands that wide reading in a variety of sources be encouraged. Children should be encouraged often to compare these sources to find contradictory accounts by different authors or opposite points of view expressed by editors of newspapers. They should be encouraged to read different accounts of history (for example, a United States history text published in the Deep South may give a slightly different interpretation of the Civil War than that given in a book published in Minneapolis) and to discuss these differences in terms of reasonable determinants. They should be led to determine the reputation of an author, to note the type of audience for which a selection was intended, to consider the time in which a selection or book was written, and to determine the purpose for which a piece of writing was done. One further step should then be encouraged: the student should make up his own mind as to what he chooses to accept or reject.

(*b*) *Considering information in terms of facts or opinions* is not difficult if the student holds in mind that facts are determined in three ways: that which has been established historically, that which is immediately observable, and that which is capable of being proven by experimentation or demonstration. If we keep in mind that most of the information with which we deal is opinion, then we realize that opinions are often worth more than isolated, irrelevant facts. They are particularly worth-while if they are based on facts. Since there is a rather general tendency among people to regard opinions as slightly less than respectable, our job as teachers of the social studies is to demonstrate that most of the content of this rich area of the curriculum is based on opinion.

Arithmetic

In dealing with arithmetic books, pupils must cope with three types of reading matter, each of which calls for specialized reading skills. In the first place, there is the material that gives the *social background* of arithmetical processes, as for promissory notes or insurance. Here the reading skills described in the social studies section of this chapter are pertinent. The second kind of material includes the *explanations* of processes, such as carrying in addition, and *directions* for work. The section on the reading of science materials will be helpful here. The third type of materials consists of the *word problems* that pupils are to solve. This section of the chapter will put stress on the reading skills involved in reading the word problems.

Vocabulary. Like any other subject in the curriculum, arithmetic has its own specialized vocabulary, for instance, *sum, multiply, fraction, decimal, percentage,* or *ratio.* If pupils are to read such terms with understanding, the teacher must make sure the pupils thoroughly understand the process that involves the term before she introduces the term itself; for example, she should have demonstrated many times the finding of a *sum,* and the pupils should repeatedly have found sums before they are introduced to the word *sum.* She should be especially careful to make clear the meaning of terms that are already familiar but with a different meaning. *Capital* (money for investment) and *principal* (base in an interest problem) are cases in point.

Attention to vocabulary has special values as pupils read their word problems, in that certain words and phrases serve as cues in deciding what process to use. "How much in all" or "how much altogether" indicate addition; "how much more or less" or "how much is left" hint that subtraction is to be used. Similarly, there are cues that indicate that multiplication or division are to be used.

Effective reading of word problems. Children should be taught to disregard the figures in their first reading of a word problem; they should concentrate on the situation, on the story the problem tells. There are several ways in which the situation in a word problem can be highlighted and the figures be disregarded. These can probably best be made clear by attacking some specific word problems.

1. Mrs. Spence bought 3 pounds of bananas at 19 cents per pound, 2 heads of lettuce at 15 cents each, and 3 quarts of milk at 24 cents each. How much change would she get from a 5-dollar bill?
2. How many yards of cloth can Mrs. Spence buy with a 10-dollar bill if it costs $2.48 a yard?
3. How much change will she get after buying this cloth?

The following methods of reading are effective: (1) Read thoughtfully, but omit the figures. (2) Read with the mind concentrated on the process (or processes) to be used. Number from 1 to 3; then write down the processes to be used in solving the three problems above.

1. ×; +; − (multiply; add products; subtract)
2. ÷ (divide)
3. − (subtract)

(3) Consider the following questions as the problem is read:

What does the problem tell me?
What am I asked to find out?
What process(es) should I use in finding out?
What would be a reasonable answer?

Pupils can also: (4) Dramatize a problem. (5) Retell a problem in the pupils' own words. (6) Draw a diagram or cartoon that makes the situation clear. (7) Read lists of problems where no figures are supplied and indicate the processes that would be used in their solution.

If teachers consistently use some of the foregoing procedures in training their pupils to read word problems meaningfully, the latter are almost sure to become independent and accurate readers who can effectively decide on the arithmetical processes that are to be used. For instance, daily practice of five minutes on writing down the processes (suggestion 2 on p. 274) will in a month's time enable the pupils to read word problems effectively.

Science

It would appear to be unnecessary to point out to the teacher that reading in science, like so much of the reading in the social studies, is not narrative in nature but quite complex for the child who has not become accustomed to a statement of laws and principles, facts and figures, and minute descriptive details; yet too often the assignments in science are made in the conventional manner: "Read the next seven pages and let's talk about them tomorrow." It is true that many of our science books in the intermediate grades are written in a delightful narrative form, but the bulk of the reference materials which children will read in the development of a single science unit may be quite difficult. The child will use the basic skills of reading which he has learned to apply to other content areas, but he must be prepared to make adjustments to science materials, both in terms of his speed of reading and his purpose for reading the material. Further adjustments will depend on the compactness of the printed materials.

Reading in science is thoughtful and often slow reading. Skimming is seldom applicable as a skill, except in searching for related ideas; directions must be read and reread, with attention directed toward the sequence of those directions and exactly what is demanded of each. And, as in all other types of reading, the student is required to establish a relationship of ideas. Fortunately, many of the concepts of science are both observable and demonstrable; many of the ideas are precise and easy to relate to laws and principles.

Mastering the vocabulary of science. Scientific terms in themselves are difficult. Moreover, so many technical terms are crowded into terse statements that the young reader is followed by careful development of the ideas presented and swamped. Note, for example, the number of ideas which are presented in this paragraph and the difficulty of the vocabulary:

> The largest bodies that revolve about the sun are called planets. Nine planets have been discovered so far: Mercury, Venus, Earth, Mars, Jupiter, Saturn, Uranus, Neptune, and Pluto. Most planets have satellites or moons that revolve around them. Between Mars and Jupiter, there are a great many small planets called asteroids. There are about one thousand of these, and each follows its own path or orbit around the sun. Comets and meteors are also members of the solar system.[3]

Since the example given is an introductory paragraph, followed by careful development of the ideas presented and explanation of the terms, the student may be directed to discuss the ideas and new words on the basis of his previous experience; further directed reading will bring clarification

[3] Warren Knox, *et al., The Wonderworld of Science,* Book Five (New York: Charles Scribner's Sons, 1952), p. 154.

of this paragraph. The slow child, however, may have reading difficulty with this mass of terms, appearing as they do in one paragraph:

bodies
revolve
planets
satellites
asteroids
orbit
comets
meteors
solar system

Illustrations, labels on objects and pictures, films, and discussion may be used to develop mastery of science vocabulary. Of course, the student will use his knowledge of pronunciation and meaning skills to attack new words. Many of the terms in science are easily understood if they are properly analyzed from the standpoint of their roots and common elements: *hemiptera, orthoptera,* and *hymenoptera* are terms used to classify insects, with a common root *pteron* (wing) from the Greek. When the student discovers that these terms are descriptive (Hemiptera, or half-wing, such as the aphid; Orthoptera, or straight-wing, the grasshopper; and Hymenoptera, or membrane-wing, the wasp), a new world of meaning is opened to him. It is reasonable to expect that the interested student will encounter technical terms as he reads a wide variety of materials which have been so well written for the young scientist.

Mastering the problem-solving technique. Reading in science is reading for solving problems, and true learning in science is never more greatly advanced than when students have learned to demand answers from what they read. Most of the content of science can be presented and mastered through a problem-solving technique:

What is stated, exactly?
What is expected? What is to be found?
What do we already know about this?

What are the possible steps which we might take to reach a solution or conclusion?
Where can we find additional information which might give further aid toward solving the problem?
Do we see clearly the steps which we must take in attempting to solve the problem?
Is our conclusion or answer reasonable?
Do we now have proof which we can present to others?

These questions indicate that the student must read directions carefully, establish a sequence in which ideas are presented, follow steps carefully, seek information at each level of the step, and demand proof. Since it may be assumed that the good science textbook is so organized as to aid the student in attaining each of these goals, the teacher has a responsibility for pointing out to the student that the author has organized his presentation of ideas to encourage good learning.

Encouraging wide reading in related materials. Most students do not have to be motivated to read the perfectly delightful science books which are to be found in abundance in the school library; our modern writers have provided us with a wealth of well-illustrated and simply written science materials. Television, radio, films, filmstrips, magazines, and newspapers are rich sources of supplementary materials for the science program. A wide range of difficulty of materials is available, from the simple and authentic *True Books* to the *The World We Live In* series from *Life* magazine.

For each child in the classroom there is available a book or a pamphlet which will meet his needs in a science unit. Collecting these materials is a responsibility to be shared by students and teacher alike. The best written science textbook can be supplemented tenfold by the use of research materials, and there is no limit to the growth children will make in vocabulary skills, reading for solution of problems, and reading for information and pleasure.

Summary

Reading in the content fields demands the development of skills which may include those general skills of reading plus specific skills for the particular subject. Wide reading is often demanded of the student, and he must constantly relate what he reads to his previous experience and knowledge. Vocabulary is introduced more rapidly, and technical terms must be mastered in order to understand the ideas which are presented. Skills of organization and retention are vital to the development of concepts which are often introduced so rapidly and in such abundance that the student needs careful guidance in comprehending his daily assignments. The teacher of homemaking, industrial arts, and music in the upper grades should know that she, too, must teach reading skills if children are to be expected to master the technical language in which these content areas are written.

Selected References

Gray, William S. (ed.). "Basic Instruction in Reading in Elementary and High Schools," *Supplementary Educational Monographs*, No. 65. Chicago: University of Chicago Press, 1949. Pp. 201–14.

——— (ed.). "Classroom Techniques in Improving Reading," *Supplementary Educational Monographs*, No. 69. Chicago: University of Chicago Press, 1952. Pp. 89–97.

——— (ed.). "Improving Reading in All Curriculum Areas," *Supplementary Educational Monographs*, No. 76. Chicago: University of Chicago Press, 1952. Pp. 125–38, 150–63, 170–82, 242–46.

———. "Improving Reading in Content Fields," *Supplementary Educational Monographs,* No. 62. Chicago: University of Chicago Press, 1947. Pp. 111–201.

TINKER, MILES A., and MCCULLOUGH, CONSTANCE M. *Teaching Elementary Reading.* New York: Appleton-Century-Crofts, Inc., 1962. Chapter 12.

16

Appraisal of the Reading Program

IN THE PRECEDING CHAPTERS, WE HAVE BEEN CONsidering the fundamentals of good reading program by stating what *ought* to be. The beginning teacher might be overwhelmed by the number of tasks which she is required to perform in aiding children to develop reading skills. Obviously, not all children need the same things nor the same types of instruction. As children progress in skills development, they typically become independent and no longer need formal instruction in word recognition, word-meaning skills, comprehension skills, and others. On the other hand, some children may have developed proficiency in one area of reading and be seriously handicapped in another. One of the most difficult tasks of the teacher, then, is appraising the needs of children as she works with them month after month.

Appraisal means many things to many people. To some it denotes the giving of standardized tests to measure the progress of children as compared to a national level of achievement at that particular grade level; to others, it denotes a diagnostic approach: just what skills are developed, and to what extent must instruction be shifted to meet the needs of the children who are below par in their development? To still another group appraisal is a means of determining the effectiveness of instruction, of measuring children's progress in a particular phase of the program, or of determining what marks should be given in reporting to parents.

We hear on every hand that our children today are reading better than they have ever read in the history of education. Teachers and administrators point with pride to the results of their standardized testing program and are quick to state that their children are reading above the national norms. While such evidence is significant, it falls far short of indicating whether all of the children are actually achieving in all of the areas of reading which they will be required to do as adults in our society. The results of standardized tests simply do not indicate problem areas, since a diagnostic test has not been devised which will yield valid results when administered to groups of children. Another question arises in this respect: Should not our children be reading better than they were thirty years ago, since the demands on a reader are more complex and materials of reading are so abundant? And should we not be very concerned with more and more growth in meeting the demands of society rather than stating joyfully that our children are reading better than the children of yesteryear's schools?

Children are still failing to learn to read. An overwhelming number of young people are graduated from high school each year with reading skills that are insufficient for effective participation in the workaday world's activities. Each year children are passed along to another grade with the fervent hope that something will happen to them within the next year to overcome their disabilities in reading. The truth of the matter is that many of the current appraisal practices which we use are obscuring the problem areas, and teachers are simply failing to realize that thousands of children are *partial* cripples in reading skills. While many are presenting dramatic accomplishment, many others are presenting dramatic retardation problems. Are not the partial cripples, then, obscured by these two extreme groups when we use mass testing techniques and nothing else to determine the achievement of our children?

The purposes of a good appraisal of the reading program are these:

1. To assess the *needs* of children in terms of the various reading skills
2. To determine the *nature of instruction* in order to meet the goals of each content area of the curriculum
3. To assess the *level of reading competency* of each child in order to predict his success in reading at more advanced levels
4. To test the *effectiveness of instruction*
5. To determine the *need for materials* of instruction
6. To aid the child's personal growth of *interests, attitudes, and tastes* in reading.

No other person is in a better position to appraise the needs of the child than the classroom teacher who works every day with that child. Hers is the task of checking periodically to find out the exact status of the child in each reading and study skill. Obviously, this means that she must know what to expect of a child's proficiency for a particular subject at any level of the curriculum. Appraisal becomes difficult, since personality factors, attitudes, interests, and capacity to learn must all be considered.

Just what can a teacher do, then, to appraise the needs of children in her classroom? There are six areas of appraisal which we shall consider: (1) standardized tests, (2) informal tests and questionnaires, (3) check lists, (4) interviews and conferences, (5) cumulative records, and (6) observations. None of these is sufficient in and of itself, but each can be an aid of great value to the teacher who really seeks information regarding the effectiveness of her reading program.

Standardized tests. Literally hundreds of thousands of standardized tests are administered each year to hundreds of thousands of boys and girls throughout the nation. Most of them are easily administered and scored, and most of them yield valid results within the realm of their limitations. When standardized tests are used, we must be aware of what they do not measure as well as what they do measure.

The standardized group test has not yet been constructed which will measure interests, motivation, attitudes, or appreciations of our children. These tests do not indicate if a child can make allowances for the content of a particular book by adjusting his speed and determining how much he should read in order to fulfill his purposes. They yield, at the most, subscores and a total score, all of which obscure the areas of difficulty which the child may experience.

On the other hand, a good standardized test should measure quite well these factors:

1. Vocabulary development in both word-recognition and word-meaning skills
2. Sentence and paragraph meaning
3. Directions
4. Main ideas and supporting details
5. Rate of reading (usually for a particular type of material)
6. Organization skills

A list of standardized tests, which may be used in the classroom, has been placed in the Appendix. In selecting a test for use in the school, apply these criteria for judging its effectiveness:

1. Does it really measure what it purports to measure? Does it merely sample a very narrow range of the total reading skills which a student needs to read in all subjects?
2. Do the results yield merely a broad picture of the child's reading ability, or do they merely indicate his ability to read silently and react to limited questions?
3. Is there provision for testing the student's ability to skim for details, to organize ideas, to react to ideas, to select relevant details, to make decisions on the basis of facts and opinions presented, and to interpret in light of personal knowledge and experience?
4. Can the tests be administered and scored easily? (Ease of administration should not be a criterion unless the test meets all other criteria. Teachers and administrators are prone to select a test which can be given in the time limit of one period; however, if a test yields valuable information regarding children's needs, and it requires two or more periods for administration, then the time element should be disregarded.)
5. Are the test results meaningful to both the teacher and the child? In other words, do the scores indicate both strengths and weaknesses with reference to specific reading skills? Can the results be used to help the child set realistic goals for improvement?
6. Does the test differentiate between the student who can profit from instruction and the student who is now working at his ability level?
7. Is the test reliable? (A common practice is to give children parallel forms of a test at the beginning and end of the year to test the effectiveness of instruction. At best, this is a poor practice, since such factors as interest, habits, attitudes, and attention are not measured. On the other hand, a reliable test does give the teacher a means of measuring the progress of the child over a given period of time.)

You may argue that no standardized test meets all of these criteria and you are right. But with such criteria in mind better selection may be made. There is a tendency to accept the results of tests on their face validity and to use the results of those tests with the assurance that they have yielded all that we need to know about the child's reading ability. Surely these criteria will point out the advisability of using standardized test results in a limited sense, and always with other methods of appraisal before a decision is reached as to what a child's needs are or into which group he should be placed.

Informal tests and questionnaires. Every teacher spends many hours preparing informal tests to measure the effectiveness of her instruction; these tests may be both valuable and practical. She determines which children have profited most from a particular type of instruction which has been aimed at the development of certain skills; she also determines which children need further instruction. From year to year, she learns to measure the progress of her children as she compares them to groups which she has taught in past years, and she refines her techniques as she learns that some areas of skills development simply cannot be measured through paper-and-pencil exercises. Several factors should be considered in constructing a test for classroom use.

1. Do not attempt to measure too wide a range of skills through any one test, but construct items which will indicate whether children have shown growth in (a) word attack skills, (b) word meaning skills, (c) knowledge of stated facts, (d) knowledge of an author's opinions, (e) ability to infer meanings, (f) ability to follow directions, (g) ability to organize ideas in a meaningful sequence, (h) ability to identify a main idea and supporting details, or (i) ability to recall important facts or details. Each question which the teacher asks should be geared to the type of evidence of skill with which she is concerned. Ideally, each elementary teacher should have taken a course in tests and

measurements, and should know the fine points of constructing test items.

2. Vary the types of tests given to children through this informal approach. At times, require them to answer questions orally, after a skimming exercise which directed their attention to specific items of information. Occasionally, test children's abilities to do research-type reading by presenting a problem and then requiring each child to give evidence of having sought and found answers to the problem. Give some open-book tests, in which the children record answers to questions which you have mimeographed or written on the board. In science, arithmetic, and the social studies, give reading tests which will yield information regarding those specific reading skills that are needed for those subjects.

3. Keep in mind that the teacher-made test may indicate the instructional levels at which children operate best. Several authorities have agreed that each student has four different levels of competency: (a) the instructional or teaching level—that level at which the student is capable of reading and receiving ideas with the aid of the teacher; (b) the independent level—that level at which the student is capable of operating independently in his reading habits; (c) the frustration level—that level at which the student can no longer read the material; and (d) the hearing-comprehension level—the highest level at which the student is capable of understanding ideas as he listens to the instructor or other students. It is obvious that the typical standardized test cannot determine these levels; it is apparent that the teacher can better determine these levels and that a knowledge of each child's levels of competency is vital to her in planning her instruction.

Occasionally, a questionnaire will yield valuable information for the teacher when she wishes to know what children like to read, their attitudes toward instruction, and their own assessment of their needs. Open-ended questions can be used, such as:

The type of book I like best is ______.
My favorite book of all time is ______.
I believe I need help in ______ if I am to become a better reader.

There are pitfalls in this technique, of course. The child will often answer in a manner which he believes to be appropriate to the teacher's expectations. This tendency to conform to a teacher's wishes can frequently be offset by asking the children not to sign their names to a questionnaire, or by inserting questions which encourage the child to react to things he does not like.

SIGHT VOCABULARY INVENTORY *

Instructions to the Teacher: Have the child read Group A orally. If he reads this group without error, disregard the remainder of the test and record a score of *4* on this diagnostic summary. If the child errs on a word in Group A, proceed immediately to Group B. Continue in this manner until a group is reached which the child can read without error. Teach those words which the child has missed until they become a part of his sight vocabulary. You may score this inventory in this manner:

If the first group read without error is	A	. . . the child earns a score of	4
	B		3
	C		2
	D		1
	None		0

* Courtesy of the Washington Unified School District, West Sacramento, California.

GROUP A

ago	always	around	ate	because	bring	buy
clean	cold	done	every	fall	green	going
ride	eight	funny	hold	light	only	our
own	don't	draw	drink	shall	sit	small
myself	hurt	pull	read	right	round	sing
six	five	fly	full	grow	these	seven
pick	start	ten	those	today	together	upon
yellow	hot	jump	kind	warm	wash	

GROUP B

after	am	ask	been	before	best	black
blue	both	brown	cut	does	eat	far
fast	find	first	found	four	gave	got
goes	has	if	keep	know	laugh	live
much	never	new	once	open	or	pretty
red	sleep	soon	stop	their	too	show
think	three	try	under	use	very	walk
white	wish	work	write	yes		

GROUP C

again	an	any	as	away	be	better
but	by	call	came	come	could	did
down	from	get	give	good	had	help
her	here	him	how	into	it's	just
let	like	long	look	made	make	many
may	must	no	now	old	over	play
please	put	ran	run	said	saw	say
so	some	take	tell	thank	then	this
two	us	want	well	were	when	where
who	why	would	your			

GROUP D

a	about	all	and	are	at	big
can	do	for	go	have	he	his
I	in	is	it	little	me	my
not	of	on	one	out	see	she
that	the	them	there	they	to	up
was	we	went	what	will	which	with
you						

4. Using the information which is available in cumulative records and the test scores of standardized tests, the teacher may want to assess the child's independent and instructional reading levels. In each of the teacher's manuals of the *Sheldon Basic Readers* (Allyn Bacon Company) there is provided a series of diagnostic paragraphs for use in making an informal inventory of the child's reading level, and detailed directions on how to administer the paragraphs to children. The teacher may prepare her own set of diagnostic paragraphs by taking sample paragraphs from old series of basal readers, making selections of one hundred words or more. To test comprehension of the paragraphs, construct five questions; one question should test the main idea of the paragraph, one should test the child's ability to draw inferences, and the remaining three questions should test the child's memory of details. An excellent standardized test for diagnosing oral reading difficulties is the *Gilmore Oral Reading Test*, published by Harcourt, Brace and World Company; this test is easy to administer and score and gives an accurate estimate of the child's independent reading level.

Check lists. Many teachers find that using a check list for day-to-day observations of children provides an accurate means of reviewing a child's progress. A check list is provided here (p. 291) which may be of value to the teacher, but she will wish to make her own modifications of this list. The value of the check list is that it gives the teacher a potential means of checking accurately her observations of a particular child; she cannot possibly remember, when she has thirty-five children, all of the areas of difficulty which a particular child may indicate from day to day. Too, the check list is a valuable source of information for the teacher who will have the child in succeeding terms.

CHECK LIST OF DIFFICULTIES IN BASIC READING SKILLS

Name ______________________ Grade ______ Year ______

I. Word Recognition Skills

A. Recognition Skills

___1. Has a limited sight vocabulary
___2. Habitually omits words ________ ________ ________
___3. Habitually adds words ________ ________ ________
___4. Habitually substitutes words ______ ________ ________
___5. Depends too much on configuration clues
___6. Does not use context clues
___7. Depends too much on context clues
___8. Habitually reverses words ________ ________ ________

B. Analysis Skills

___1. Does not look for familiar parts (roots, prefixes, suffixes)
___2. Uses only initial consonant attack
___3. Confuses final consonants
___4. Omits structural endings
___5. Confuses consonant blends
___6. Confuses consonant digraphs
___7. Confuses diphthongs
___8. Makes frequent errors on long vowels
___9. Makes frequent errors on short vowels
___10. Does not recognize silent letters in words
___11. Lacks skills of breaking words into syllables

C. Meaning Vocabulary

___1. Has a limited speaking vocabulary
___2. Does not use context to determine meanings of new words
___3. Lacks skill in use of dictionary

II. Phrasing, Fluency

____1. Ignores punctuation when he reads orally
____2. Reads word by word
____3. Habitually repeats words or phrases
____4. Reads too slowly, ploddingly
____5. Reads too fast, carelessly

III. General Observations

____1. Does not understand, but reads fluently
____2. Does not show interest in reading
____3. Reads too literally
____4. Is not accurate in interpretation
____5. Grasps details but misses the main idea
____6. Has poor work habits
____7. Cannot relate sequence of events or ideas
____8. Does not follow directions well

Interviews and conferences. At various times the teacher will have an opportunity to interview individual children and perhaps have a conference with their parents. The interview can be structured so that the teacher poses definite questions and seeks specific information, or it can be totally unstructured. In either case, it may be important for the teacher to find out the answers to these questions:

1. How does the student feel about his reading problems? What does he feel his problem is? When did he begin to have difficulty?
2. What evidence is there of causal factors, either in the home or the school?
3. What are the feelings of the child toward reading? Does he have definite interests in some area? Does he feel that learning to read is important?
4. Is he willing to accept the responsibility for improving his skills?
5. What are his interests and aspirations? How much do parents influence his goals?

6. Has he adopted the "what's the use" attitude after many failures?
7. What does the child do with his spare time? his week ends? What TV shows does he regularly watch? What types of materials does he read outside of school? What movies, excursions, and out-of-school activities does he prefer?

These are but a few suggestions, and the teacher will add other areas which are of concern to her and to the child. If the child has a problem in school, it is many times minimized when he finds that the teacher is interested in his problem and wants to talk sympathetically with him.

Cumulative records. The cumulative record of a child often yields information which cannot be obtained from any other source. Although cumulative records are often poorly kept and statements from teachers sometimes reveal practically nothing specific regarding a child, there may be items of information available which can reveal to the teacher the real reasons for a child's behavior in a classroom. Each teacher has a responsibility for adding anecdotal records to the child's folder if she feels that her information might aid another teacher in working with the child. Good records should yield the following kinds of information which are of value to the classroom teacher of reading:

1. Subjects in which the child has succeeded and failed. Evidence of previous success, followed by dramatic failure.
2. The number of schools which he has attended. Evidence of lack of continuity in training. Times of year in which his training has been interrupted by moving to another school.
3. Health status. Evidence of visual and/or auditory acuity. History of physical or mental illness over a prolonged period of time.
4. Previous testing record. Evidence of intellectual capacity. Consistency of pattern in achievement testing in all content areas.

5. Previous history of special help. Has this child been singled out previously for his achievements or failures? Is there evidence that he has not responded to special help?
6. Teachers' attitudes toward the child. Are these consistent? Is there evidence of mishandling of the child's problems?
7. Family background. Parents' occupations. Language spoken in the home. Evidence of family pressures or interests in the child's progress. Evidence of academic achievement of brothers and sisters. Education of parents.

If each teacher had all of this information on each child in her classroom, she would be much better prepared to meet the needs of that child. Not all of this information is available in cumulative records however. It is advisable that each teacher add what information she has to the record in order that the next teacher may profit from her experience with the child.

Observations. It is probably true that more teachers depend upon their observations of the child in the classroom setting to determine his needs than on any other method of appraisal. Day-by-day observations are very important, since they reveal the persistence of behavior which a child may evidence. Here are some examples of the types of observations which may be of value to the teacher:

1. Completion of assignments
2. Ability to follow directions
3. Independence in reading assigned materials
4. Amount of reading which is done in addition to assigned lessons
5. Oral reading as contrasted or compared to silent reading abilities
6. Participation in group planning and work
7. Evidence of good study habits
8. Interests in other content areas
9. Social and emotional adjustment
10. Physical well-being

11. Persistence of problem areas with reference to specific reading skills
12. Motivation for learning
13. Evidence of growth in each of the reading and study skills

Each of us has a tendency to look for negative aspects of children's behavior; these are important in that they indicate problem areas. On the other hand, the teacher observation can serve to indicate areas of real strength, on which can be built sound skills.

Summary

No program of appraisal is perfect, nor is it a simple process which can be reduced to one or two techniques. Good appraisal includes standardized testing, interviewing and observing the child, consulting cumulative records and contributing information to the records, constructing teacher-made tests which measure the effectiveness of instruction and indicate areas which need further emphasis, and frequent checking on the child's status with reference to his interests, attitudes, and capacity. No technique of appraisal is sufficient alone. Reading is a complex process, associated with emotional and social aspects of development, and the attainment of reading skills cannot be measured by a single testing instrument.

Selected References

BETTS, EMMETT. *Foundations of Reading Instruction.* New York: American Book Co., 1954. Pp. 438–87.

HILDRETH, GERTRUDE. *Readiness for School Beginners.* Yonkers, N.Y.: World Book Co., 1950. Pp. 64–87.

MCKIM, MARGARET. *Guiding Growth in Reading in the Modern Elementary School.* New York: The Macmillan Co., 1955. Pp. 453–91.

Monroe, Marion. *Growing into Reading.* Chicago: Scott, Foresman and Co., 1951. Pp. 229–54.

Russell, David H. *Children Learn to Read.* 2nd ed. Boston: Ginn and Co., 1961. Chapter 16.

Strang, Ruth. "Evaluation of Growth in and through Reading," in *Development in and through Reading,* Sixtieth Yearbook, Part I, National Society for the Study of Education. Chicago: University of Chicago Press, 1961. Chapter 21.

17

Parents and the Reading Program

Any consideration of the reading program in the elementary school would be incomplete unless we discussed the vital role which parents play in the development of the child's reading skills. For inexperienced teachers, the task of meeting and discussing a child's progress with parents is a formidable task. It need not be, if we adopt the attitude that parents are very much a part of the educational processes which we, as teachers, attempt to foster in the classroom. Each parent has an emotional investment in the child whom we teach; most parents are both interested in the child's progress and eager to aid the school in furthering that progress.

The kindergarten teacher can easily pick out those children in her group whose parents have played a role in their preschool development of language skills. These are the children who have already learned to treasure books and to handle them properly; they speak in complete sentences and participate freely in discussions. They attempt to use good grammar and are aware of accurate enunciation and pronunciation of words. How fortunate would we be if we could depend on each child's being at these stages of development when he enters the school!

Even before the recent publicity which has been given to reading in our public schools, parents held reading as the most important activity of the school. Many parents who have never been good readers themselves desire a higher level of attainment for their children.

The happiest and most successful teacher in the school is most often the one who regards parents as helpmates and friends to education. She invites parents to visit her room to observe a reading activity; she is available for conferences on each of the children in her room. She keeps parents informed of their children's progress. In the case of a problem area, she enlists the aid of parents in attempting to discover the cause of the difficulties, and perhaps she asks them to work with the child under her guidance.

Many of our parents today are confused over what their role in helping their children should be. Not too many years ago leaders in education were asking parents not to be concerned about their children in the school. It was assumed that the school could meet the needs of the child, and it was thought best that parents not be involved. We do not believe these things today; we have realized that the school has the child but a small part of the day. Someone has estimated that the total time a person spends in school, from kindergarten through a Ph.D., in actual classroom participation would amount to less than eleven months, if we added the hours throughout the day and night! What the parent thinks of the school, how much he knows about helping the child with difficult educational tasks, what he does to stimulate the child to learn, and how he handles the child's successes and failures are all vital to the child's development. Through the Parent-Teachers Association, numerous conferences with parents, articles in magazines and newspapers, and increased social contacts with parents through the school, we are fostering *more* participation by parents in the child's education. Our biggest job is to interpret modern education to these parents in such a way that they will realize that the changes which have been made are best for their children. And we must be prepared to answer the questions which arise each time a parent meets a teacher or administrator.

What parents want to know. At no time in the history of education has the value of education for every child been more emphasized than in today's society. Nearly every child goes to high school, and more and more young people are seeking a college education. Consequently, young parents view their children's education as a vital issue. They are asking questions regarding their children's progress in the school, and they have a right to demand answers. Where we often fail in dealing with parents is in our own inability to interpret the modern school and its curriculum to them. Parents are not satisfied with such answers as, "Just don't worry about it; Jimmy will read when he decides it is important to him," and, "We are concerned with the *whole* child in our school, not just the individual skill." Each of these answers has its merits, if it is clearly understood by the person who is giving the answer and by the person who is receiving it. No teacher can at any time afford to use circumlocution merely to dodge an embarrassing issue which concerns the welfare of a child. We need as much specific information as we can get, and we must relate this information to parents as honestly and frankly as possible. What types of questions do parents ask? Obviously, we cannot pretend that we have anticipated all of the questions, but experienced teachers have listed certain areas which are causing rather widespread concern and confusion:

1. What is meant by readiness, and how can we help in preparing our child for reading?

2. Is it true that we no longer teach phonics but depend on sight recognition for the words which the child learns?
3. Why are children not started with books, rather than with the reading charts which are used so widely in the first grade?
4. What books can I read to help me understand the curriculum of today's schools?
5. How can I help my child to become interested in reading good books rather than comics?
6. Why are children grouped as they are for reading instruction? Does grouping really give children feelings of inferiority?
7. Why was I not told that my child was failing before the report cards were issued?
8. My child wants to learn the alphabet. Will I harm him if I teach the alphabet?
9. Is special help available for the child who is failing in his reading? Do our schools provide remedial help?
10. Why must my child be held back with the rest of the class? Are all of the children expected to learn at the same rate?
11. Why don't teachers assign homework for our children?
12. Why is it that my child can read very well in his reader and not get anything out of reading his science and arithmetic books?

These, and many more, are the questions which teachers must be prepared to answer, and there are no "pat" answers. Throughout the preceding chapters in this book, however, we have attempted to anticipate these questions. There are good reasons for our methods of teaching in our modern schools. We are learning more and more about the total development of children, and we are providing education for living in a complex society; hence we do not teach the same things in the same way that we did twenty or thirty years ago.

What teachers can do to help parents. Every teacher wants to be able to help each child who comes to her and to challenge him to learn and prepare himself for more complex tasks. Her desires for the child are fundamentally the same as the parents' desires; each party can contribute both knowledge and skills to the child's progress. Here are some suggestions for teachers who wish to enlist the aid of parents in their reading program:

1. At the beginning of each year, interpret the reading program to the parents, explaining what is expected of the child at this level of the curriculum.
2. Invite parents to visit the school to observe reading activities. Give them time for questions, when the children are not around, in order that you may determine that they have interpreted accurately what they observed.
3. With the aid of other teachers, compile reading lists for children and send them to the parents with the suggestion that they may wish to purchase a few books and get others from the library. The teacher is in a much better position to recommend appropriate books for the individual child.
4. Hold frequent parent conferences and be prepared to answer questions regarding the child's ability to learn, his achievement, and his behavior in the classroom learning situation.
5. When a child needs extra help and you have the confidence that the parent can help, outline carefully what can be done at home.
6. With the aid of other teachers and interested parents, organize a child study group for consideration of problems which are common to most children. Invite competent speakers (psychiatrists, subject-matter specialists, medical doctors) to conduct the discussions.
7. Explain the reasons for grouping children and give detailed information on the criteria which have been used for determining those groups.
8. Suggest activities in which parents can help you and other teachers in broadening the experiences of children: field trips, excursions, talks by the parents about their interesting work.

Parents so often complain that information has been withheld or that they were simply not informed of the progress of their child. They frequently state that they want to be of service to the school, but the teacher never suggests activities in which they can become involved. The answer is, obviously, to make every effort to involve the parents in the child's reading, within the safe limits which you, as a teacher, have determined for the child.

What parents can do. What do we suggest to parents that they may do at home to help the child? There are many constructive activities in which any family can participate and contribute to the educational progress of the child. Make suggestions on the basis of what you know of the child in your classroom when you have opportunities to confer with parents.

1. Give the child wide experiences—experiences which are shared with the family and discussed in such a way that the child actually understands what he is seeing or doing.
2. Provide a rich background of language development by allowing children to use their parents and brothers and sisters as sounding boards for their ideas. Answer questions, remembering that children's concepts are very often vague and inaccurate.
3. Have a family reading hour each day. Read books, poetry, and articles from magazines and newspapers. Encourage the child to read, too.
4. Praise progress, even though it appears to be slight.
5. Teach the child to handle a book: to turn pages, to hold the book properly, and to put it away in a safe place when he has finished with it.
6. Help him develop a sense of responsibility for correcting his own errors; do not be quick to criticize nor too quick to help him if there's a possibility he can work it out for himself.
7. Surround the child with books. So many lovely but inex-

pensive books can be purchased today. Encourage him to read them by reading them with him.

8. Keep him in good health. Have frequent checks on his visual and auditory acuity. Be certain that he gets plenty of rest, since a day at school demands much energy.
9. Refrain from pushing the child into too many activities. Many parents feel that they were denied dancing lessons, music lessons, membership in clubs, and other extracurricular activities, and push their children into so many activities that the child cannot possibly keep up with his school work.
10. If there is something which you do not understand about the methods or goals of the school, confer with the teacher or the principal.
11. Assume responsibility for helping the child if he is failing. With the teacher's help, ascertain what the prediction for his success is on the basis of his capacity to learn. Ask the teacher for suggestions on how you might help him with his skills development.
12. Encourage the children in the family to help each other; refrain from making comparisons among older brothers and sisters and the younger child.
13. Help your child to understand that, in addition to reading, many other learnings are important in life. Not all children will excel in reading, but they may excel in other areas.
14. Refrain from projecting your own feelings of failure in reading or other areas of the school upon your child; give him a chance to make up his own mind about how he feels about his teacher and the school.

We have suggested no panaceas simply because there are none. In each combination of a child and a teacher and parents, there are elements which are perhaps unique. They are all involved in a very important role which has implications for success and happiness for each of the persons involved. The young parent in our country today wants to be able to help his child and to contribute to his general well-being. He holds reading as an important life process, and he expects the teacher to keep him informed on the limits of the child's expected behavior. Many parents are neither interested nor cooperative; many are critical of all schools and all teachers. But for each of these negative persons, there are one hundred young parents who esteem their home and their children and their futures together. That's our challenge as teachers. How well can we face it?

Selected References

ARTLEY, A. STERL. *Your Child Learns to Read.* Chicago: Scott, Foresman and Co., 1953. Entire book.

LARRICK, NANCY. *A Parent's Guide to Children's Reading.* New York: Doubleday and Co., 1958.

MONROE, MARION. *Growing into Reading.* Chicago: Scott, Foresman and Co., 1951. Entire book.

OVERSTREET, BONARO. "The Role of the Home," in *Development in and through Reading,* Sixtieth Yearbook, Part I, National Society for the Study of Education. Chicago: University of Chicago Press, 1961. Chapter 5.

"Parents and the Reading Program," *The Reading Teacher,* VII (April, 1954), entire issue.

RUSSELL, DAVID H. *Children Learn to Read.* 2nd ed. Boston: Ginn and Co., 1961. Chapter 17.

APPENDIX A

Reading Aids

Cards and Games

Doghouse Game. Kenworthy. Intended to teach fusion of phonetic elements quickly and correctly; 117 phonograms included; 1–12 players.

Dolch Teaching Aids. Garrard.

Basic Sight Cards: The basic 220 sight vocabulary words.

Consonant Lotto: Eight lotto cards, each containing six pictures of familiar objects. For teaching beginning sounds.

Group Sounding Game: Bingo-type game, covering all stages of phonetic analysis, including syllabication.

Match Games: For grades K–1; matching of 95 commonest nouns with picture cards.

Picture Word Cards: For teaching the 95 commonest nouns; word is pictured on opposite side.

Popper Words: Two sets; set one introduces the first 110 sight words, and set two gives the harder half of the basic sight vocabulary.

Syllable Game: Three decks of 64 cards for teaching hundreds of common syllables; can be used from grade 3 upward.

Take: Matching the sounds of the beginning, middle, and ending of words.

Vowel Lotto: Gives practice in hearing and learning short vowels, long vowels, vowel digraphs, and diphthongs.

What the Letters Say: A beginning phonics game; matching pictures to letters.

Who Gets It: Matching of pictures and of two types of the same object; for K–1.

Embeco Phonetic Drill Cards. Bradley. Aid for learning common phonograms.

Grab. Order directly from Dorothea Alcock, 324 East College Street, Covina, California.

Six decks of cards, for matching words, for grades 1–6; teaches phonetic elements, structural analysis, and syllabication; good for basic sight vocabulary.

Parent-Teacher Aids. Gelles-Widmer. Four boxes of cards: Alphabet, Phonics, Pre-primer Words, Primer Words. Story tests with each set of cards.

Phonic Lingo. King. A bingo-type game, designed to teach discrimination of initial consonants.

Phonic Rummy Games. Phonovisual. Four sets of cards: Short Vowels, Long Vowels, Phonograms, Miscellaneous Sounds.

Phono-Word Wheels. Steck. Five sets; total of 81 wheels for teaching phonetic and structural elements.

Phrase-O Game. Steck. Rapid recognition of phrases. 71 master cards, containing 375 phrases.

Reading Essentials Teaching Aids. Steck. Three separate kits, for grades 1, 2, and 3. Excellent teaching aids, encompassing word-attack and word-meaning skills.

Webster Word Wheels. Webster. 63 word wheels; consonant blends, prefixes, and suffixes.

Charts for Teaching Word Attack Skills

ABC Sounds, Consonantal Blends, Vowel Blends. Hammond. Three sets of large cards, in color.

Horrocks-Norwick Word Study Charts. Ginn. Twenty large full-color charts, for teaching phonetic and structural analysis. 48-page manual.

Phonics Key Cards. McCormick-Mather. 78 cards, illustrating phonic units.

Phonovisual Wall Charts. Phonovisual Products. Two charts, illustrating phonic units.

Word Analysis Charts. Webster. Five large charts, for teaching phonetic and structural analysis.

Filmstrips

Comprehensive Reading Lessons. Curriculum. A total of 63 filmstrips and 21 charts which are designed to parallel topics or stories in any basal reading series.

How to Read: To Understand, To Evaluate, To Use. SVE. Outlines principles for effective reading.

Filmstrip Reading Series. Pacific Productions. 42 strips, in color, covering phonetic analysis, structural analysis, syllabication, reading to understand, learning to use the dictionary, learning to use the library, and effective use of books.

New Spelling Goals Filmstrips. Webster. Series of 7 filmstrips, designed to develop both auditory and visual perception.

Reading for Meaning: What's the Word. Houghton Mifflin. Series of 12, featuring word analysis, word meanings, and use of the dictionary.

Filmstrips for Phonetic Skills. Scott, Foresman. Four filmstrips, for developing auditory and visual discrimination.

Row, Peterson Reading Series. Row, Peterson. Filmstrips at preprimer, primer, first-reader, second-reader, and third-reader levels; good background for social studies and training in word analysis.

Sounds We Use. Ginn. Series of 16 filmstrips, full color, to develop and reinforce the auditory and visual recognition of the sounds of letters.

Enrichment Film Strips. Enrichment Teaching Materials. Color. Correlated with the Landmark Reading Series.

Films

"Background for Reading and Expression Films." Coronet. B & W, $55.00; Color, $110.00. 10 minutes.

"Cues to Reading." C-B Educational Films. B & W, $396.00. 6 minutes each.

Why Read?—Sets purpose for reading.
How to Read—Covers word recognition, vocabulary, and phrase reading.
What Did You Read?—Elements of comprehension.
Was It Worth Reading?—Evaluation of what is read.
What Is A Book?—How to use a book effectively.

"Encyclopedia Britannica Primary Reading Series." Color, $50.00 each; 6 for $270.
Set I of 6 films, giving rich background in home and family living; first grade.
Set II devoted to American holidays; second grade.

"Film Readers." Encyclopaedia Britannica Films. B & W, $50.00. 10 minutes.
D.C. Heath, publisher of 16 books intended for grades 1–3, dealing with animals, community workers, and children's familiar activities.
Row-Peterson, publisher of 8 books at easy fourth-reader level, dealing with children in foreign lands.

"It's All Yours." Teen Age Book Club. B & W, $25,00. 11 minutes. Ralph Bellamy narrates as scenes from familiar children's books are shown in illustrating the information, fun, and inspiration that books afford.

"It's Fun to Read Books." Coronet. B & W, $55.00; Color $110.00. 10 minutes.
Shows how to care for books, where to get them, and how to read them for pleasure.

"Let's Read Poetry." Bailey Films. B & W, $50.00. 10 minutes. By using three familiar poems, the narrator demonstrates good oral reading.

"They All Learn to Read," B & W sound, Syracuse University. Effective teaching in third grade where each of four groups reads on appropriate level.

"Why Can't Jimmy Read?" Syracuse University. B & W, $75.00. Intended as a film for training the teacher of reading in steps involved in diagnosing a severe reading difficulty.

APPENDIX B

Tests and Evaluation Instruments

Name of test	*Level or grade*	*Skills measured*	*Publisher*
READINESS:			
Gates Reading Readiness Tests	1	Picture directions, word matching, word-card matching, rhyming, letters and numbers	Bureau of Publications Teachers College Columbia University
Harrison-Stroud Reading Readiness Tests	K–1	Visual discriminations, attention span controlled; visual discriminations, attention span uncontrolled; using context clues; making auditory discriminations; using context and auditory clues; using symbols	Houghton Mifflin
Lee-Clark Reading Readiness Tests	K–1	Letter symbols, concepts, word symbols, total	California Test Bureau

Name of test	*Level or grade*	*Skills measured*	*Publisher*
Metropolitan Readiness Tests	K–1	Reading readiness, number readiness, drawing-a-man, total	Harcourt, Brace and World
Monroe Reading Aptitude Tests	K–1	Visual, auditory, motor, articulation, language, and preference	Houghton Mifflin
Murphy-Durrell Diagnostic Reading Readiness Test	1	Visual discrimination, auditory discrimination, learning rate	Harcourt, Brace and World
Checklist for Reading Readiness	K–1	Physical development, work habits and attitudes, skills, language abilities	Seattle Public Schools
ACHIEVEMENT:			
California Reading Tests	1–3, 4–6, 7–9, 9–14	Reading vocabulary, reading comprehension	California Test Bureau
Durrell-Sullivan Reading Achievement Test	2–4, 3–6	Word meaning, paragraph meaning	Harcourt, Brace and World
Gates Primary Reading Tests	1–2	Word recognition, sentence reading, paragraph reading	Bureau of Publications Teachers College Columbia University

Gates Advanced Primary Reading Tests	2–3	Word recognition, paragraph reading	Bureau of Publications Teachers College Columbia University
Gates Basic Reading Tests	4–8	Reading to (1) appreciate general significance; (2) predict outcomes; (3) understand directions; (4) note details	Bureau of Publications Teachers College Columbia University
Gates Reading Survey Test	3–10	Vocabulary, comprehension, speed of reading, accuracy	Bureau of Publications Teachers College Columbia University
Iowa Every-Pupil Tests of Basic Skills			
Reading Comprehension	3–5, 5–9	Comprehension, vocabulary, total	Houghton Mifflin
Work-Study Skills	3–5, 5–9	Map reading, use of references, use of index, use of dictionary, alphabetization	Houghton Mifflin
Metropolitan Achivement Tests: Reading	1–8	Paragraph Comprehension and Vocabulary	Harcourt, Brace and World
Sequential Tests of Educational Progress: Reading	3–College	Comprehension	Educational Testing Service

Name of test	*Level or grade*	*Skills measured*	*Publisher*
SRA Achivement Tests: Reading	1–9	Comprehension, Vocabulary, Study Skills	Science Research Associates
Stanford Achievement Tests: Reading	1–9	Vocabulary, Comprehension	Harcourt, Brace and World
DIAGNOSTIC:			
Botel Reading Inventory	1–4	Word recognition, listening, phonetic skills	Follett
Diagnostic Reading Tests	K–4, 4–8	Word attack and comprehension, oral and silent reading, vocabulary	Committee on Diagnostic Reading Tests, Inc.
Durrell-Analysis of Reading Difficulty	0–6	Oral reading, silent reading, listening comprehension, word recognition and analysis, visual memory, auditory analysis, spelling and handwriting	Harcourt, Brace and World
Durrell-Sullivan Reading Capacity Test	1–6	Capacity for vocabulary and paragraph meaning	Harcourt, Brace and World

Gilmore Oral Reading Test	1–8	Individual test, containing 10 paragraphs of increasing difficulty; word attack-meaning skills, comprehension	Harcourt, Brace and World
Gray Standardized Oral Reading Paragraphs Test	1–8	12 paragraphs of increasing difficulty; word attack skills, oral reading efficiency	Public School Publishing Co.
Gates Reading Diagnostic Tests	1–12	Silent reading, oral reading, vocabulary, reversals, phrase perception, word perception	Bureau of Publications Teachers College Columbia University
McCullough Word Analysis Tests	4–College	Seven types of word analysis skills	Ginn

APPENDIX C

Selected Series of Books

These books may be used for enrichment or, in many cases, as materials for the reluctant reader whose needs are best met through high-interest, low-vocabulary content. Where it is possible, both the difficulty level and the interest level have been given.

All About Books. Random. Level: 4–5. Interest: 3–12.
American Adventure Series. Wheeler. Level: 2–6. Interest: 3–12.
American Heritage Series. Aladdin. Level: 5–6. Interest: 5–10.
American Indians. Benefic. Level: 3–4. Interest: 2–6.
Around the World Today Books. Watts. Level: 3–6. Interest: 3–8.
Basic Goals in Reading. Webster. Level: P–4. Interest: K–4.
Basic Vocabulary Series. Garrard. Level: 2–3. Interest: 1–6.
Beginner Books. Random. Level: 1–2. Interest: K–6.
Button Books. Benefic. Level: 1–3. Interest: 1–6.
Childhood of Famous Americans. Bobbs-Merrill. Level: 4–5. Interest: 3–12.
Cowboy Sam Series. Benefic. Level: 1–3. Interest: 1–6.
Dan Frontier Series. Benefic. Level: 1–4. Interest: 1–6.
Deep Sea Adventures Series. Harr Wagner. Level: 2–4. Interest: 3–10.
Discovery Books. Garrard. Level: 2–4. Interest: 2–8.
Dolch Pleasure Reading Series. Garrard. Level: 1–4. Interest: 1–8.
Easy Reading Series. Houghton. Level: 1–8. Interest: 1–10.
Every-Reader Series; Junior Every-Ready Series. Webster. Level: 4–5. Interest: 3–12.
First Books. Watts. Level: 3–5. Interest: 3–8.

Folklore of the World Books. Garrard. Level: 3. Interest: 2–8.
Getting to Know Books. Coward-McCann. Level: 4–6. Interest: 4–8.
How and Why Wonder Books. Grosset-Dunlap. Level: 3–6. Interest: 3–8.
I Can Read Series. Follett. Level: 1–2. Interest: K–4.
I Want To Be Books. Children's Press. Level: 2. Interest: 1–4.
Jerry Books. Benefic. Level: 1–2. Interest: 1–4.
Jim Forest Series. Harr, Wagner. Level: 1–3. Interest: 1–8.
Junior Library Series. Morrow. Level: 3–5. Interest: 4–12.
Junior Science Series. Garrard. Level: 3. Interest: 2–6.
Landmark Books. Random. Level: 4–5. Interest: 3–12.
Morgan Bay Mysteries. Harr Wagner. Level: 2–3. Interest: 2–8.
North Star Series. Houghton. Level: 4–6. Interest: 4–12.
Piper Series. Houghton. Level: 3–4. Interest: 3–8.
Real People Series. Row, Peterson. Level: 4–6. Interest: 3–9.
Rivers of the World Books. Garrard. Level: 4–5. Interest: 4–12.
True Books. Children's Press. Level: 2–3. Interest: 1–6.
What Is It Series. Benefic. Level: 1–2. Interest: 1–4.
Wonder-Wonder Series. Steck. Level: 1–3. Interest: 1–6.
Woodland Frolics Series. Steck. Level: 1–6. Interest: 1–8.
World Landmark Books. Random. Level: 4–6. Interest: 4–12.

APPENDIX D

Magazines and Newspapers

American Childhood. 74 Park Avenue, Springfield, Mass.
Suitable for primary grades.

American Girl. Girl Scouts, Inc., 155 East 44 Street, New York 17, N.Y.
Emphasis is upon reporting activities of Girl Scouts; good stories for girls, dealing with real life problems.

Boys Life. Boy Scouts of America, New Brunswick, N.J.
News of Scout activities; some very good stories and highly interesting materials on science and boys' hobbies.

Child Life. O. H. Rodman, 30 Federal Street, Boston, Mass.
Good stories and many activities for young children. Excellent photographs and illustrations.

Children's Activities. Child Training Association, 1018 South Wabash Avenue, Chicago 5, Ill.
Wide selection of stories and activities for young children. Some good developmental tasks in reading are given in each issue.

Children's Digest. Children's Digest, Inc., 52 Vanderbilt Avenue, New York, N.Y.
Excellent selection of children's literature; good illustrations; book review section is valuable for teachers.

Highlights for Children. Highlights, P. O. Box 269, Columbus 16, Ohio.
Fine stories for primary children. Activities in each issue which are provocative and challenging for children.

Humpty-Dumpty's Magazine. Parents Institute, 52 Vanderbilt Avenue, New York, N.Y.
Good stories for preschool and primary children.

Jack and Jill. Curtis Publishing Company, Independence Square, Philadelphia 5, Penn.
Good science stories, mysteries, poems, puzzles, songs, games, and informative articles. For ages 6–12.

Junior Natural History Magazine. American Museum of Natural History, New York, N.Y.
One of the outstanding magazines for the child who is interested in natural history; for ages 8–14.

Junior Scholastic, News Explorer, News Ranger, News Time, News Trails, Scholastic News Pilot. Scholastic Magazines, 33 West 42 Street, New York 36, N.Y.
Consistently interesting and stimulating materials for youngsters in grades 1 through 9.

My Weekly Reader. American Education Publications, Education Center, Columbus 16, Ohio.
For grades 1 through 6, each issue contains news reading and reading exercises for the particular grade level. Excellent materials for social studies and science.

Nature Magazine. American Nature Association, Washington, D.C.
Excellent science materials for good readers; illustrations appeal to children of all ages.

Outdoor Life. Popular Science Publishing Company, 353 Fourth Avenue, New York 10, N.Y.
Stories of the out-of-doors, particularly hunting and fishing experiences, for the junior high school boy.

Popular Science. Popular Science Publishing Company, 353 Fourth Avenue, New York 10, N.Y.
Abundant suggestions for boys who love to tinker and experiment. Good informational articles.

Read. American Education Publications, Education Center, Columbus 16, Ohio.
Good material for the English and social science classes. Teacher's edition available with each issue. Junior high school level.

APPENDIX E

Index of Publishers

Abingdon Press, 201 Eighth Avenue, South, Nashville 3
Aladdin Books, 55 Fifth Avenue, New York 3
Allyn and Bacon, Inc., 150 Tremont Street, Boston
American Book Company, 55 Fifth Avenue, New York 3
American Council on Education, 1785 Massachusetts Avenue NW, Washington 6, D.C.
American Library Association, 50 East Huron Street, Chicago 11
Appleton-Century-Crofts, Inc., 35 West 32 Street, New York 1
Association for Childhood Education International, 1200 15 Street, Washington 5, D.C.
Barnes and Noble, 105 Fifth Avenue, New York 3
Beckley-Cardy Company, 1900 North Narragansett, Chicago 39
Bobbs-Merrill Company, 730 North Meridian Street, Indianapolis 7
Bureau of Publications, Teachers College, Columbia University, 525 West 120 Street, New York 27
Burgess Publishing Company, 426 South 6 Street, Minneapolis 15
California Test Bureau, 5916 Hollywood Boulevard, Los Angeles 28
Children's Press, Jackson Boulevard and Racine Avenue, Chicago 7
Committee on Diagnostic Reading Tests, Mountain Home, North Carolina
Coward-McCann, Inc., 200 Madison Avenue, New York 16
Crowell, Thomas Y., Company, 432 Park Avenue South, New York 16
Dodd, Mead and Company, 432 Park Avenue South, New York 16

Doubleday and Company, 575 Madison Avenue, New York 22
Dutton, E. P., and Company, 300 Fourth Avenue, New York 10
Economy Company, Oklahoma City, Oklahoma
Educational Publishing Corporation, Darien, Connecticut
Educational Testing Service, Princeton, New Jersey
Encyclopaedia Britannica, Inc., 425 North Michigan Avenue, Chicago 11
Follett Publishing Company, 1010 West Washington Boulevard, Chicago 7
Funk and Wagnalls Company, 153 East 24 Street, New York 10
Garrard Press, 510–522 North Hickory Street, Champaign, Illinois
Ginn and Company, Statler Building, Boston 17
Globe Book Company, Inc., 175 Fifth Avenue, New York 10
Grosset and Dunlap, Inc., 1107 Broadway, New York 10
Harcourt, Brace and World, Inc., 750 Third Avenue, New York 17
Heath, D. C., and Company, 285 Columbus Avenue, Boston 16
Heritage Press, 595 Madison Avenue, New York 22
Holiday House, 8 West 13 Street, New York 11
Holt, Rinehart and Winston, Inc., 383 Madison Avenue, New York 17
Horn Book, The, 585 Boylston Street, Boston 16
Houghton Mifflin Company, 2 Park Street, Boston 7
Laidlaw Brothers, Thatcher and Madison Streets, River Forest, Illinois
Lippincott, J. B., Company, East Washington Square, Philadelphia 5
Lyons and Carnahan, 2500 Prairie Avenue, Chicago 16
McCormick Mathers Publishing Company, P. O. Box 2212, Wichita 1, Kansas
McGraw-Hill Book Company, 330 West 42 Street, New York 36
McKay, David, Company, 119 West 40 Street, New York 18
Macmillan Company, The, 60 Fifth Avenue, New York 11
Merriam, G. and C., Company, 47 Federal Street, Springfield 2, Massachusetts
Merrill, Charles E., Books, 1300 Alum Creek Drive, Columbus 16, Ohio
Morrow, William, and Company, 425 Park Avenue South, New York 16

National Council of Teachers of English, 508 South Sixth Street, Champaign, Illinois
National Education Association, 1201 16 Street, N.W., Washington 6, D.C.
Noble and Noble, 67 Irving Place, New York 3
Norton, W. W. and Company, 55 Fifth Avenue, New York 3
Odyssey Press, 55 Fifth Avenue, New York 3
Owen, F. A., Publishing Company, Dansville, New York
Prentice-Hall, Inc., Englewood Cliffs, New Jersey
Public School Publishing Company, 204 West Mulberry Street, Bloomington, Illinois
Putnam's Sons, G. P., 210 Madison Avenue, New York 16
Rand McNally Company, 8255 Central Park Avenue, Skokie, Illinois
Random House, Inc., 457 Madison Avenue, New York 22
Ronald Press, 15 East 26 Street, New York 10
Row, Peterson and Company, 2500 Crawford Avenue, Evanston, Illinois
Sanborn, B. H., and Company, 249–259 West Erie Boulevard, Syracuse 2, New York
Science Research Associates, Inc., 259 East Erie Street, Chicago 11
Scott, Foresman and Company, 433 East Erie Street, Chicago 11
Scribner's, Charles, Sons, 597 Fifth Avenue, New York 17
Silver Burdet Company, Park Avenue and Columbia Road, Morristown, New Jersey
Simon and Schuster, Inc., 630 Fifth Avenue, New York 20
Singer, L. W., Company, 249–259 West Erie Boulevard, Syracuse 2, New York
Steck Company, P. O. Box 16, Austin 61, Texas
Wagner, Harr, Publishing Company, 609 Mission Street, San Francisco 5
Watts, Franklin, Inc., 575 Lexington Avenue, New York 22
Webster Publishing Company, 1154 Reco Avenue, St. Louis 26
Wesleyan University Press, Middletown, Connecticut
Westminster Press, Witherspoon Bldg., Philadelphia 7
Wheeler Publishing Company (See Row, Peterson)
Wonder Books, Inc., 1107 Broadway, New York 10

Index

(*Boldface type indicates major treatment.*)